ROUTLEDGE LIBRARY EDITIONS: POLICE AND POLICING

Volume 9

RACE, RIOTS AND POLICING

RACE, RIOTS AND POLICING

Lore and Disorder in a Multi-racist Society

MICHAEL KEITH

LONDON AND NEW YORK

First published in 1993 by UCL Press

This edition first published in 2023
by Routledge
4 Park Square, Milton Park, Abingdon, Oxon OX14 4RN

and by Routledge
605 Third Avenue, New York, NY 10158

Routledge is an imprint of the Taylor & Francis Group, an informa business

© 1993 Michael Keith

All rights reserved. No part of this book may be reprinted or reproduced or utilised in any form or by any electronic, mechanical, or other means, now known or hereafter invented, including photocopying and recording, or in any information storage or retrieval system, without permission in writing from the publishers.

Trademark notice: Product or corporate names may be trademarks or registered trademarks, and are used only for identification and explanation without intent to infringe.

British Library Cataloguing in Publication Data
A catalogue record for this book is available from the British Library

ISBN: 978-1-032-41114-9 (Set)
ISBN: 978-1-032-42194-0 (Volume 9) (hbk)
ISBN: 978-1-032-42205-3 (Volume 9) (pbk)
ISBN: 978-1-003-36168-8 (Volume 9) (ebk)

DOI: 10.4324/9781003361688

Publisher's Note
The publisher has gone to great lengths to ensure the quality of this reprint but points out that some imperfections in the original copies may be apparent.

Disclaimer
The publisher has made every effort to trace copyright holders and would welcome correspondence from those they have been unable to trace.

Race, riots and policing

Lore and disorder in a multi-racist society

Michael Keith
*Goldsmiths' College,
University of London*

© Michael Keith 1993

This book is copyright under the Berne Convention.
No reproduction without permission.
All rights reserved.

First published in 1993 by UCL Press

UCL Press Limited
University College London
Gower Street
London WC1E 6BT

The name of University College London (UCL) is a registered
trade mark used by UCL Press with the consent of the owner.

ISBN:
1-85728-109-8 HB
1-85728-110-1 PB
British Library Cataloguing-in-Publication Data
A catalogue record for this book
is available from the British Library.

The photograph appearing on the paperback front cover,
entitled *Prejudice*, is reproduced by kind permission of
Don McCullin, Mugshots Model Agency,
Collett Dickenson Pearce and the Metropolitan Police.

Typeset in Palatino.
Printed and bound by
Biddles Ltd, King's Lynn and Guildford, England.

ii

CONTENTS

Preface and acknowledgements	iv
Abbreviations and acronyms	viii

PART ONE *Lost times, forgotten places*

1	From bad to worse? Policing and British Black communities	2
2	Contested fictions: local histories and glimpses of the past	19

PART TWO *1981:* That summer *in London*

3	Shaggy dog riots and copycat rioters: the "riots" in London as a moral panic	52
4	Blame, guilt and "causes" of "riots"	72
5	The reality of insurrection? Empiricism and the search for the "average" rioter	96

PART THREE *"Grief"*

6	Front Line policing in the 1980s	122
7	Building stages for confrontation: power relations and policing	147
8	Misunderstandings? The resolution of conflict by consultation: assumptions and contradictions	171

PART FOUR *Discipline and punish?*

9	Strategies of control: the local reality of racial subordination	188
10	Policing reconstructions of reality	208
11	Constructing characters: racialization and criminalization into the 1990s	231

Appendix	257
Bibliography	259
Index of authors cited	275
Subject index	277

PREFACE AND ACKNOWLEDGEMENTS

In 1988 Roald Dahl, the author of didactic horror stories for children and adults was witness to a young Black man being beaten up by police officers. In an outraged description given to a not very liberal newspaper (*Daily Mail*, 28 April 1988) he expressed extreme shock that the traditions of British justice and the conventions of British policing could be transgressed in such a public manner.

In one of the more effective recruitment posters run by the Metropolitan Police in London in the past few years, a Black man is shown in a photograph being chased by a White police officer in uniform. Confounding the reader's expectations, the text of the advertisement reveals that the Black man is not a criminal but is instead a police officer in plain clothes leading a chase which has left the uniformed constable in his wake.

The two images are symmetrically similar and exemplify a recurrent feature in the popular understanding of policework. Fragments of action, they invite the decorative rationalizations of a chronology and moral cast list. A preferred explanation is attached to a particular set of circumstances. Divorced from any meaningful context, they become empirical evidence that in turn confirms our own presuppositions.

If this book does anything at all, I hope in some small way it disrupts the easy logic of this sort of slippage. It is a book about the institutional racism that defines the criminalization of Black communities. Appallingly large numbers of Black citizens have had their lives blighted by their encounters with the British criminal justice system. Yet if the evil of racism becomes the central analytical focus of the work, and and a constructive engagement with institutional racism its primary rationale, it is equally the case that the perpetrators of such evil are no more easily identified at the end of the book than at the beginning. The scandals that have coalesced around policing in recent years can prompt simplistic explanations of police malpractice, not least in mainstream academic analysis. A clear division of good and evil is always neater and on some level more appealing and it is always easier to portray the police as either heroes or villains in such narra-

PREFACE AND ACKNOWLEDGEMENTS

tives, though in reality of course they are neither.

The systematic racism that works through the British criminal justice system is no worse than its counterpart that pervades the educational institutions in which the author has spent most of his professional career. Only the social settings and the power to affect the lives of the subjects of iniquitous practice differ. Personally, I find myself and other White researchers always throwing stones from ivory towers that bear more than a passing resemblance to greenhouses. In the same way, the picture on the paperback cover of this book invites a certain complicity, assumes that the meaning is read stereotypically, and almost implies a White gaze that translates the image into a specific understanding of police–Black relations. An understanding of policework would be impossible if it were completely alien to the rest of society, but unnecessary if it were not alien in some important ways. Such is the nature of interpretation, at least in the ethnographic work reported here in Stoke Newington and Brixton police stations, two places that have featured in some of the more striking policing controversies of the past decade.

Yet it remains the case that, outside the sociology of policework, it seems easier to get away with cruder and more simplistic understandings of the police force than of almost any other institution in contemporary society. This is not least the case in the field of studies of race and racism. Consequently, in part I have tried to highlight the always disturbing cliché that it is all more complicated than academic common sense frequently suggests. More specifically, it is argued that meaningful understandings of the relationships between police and Black communities depend on situating detailed accounts of police practices firmly within the social and political context in which the police operate.

What I have tried to do here is to unravel just a few of the processes by which conflict and its consequent injustices have become built into the institutional fabric of contemporary policework, become a part of the everyday practice of policing and the everyday experiences of Black communities. The suggestion is that confrontations between police and local communities do not occur randomly in some places and not others. Instead, such places have been produced and defined by their histories which in turn structure the actions of people who live and work there. In this sense the text often refers to the manner in which social relations are *inscribed* in space. The spaces in which police and Black communities have clashed are not just a container of these conflicts, they are a constitutive part of them. If we want to understand how conflict has evolved, we have to understand how histories are written and geographies imagined on both sides of this divide. So although the protagonists referred to throughout the book are most often White police and Afro-Caribbean communities, ethnicity as such is less relevant than the manner in which migrants

v

PREFACE AND ACKNOWLEDGEMENTS

experiencing racism come into contact with one of the institutions of the British criminal justice system, and how "blackness" becomes defined as a sign of criminal otherness. In order to explain this, the theoretical work of the text argues that particular parts of cities have come to signify particular and contested sets of meanings to different people at different times, meanings that are spatially rooted and which come to serve as rationalizations for both policies by all the institutions of the state and popular mobilization by local communities. Crudely put, the good news is that the police force is no worse than any of the other White-dominated institutions of British society. The bad news is that it is no better.

The book attempts to synthesize several different pieces of research carried out over the past ten years in order to provide an account of racialized criminalization in Britain in the hope that the final whole might turn out more worthwhile than the sum of the constituent parts. Without the support of three people in particular – Harbhajan Brar, Karim Murji, and John Solomos – over a considerable period of time, and their belief in the value of the project, it would never have been completed. I owe them. I am also in debt to many other colleagues who have been kind enough at various times either to take an interest in the work or else offer other forms of advice. There are too many to list here, but Les Back, Malcolm Cross, Paul Gordon, Eugene McLaughlin, Ceri Peach and Mel Thompson are particularly worthy of mention, as is Justin Vaughan at UCL Press for his belief in the project. Much of the book is based on research that would have been impossible without the co-operation of the many informants inside and outside the police force who agreed to be interviewed and others who were "observed" in ethnographic work. Many of these people are anonymized in this book, particularly almost all junior police officers (for obvious reasons) and also those senior officers whose actions or statements the author found most objectionable. Those officers named are generally both individuals whose "anonymity" would have been disingenuous and whose commitment, integrity and personal courage I have greatly admired at first hand. Of course none of the above bears any responsibility for the flaws in the book. Most of all, this book is dedicated to my family, whose faith has been unwavering and who were kind enough to keep occasional scepticism largely muted.

What I have tried to do is to to place the horrific process of racialized and racist criminalization in a particular rather than exhaustive context. Such a complex story can be told only in part; the book does not pretend to tell the whole story of criminalization. I am not sure if such a task could ever be feasible. Instead, the work attempts to demonstrate how the systematic reproduction and amplification of conflict between the police and Black communities has a specific geographical and historical provenance that confounds both the more seemly image people (Black and

PREFACE AND ACKNOWLEDGEMENTS

White) like to have of their own society and the more simplistic under-standings of policing that often pass for common sense among the enlightened classes. Only by understanding the manner in which this provenance becomes inscribed in the routine of particular times and places is it possible to make comprehensible the sort of fleeting images that confronted Roald Dahl and are manipulated in that recruitment poster.

All of this is done in the firm belief that the old aphorism is wrong: to know all is not to forgive all. Yet this can be said only in the context of academic work that has been far from innocent in the reproduction of racism, in acknowledging the force of Steven Biko's remark that Black communities were "tired of being spectators standing on the sidelines in a game we should be playing", and in the spirit of Geoffrey Hill's wry assessment that could be taken as the epigraph of most social observation:

> We are the occasional just men who sit
> in gaunt self judgement on their self-defeat,
> the elite hermits, secret orators
> of an old faith devoted to new wars.

London, 1993

ABBREVIATIONS AND ACRONYMS

ACCA Afro-Caribbean Community Association
ACCE Afro-Caribbean Cultural Centre
ACPO Association of Chief Police Officers
AFFOR All Faiths For One Race
CCCS Centre for Contemporary Cultural Studies
CID Criminal Investigation Department
CIO Community Involvement Officer
CPCGL Community Police Consultative Group for Lambeth
CRE Commission for Racial Equality
DAC Deputy Assistant Commissioner
DI Detective Inspector
DS Detective Sergeant
DSU District Support Unit
GLC Greater London Council
HCRE Hackney Commission for Racial Equality
IC1 Identification Category 1: White
IRR Institute for Race Relations
JCAO Joint Council of Asian Organisations
LVSC London Voluntary Services Commission
MP Member of Parliament
MPD Metropolitan Police District
NCCL National Council for Civil Liberties
PACE Police and Criminal Evidence Act
PC Police Constable
PR public relations
PROD photographic retrieval from an optical disk
PSI Policy Studies Institute
QC Queen's Council
RAAS Racial Adjustment Action Society
RRYCC Railton Road Youth and Community Centre
SPG Special Patrol Group
SUS Arrest on Suspicion
TA Tenants' Association
TSG Territorial Support Group
VAP Violence Against the Person
WPC Woman Police Constable

PART ONE

LOST TIMES, FORGOTTEN PLACES

CHAPTER 1

From bad to worse?
Policing and
British Black communities

The first step in liquidating a people is to erase its memory. Destroy its books, its culture, its history. Then have somebody write new books, manufacture a new culture, invent a new history. Before long the nation will forget what it is and what it was. The world around will forget even faster.

Milan Kundera (from *The book of laughter and forgetting*)

For the vast majority of people in civil society, the mechanics of police practice are an irrelevant fiction. The same is not the case for British Black communities of many centuries' residence in this country, and few people, if any, would suggest that the same can be said about the lives and life–chances of those people who either migrated from the Caribbean in the post-war era or else are descended from that population.

There is a strong case for arguing that the relationship between the police and the British Black community is one that can be understood only in terms of premeditated repression by the British state. Changes in the techniques, motivation and ideology of that repression may lie at the heart of changes in police practice, but are irrelevant to the anti-racist struggle precisely because they make such little difference to the lived experience of those "at the sharp end".

If such neat and simple reasoning is accepted as adequate, then there is little point to this book. However, there seem to be certain flaws in such a simplistic rhetoric. In particular, looking back at the 1980s, it would appear to be a decade when a whole series of political, economic and ideological processes were operating that were reshaping the way in which both socially powerful groups and institutions conceptualized notions of "race" and the commonly oppressed minority groups characterized "racial" mobilization. The very ground on which discussion of racism and racial equality had been consensually based in the preceding decade appeared to be shifting under everyone's feet.

Alarmingly, in a decade that witnessed two more Nationality/Immigration Acts, one new Public Order Act and a popular resurgence of jingoistic nationalism tied to violent armed conflict in the Falklands, some concepts of rights and dignity, previously taken for granted, seemed to be questioned. In political debate the all-too elliptical nature of what was not being said was at times almost as alarming as the all-too invidious nature of what *was*. Specifically, one of the organizing themes through which many of the old debates about racial equality seemed to be refashioned was a field of discussion which gained prominence through the symbolically powerful incidence of rioting, with which the decade opened in the spring and summer of 1980 and 1981.

Shaped as much by historical coincidence as by teleological predictability, this field of discussion in domestic British politics was characterized by the conjunction of the related subject areas of policing, civil disorder and race. It is this terrain that this book attempts to explore, hopefully not as a purely self-indulgent exercise in academic meditation, but in an attempt to expose the way in which the reproduction of racial subordination and inequity in British society in the 1980s has occurred, in part through the manner in which these three arenas came together in theory and in practice. It is a field of discussion that for convenience is here described as the discourse of "lore and disorder".

Mapping the book

In short, the case I am arguing is that representations of "Blackness" as innately criminal – in part reproduced through a constellation of debates owing their lineage to the uprisings of the 1980s – have played an instrumental rôle in the naturalization of the systematic racist criminalization of Black communities in Britain. This case is advanced through five related projects: a juxtaposition of theories of police/Black antagonism with localized realities of conflict; an analysis of the uprisings themselves; a largely ethnographic study of policing in three parts of London; a contextualization of this evidence in terms of national developments in policing and police rationalizations of their own practices; and finally an attempt to draw these themes together through an understanding of how the reproduction of conflict transcends

POLICING AND BRITISH BLACK COMMUNITIES

individual integrity to emerge as institutionalized racial subordination. In Part One of the book I try to suggest that there is a common-sense understanding of the function and potential of academic theorization that has commonly misrepresented the nature of writing in the social sciences. Specifically, this can lead both to a false expectation of the potential of theoretical analyses of police racism and, more significantly, a systematic forgetting of the manner in which struggles and conflict are deeply rooted in the local experiences of particular communities. Chapter 2 looks briefly at just a few of the incidents and trends that have lent the conflict between police and Black communities historical depth and locational specificity, in order to provide not definitive histories of these places, but instead a contrast with the timeless, placeless theories of racism and police/Black conflict alluded to in Chapter 1.

The second part of the book is an attempt to re-examine the disorders of 1981 which placed rioting on the political agenda for the following decade. It is not easy to cloak discussion of such powerfully emotive events in the scientific language of academic objectivity. Quite possibly it is not proper to do so. The very vocabulary used to describe riots at once implies an accompanying set of values and preconceptions. The terms "riot", "uprising", "disorder" and "rebellion" have all been used to define these events, and all connote very different understandings about the nature of this particular form of conflict. In this context it seemed important both to unravel the way in which these events were conceptualized and to subject them to some sort of empirical scrutiny.

In order to do this, Part Two of the book attempts to make several points. The first is to demonstrate that in 1981 the incidence of violent disorder created a moral panic in which a set of common-sense understandings about the nature of violent conflict was just as important in determining the way people reacted as the events and processes that generated the riots themselves. People conceptualized rioting as a form of pathological contagion, commonly associated with Black communities, a contagion that threatened to spread like an epidemic from those points at which disorder had first erupted.

So, in a sense, civil disorder can be seen as a two-faced phenomenon: a set of preconceptions about violent conflict co-exist alongside the empirical reality of rioting. Although not completely divorced, the processes behind the generation of the former are not the same as those that determine the incidence of the latter.

Chapter 4 tries to take this concept further by looking at the way in which those who speak with the authority of the academy have attempted to explain the events of 1981. It is suggested that academic explanations commonly appropriated the symbolic power of rioting in order to vindicate preferred explanatory frameworks. This was in part possible

4

MAPPING THE BOOK

because of the dearth of empirical material available on the fleeting and momentary form of popular mobilization witnessed in violent disorders. Chapter 5 attempts to provide an alternative conceptualization of the same events, one that is both empirically rooted and aware of the problem of attempting to reproduce faithfully angry scenes in dispassionate prose. I try to provide both some sort of empirical description of the events of 1981 in London and an outline of the key theoretical problems which bedevil alternative conceptualizations of these events.

The empirical description accepts that the accuracy of any such picture is strictly limited by the data used. However, it does seem to be possible to demonstrate that at the heart of almost all serious riots was a conflict between British Black communities and the police, not just a clash between the police and a subgroup that can be neatly catalogued as "Black youth" or "the young", or romanticized as a trans-racial unification, but instead involved violent clashes with a broad cross-section of the Black communities of specific neighbourhoods. Although such a conclusion might appear self-evident to many, it contradicts many of the images of "the average rioter" that populated many of the explanations of violent conflict in both popular press and supposedly serious academic writing.

Just as the manner in which this conflict was realized in violent disorder is obvious to everyone until alternative explanations are subjected to closer scrutiny, so it is suggested that the common-sense set of understandings in which descriptions of the events of 1981 are placed is similarly self-evident at one level, but much more problematic on closer inspection. In particular it is difficult, even within more progressive literature, to see how the essentially spontaneous nature of collective protest is retained, avoiding notions of conspiratorial insurrection, without reducing those who took part to either passive respondents to a transcendent social logic or conspiratorial plotters of incipient revolution.

In Part Three an answer to some of these problems is sought through a focus on the manner in which the depth, sincerity and significance of antagonism between the police and British Black communities is embedded in the histories of particular communities. The analysis is based on ethnographic work carried out in the mid- and late 1980s.

There is a certain contradiction here, quite possibly even a betrayal on the part of the author, and I have discussed elsewhere the ethical and methodological issues that ensue from this "betrayal" (Keith 1992). Policing has been and remains a principal focus for Black community mobilization. It is undoubtedly the case that the police have featured prominently in many of the most horrific moments of British racism; the grim list of deaths of Black people in police custody belies glib

5

euphemism. Yet much of this work would not have been possible without the help of serving police officers whose integrity I wholly respect and whose conduct I have admired. The intention is instead to situate such individuals in their institutional context, not in any way to suggest that they were exceptional, but instead to highlight the situations, not necessarily of their own making, in which they and others found themselves.

Once placed in their historical and geographical context, some of the generalized theorizations of police/Black antagonism begin to look even less plausible. Specifically, the text attempts to suggest that, although it would be misleading to underestimate the salience of police occupational culture, the causal powers attributed to it, both inside and outside the police service, can be exaggerated too easily in understanding the nature of police racism.

Crudely, the police force has become trapped in a position where the public face of policing is sustained only by deception, not by the police alone but by society more generally. We commonly prefer to regard the job of upholding the law as unproblematic. The rôle of the police has traditionally been legitimated by a pervasive emphasis on the collective interest in the rule of law, combined with a public reticence on the necessarily contested nature of the social order that such laws embody. Although this may sometimes have been sustainable for a White majority at a time of national political consensus, it has never been so credible to Black British communities who have suffered systematic institutional racism. It has also become a progressively less tenable definition of *the job* within the context of the controversial restructuring of British society in the past decade.

This book strives quite consciously not to be a crude anti-police text, but tries instead to set the institutional racism of the police service alongside the institutional racism of all other facets of British society. The essential problem is one of policing a multi-racist society.

To this end I have tried to demonstrate that the roots and reality of the conflict between police and British Black communities are far deeper and more insidious than popular understandings of society can countenance. Hence in the final part of the book there is an attempt to demonstrate that a series of policies which have sustained the systematic racial subordination of one class of British citizens, have become built into the daily routine of British policing and yet are understood as a normal facet of daily life. This can be traced neither to the conspiratorial malice of senior police officers, nor to the ubiquitous bigotry of their junior colleagues, but instead to the changing position of the police as an institution within the criminal justice system of the state in the 1980s (Ch. 11), rationalized in terms of a set of understandings of the nature

MAPPING THE BOOK

of society that mystify precisely these changes (Ch. 10). The latter is by and large made possible by the growth of a series of quasi-scientific explanations of police/Black conflict tied to liberal notions of racial inequality and supported by a less than flattering portrayal of rank-and-file PCs and junior officers, which some senior police themselves readily use to explain clashes with Black communities.

The conclusion cannot avoid pessimism because it is suggested that, through the combined influences of all the institutions of the penal system, not just the police, an abstract criminalized subject position of "Blackness" has been constructed which in its specific realizations can systematically blight the life-chances of whole communities. The conclusion also attempts to locate this process within some sort of theoretical conceptualization of contemporary British society and the naturalization of "civil disorder" or, more generally, rioting in the early 1990s.

There is also a particular point that I am trying to make about the empirical material in this book. Although the focus of the subject matter is on the 1980s, and particularly the uprisings of that decade, the attempt is to understand the genesis and reproduction of police/Black conflict as a whole. To do this I have tried to combine empirical and abstract material drawn from several different times in the 1980s: the material on the uprisings concentrates on 1981 rather than 1985; the ethnographic material relates to two different ethnographic periods in the mid- and late 1980s (Keith 1992); the final part is much more catholic in its delimitation of time. Likewise, three loosely defined London locations are introduced early in the text that they can be returned to in the ethnographic account.

With both historical and geographical boundaries, it needs to be strongly emphasized that choices and omissions were often necessarily arbitrary. It would have been just as easy to focus on the nature of criminalization in the 1970s as the 1980s. It would have been equally valid to chose Wolverhampton, Liverpool and Birmingham as the three locations discussed here. The three locations in fact owe their selection in large part to a definition of police/Black confrontation voiced by Kenneth Newman when Commissioner of the Metropolitan Police, as Chapters 6 and 9 explain. It is also germane to note that there are definitive geographies of the conflict between police and British Black communities to be written, just as there is a need for authoritative histories of this confrontation in particular places to be recorded. This work pretends to be neither.

Instead, it is because of the need to combine the abstract and the empirical that I believe it is important to synthesize specific historical and geographic realizations within a broad theoretical framework. I

7

POLICING AND BRITISH BLACK COMMUNITIES

passionately believe that one of the constructive contributions the academy can make to anti-racism is to prompt people to think through the apparent self-evidence of racist institutions and glib assumptions about the tasks of anti-racism. If this is no more than making the familiar appear strange, it may still have a value. There are inevitable shortcomings to such an approach; no location is exhaustively described, and there is a great deal of historical and ethnographic material I have, selectively, omitted. Although the choice of the omissions was the author's, it is for the reader to judge if they were justified in terms of what remains.

The intention behind this book was to write a work that would help me, and hopefully other people, to examine the particular manifestations of racism that have underscored both the incidence of major riots or uprisings in Britain in the 1980s and also our understanding of those events.

In this sense I have in this book rejected any notion of academic work as no more than a form of cerebral hard labour at the coalface, producing a steady exposure of a product that we call knowledge. I have attempted to write about both the empirical reality of one aspect of 1980s Britain and the way in which that reality comes to be represented by people who claim the right to speak about those events, and to offer an authoritative account of a particular history; in short, *to know what happened*.

Knowledge is socially constructed, and academic research is one set of social practices that is inseparable from all that is good and all that is bad about the institutions of British academic life in which they are set, institutions which have themselves been both the site and the cause of processes of systematic institutional racism.

Trotsky once claimed that theory without practice is empty, but equally that practice without theory was blind. It is in this sense, I hope, that this text can make some contribution to the countering of racist practices in society by combining theoretical synthesis with empirical description. Both may fail, but I do feel that both are essential to any understanding of those highly charged events that are sometimes called riots.

Finally, it is questionable whether White academics, socialized to the ivory tower, are necessarily in the best position to analyze and theorize racism. Their right to speak is quite rightly subject to question. This is a problem that can be answered only provisionally, just as Salman Rushdie once pointed to exactly the same phenomenon when writing a thinly disguised treatise about another land.

"Outsider! Trespasser! You have no right to this subject! . . .
Poacher! Pirate! We reject your authority. We know you with your

8

foreign language wrapped around you like a flag: speaking about you in your forked tongue, what can you tell but lies? I reply with more questions. Is history to be considered the property of the participants solely? In what courts are such claims staked, what boundary commissions map out their territories? Can only the dead speak?" (Rushdie 1983: 28)

So the justification for the book is thus tied to some loosely defined claim of anti-racism based on the value of rediscovering and exposing the historically traced paths through which some of the more invidious practices of racial subordination have come to be seen as *normal* or *natural* in today's Britain. The argument is that it has been necessary for society to do a great deal of forgetting in covering up these traces of history.

Forgetting

A central theme of this book is that the writing of academic texts cannot be divorced from the social context in which they are situated. In this context the remainder of this chapter attempts to make two points. First, that literature may feed into policy and practice in ways which are significant but not necessarily controlled by the authors of such a work. Secondly, I want to suggest that there is a commonly held conception of social theory which is instrumental in mystifying and misrepresenting the evolution of conflict between police and British Black communities. For although much of this work may be valuable in its own terms, it can at times contribute to a wider process of social amnesia. Historical reality is lost in the search for *theoretical truth*.

The antagonism up and down the country between Black communities and local police forces is widespread, historically mature and well documented (Gordon 1985a,b, Humphry 1972, John 1970, MacDonald 1973, Pullé 1973, Reiner 1985b, Holdaway 1979, 1987). The best reviews of the academic literature are found in Paul Gordon's two bibliographic essays (1985a,b), although Reiner (1985b) also provides a comprehensive and concise summary of much of the same material as well as a brief examination of similar issues in the USA. Significantly, Jefferson (1988), in an updated version of the same literature has argued for a more historically informed research problematic.

Research in this field is most succinctly summed up by Robert Reiner's comment that, "The now vast literature on police/Black relations in Britain is a depressing chorus of unheeded prophecies of doom." (Reiner 1985a: 149) Rather than systematically review this vast literature, it is intended here only to draw out some of the connections between theory and practice, to demonstrate the rôle of academic work in sustaining a process of official forgetting.

Most of this literature has attempted to explain the roots of the pessimism Reiner outlines, normally focusing on one of the key players in this interaction, either the ethnic communities or the police. An alternative approach, exemplified by the work of Phil Scraton and Tony Bunyan has preferred to look at the changing tasks demanded of the police by the British state. The value of such analysis is considered below in Chapters 4 and 9.

Black communities and pathology sociology

The notion that newness to British society was the root cause of misunderstanding and antipathy between Black communities and a whole host of White institutions was a theme that recurred in much political and academic discussion throughout the 1960s and early 1970s. A tendency to consider any confrontation between police and Black people as a product of *cultural difference*, however this *difference* was construed, likewise dominated discussion of *police–immigrant relations* in this period.

Such notions, which imply that migrant groups and their future generations pose *problems* to host societies, led to a popular and academic focus on the Black populations rather than on the societies in which those communities found themselves. Studies of Black communities, epitomized by the early work of Banton (1955), Little (1947), Patterson (1961) and Richmond (1954), attempted to describe particular cultural milieux. In such work, and perhaps more importantly in the common-sense assumptions that such work inadvertently perpetuated, acknowledgement of the existence of racism tended to be downplayed by seeing it as an essentially irrational reaction to the strangeness of new cultures. Implicitly, strangeness generated a passing hostility which was a temporary aberration that would pass with the onset of *assimilation*.

The manner in which this sort of work has contributed to an invidious pathological conception of Black culture generally, and played a contributory rôle, if only accidentally, in the reproduction of racist stereotypes of Black communities specifically, has been more than adequately described in several works throughout the 1980s (e.g. Lawrence 1982, Solomos 1988).

Yet it is important to realize that it was in no small way through these early academic exercises in "race relations sociology" that, in 1967, the Home Office called for the appointment of liaison officers to help overcome the "cultural barriers" between police and "coloured" communities (Solomos 1988: 90). The link between academic theory and policing practice is sometimes closer in time than notions of "ivory tower" remoteness might suggest.

"Theories" of police racism

If it is accepted that the roots of police/Black antagonism are not found in the salient features of "immigrant culture", one obvious reaction is to locate the "blame" for conflict in the particular nature of British policing. Most obviously, such a stance must take on board the catalogue of complaints by Black communities about policing that have recurred throughout the past 30 years (e.g. IRR 1979, 1988, AFFOR 1978), which have tended to cite both manifold forms of "over-heavy policing" (overt discrimination, saturation policing of Black communities, over-policing Black social and political institutions, and police abuse) and the failure to police racial attacks effectively.

The intensely disturbing perennial reappearance of similar types of complaint over a long period of time may lead, ordinarily, to an attempt to explain these complaints within the comprehensive analytical concept of police racism. Yet, while accepting that this change of emphasis is as much political and moral as it is analytical, it is essential to recognize the wide variety of diagnoses that co-exist within this concept.

Rotten-apple racism

A method much used to rationalize specific demonstrable cases of racist behaviour by police was the practice, commonly reflected in official accounts, of attributing the failings of particular incidents to the proclivities of a small minority of "rotten apples" within the police force. At one level this obviously does no more than reflect the historical misconception of individualized racism, conceived purely in terms of personal attitudes, that has dogged British social policy through much of the past 20 years (Jenkins & Solomos 1985). At another it suggests that the antagonism between police and Black communities is the product of the popular misrepresentation of the misdeeds of a small minority of police officers.

Police pathologies

There is a certain consistency in the findings of ethnographic work on policing in Britain. From the early work of John Lambert (1970), Maureen Cain (1973) and Robert Reiner (1978) to the later studies carried out by Holdaway (1983), Smith & Gray (1983), Foster (1990) and Young (1991), revelations, in the idiom of "dirty realism", have highlighted not only commonly held racist attitudes and beliefs but also a less than Utopian image of something often referred to as "police subculture".

Again, the context in which such portraits are placed – rather than their accuracy *per se* – is frequently problematic. At times there has been a suggestion that it is possible to identify certain personality traits which are more commonly found among police than among the public generally. A debate that centred on the putative authoritarian attitudes apparently characteristic of those who wished to join the police is just one example of this (cf. Colman & Gordon 1982, with Butler 1982). Within such debates there is an obvious possible extension to notions of racism; hypothetically it might be argued that police are in some way more racist than other groups in society.

Yet, besides incorporating a distorted notion of what constitutes racism, locating it as some form of personality defect, such a line is particularly misleading. For what remains less readily identifiable is any notion of placing the quantity of ethnographic work within any sophisticated theoretical context. This is at least as much the case for scholarly ethnographic reports of the police as for more populist, less analytical, exercises in the genre (e.g. Chesshyre 1989). The most glaring example of the priority given to description is the much-quoted PSI study of the Metropolitan Police by Smith & Gray in the early 1980s in which, perhaps for understandable reasons, a wealth of empirical observation is matched with no theoretical comment at all beyond a certain level of crude generalization.

Roger Graef's book *Talking Blues* (1990) is another case in point. An important book, it is invaluable for its extensive coverage of twelve different police forces and five hundred officers, but in its desire to let the police themselves describe "an emotional mosaic . . . of what it is like to police Britain today", a search for the universal generalization necessarily obscures the salience of the particular. Heavily influenced by Studs Terkel (Graef 1990: 11), the style of reportage – long excerpts of quotations from police officers framed by the brief explanatory notes of the author – aims at social realism by letting the police speak for themselves. Yet the product is inevitably ambiguous. Although well written, by their very nature the explanatory notes often confuse as much as explain, advancing a simplistic split between "'hard' and

"THEORIES" OF POLICE RACISM

'soft' policemen" (Graef 1990: 12–13), forgetting scares and confrontations with the police in a misleading description of Handsworth as "a multi-racial area of Birmingham, previously noted for its good community relations" (Graef 1990: 76) and accepting as race-neutral and unproblematic terms such as steaming, rioting and looting (Graef 1990: 158). Significantly, the result is a text that is not so much objective as ambiguous. The extended interview extracts have proved a treasure trove for those looking for evidence to support a pathological view of police culture and yet, on its cover, the book is praised by John Stalker, the former policeman, who has been vociferous in his reactionary condemnations of what he sees as the Scarman agenda for policing (e.g. his article in the London *Evening Standard*, 9 May 1988).

This ambiguity is intrinsic rather than incidental. Although the framing of the ethnographic report, whether of participant observation or depth interviews, structures interpretation, the apparent lack of theoretical content in such work does not make it descriptively neutral. Left relatively unscathed by ostensible "theory", the reader instead confirms her or his own worst fears or best hopes in such a text. Theory is imposed on the verité genre in the form of the reader's own preconceptions or common sense.

It is precisely this malleability of well reported high-quality material, such as the PSI study and Graef's work, that demands a more explicit theoretical and empirical contextualization by the authors. Yet, with the exception of the work of Jefferson & Grimshaw (1984, 1987), and to some extent Holdaway (1983), ethnographic work rarely receives such treatment. Certainly, my own ethnographic work confirmed the existence of an identifiable set of common values – the clichéd canteen culture – that many other studies have highlighted. Left alone with little theoretical deconstruction, however, the all-too-real accounts of racist rationalizations and commentaries, which fill the narratives of many ethnographies of police work, can find a causal root only in a loose and dangerously defined pejorative categorization of police subculture.

Ironically, such a conceptualization of a racist, sexist, authoritarian police subculture dominated by machismo and alcohol has become the routine grist of much progressive Left political rhetoric, even though in its genesis it replicates very many of the insidious stereotypes that were once purveyed, if at times inadvertently, by studies of immigrant culture.

Even the patronising, but less obviously malevolent, stereotypes of Afro-Caribbean people as carefree, sociable, musical and athletic, or of people from the Indian subcontinent as thrifty, family-orientated and cultivated were and are dangerous, not so much because of their de-

POLICING AND BRITISH BLACK COMMUNITIES

grees of inaccuracy as for their usage (see below Ch. 10). Likewise, it is in large part less relevant to know the degrees of masculinity, alcohol abuse and sexism (or equally bravery, social conscience and fitness) that prevails among police officers as to know what explanatory power such alleged cultural proclivities are being given (cf. McConville & Shepherd 1992: Ch. 6).

As later chapters in this book suggest, in the late 1980s it was also not unusual for senior police to use variations on the subcultural theme in explaining their own junior officers' behaviour. So at issue is not just the existence, at some level of generalization, of a "professional culture" as such. What is contentious is the causal significance attributed to this police subculture. Notwithstanding some notable exceptions (Brogden et al. 1988, Jefferson & Grimshaw 1984, 1987), there is a danger that ethnography, frequently "under-theorized", culminates in cultural generalizations of junior police officers which either provides a rhetorical let-off for their senior colleagues or a convenient scapegoat for analysis of police/Black antagonism. And certainly, although it is not irrelevant, the subcultural theme is woefully inadequate as the sole explanation of police racism.

Reflecting society

An alternative construction of "police racism" has been to cast it in the context of the social groups from which police are drawn. It is commonly argued that police will do no more than reflect the attitudes, presuppositions and bigotries of their communities. A racist-majority society produces racist police officers.

As elementary logic this argument is important and strong, if rather a truism. Yet it also potentially perpetuates the misleading conceptualization of racism which focuses on the proclivities of individuals, although as Pearson et al. (1988) have pointed out, "bad apples theory" and reflection theory are clearly not the same thing.

In a sense, the circular nature of the argument that police racism reflects society highlights the limitations of any analysis of racism which separates the police from the social context in which they are operating. Indeed, the shortcomings of attempting to isolate racism as a problem has more recently led Pearson et al. (1989) to prefer a more nuanced notion of "policing racism", although, at time of writing, their own developments of this concept, which appear important, do not seem to be fully developed.

Very often it is not that analysis of police racism has been unproductive or worthless in its own right; it is rather that the context in which it may enter into political debates and common-sense understandings has particular ramifications that may either mystify or misrepresent the nature of policing. Most obviously, the construction of police pathologies lends itself to a critique of policing based on stereotypes of police work which are as inaccurate as they are sterile avenues for reform. A notion of police racism in this vein channels debate into a dead-end. If police racism can be isolated, the logical questions to ask run along the lines of "How much racism is there?", "Are things better now or worse than they were at some unspecified time before?" (cf. Scarman 1987), "Is there greater or less antagonism between police and Black people in 1990 than in 1980?". It is precisely these sorts of questions that must be negated before they are asked, because they incorporate both a clichéd metaphor of racism as a disease or infection and because they turn both police and Black communities into material objects to be scrutinized rather than living and contingent groups of real people.

It is the academic metaphoric equivalence made between racism and contamination that leads logically to the notion that this *disease* can be purged by the treatment of individual souls. The misbegotten production of Human Awareness Training and Race Awareness Training for the police (Southgate 1984, Oakley 1988, 1989) thus reproduced all the canards that were so incisively pointed to by Sivanandan (1985) in the early 1980s and by many across the political spectrum who, subsequently, imitated his critique.

Different forms of analysis serve different purposes. There is an intuitive usefulness, in attempting to formulate anti-racist strategy and/or policy by seeking out the nature of police racism. Yet the very search for generalization may have consequences of its own. The structural position of police forces within society as a whole is frequently suppressed by reifying a problem of police racism; less obviously, the historical change in the nature of conflict cannot be addressed.

There are notable exceptions to this. Solomos (1988) has analyzed the historical change in police/Black relations in the context of Black youth, in terms of three themes: the supposed link between race and criminality, mugging and street crime, and policing law and order. However, the historical depth to Solomos's work remains a rarity in most analysis of policing Black communities.

Police / race relations?

If it is accepted that an understanding of the antagonism between police and British Black communities must look beyond the salient characterizations of either party, then:

The re-occurrence of similar patterns of complaint and conflict in a

POLICING AND BRITISH BLACK COMMUNITIES

variety of social contexts certainly implies that . . . police–minority relations are not so much a problem of individual attitudes or prejudices as one with structural roots in the rôle of the police and the position of minorities. (Reiner 1985: 148)

This unexceptionable comment by Robert Reiner has led some to proffer alternative accounts of this conflict, couched in terms of *the interaction* between police and Black people.

However, if what is addressed are the "relations" between police forces and all minority groups, there is a temptation to highlight the similarities between examples through time and between countries. Typically, Britain looks repeatedly to America for enlightenment concerning problems of race relations. Academics search for historical generalization. In this process, although not in Reiner's own work, the specific historical development of policing Black communities in Britain may again be played down in the search for a particular vision of academic "theory".

The danger with such work is that too often the antagonism between police and Black communities is cast in the vocabulary of criminality. In the most notable school of explanation in this vein, Left Realist criminologists, associated at various times with Jock Young and his associates, have attempted to trace this antagonism back to the disproportionate representation of Black people among the poorest sections of society (Lea & Young 1981, 1984, Kinsey et al. 1986, Matthews 1987, Matthews & Young 1986, Young 1987). This is suggested to produce a commensurately disproportionate involvement of young Black people in certain crimes, an involvement that is exaggerated by police stereotyping and racism. The explanation takes "Black criminality" as given, and excuses it on the grounds of racial deprivation. The "mugging" debates of the late 1970s and early 1980s (Deutsch 1982, Runnymede Trust 1982, Smith 1982), supported by a fraudulent manipulation of crime statistics, are echoed in academic prose. Crucially, for the Left Realists, the conflict that was seen at its most dramatic in the uprisings of the 1980s owes its roots to an apologetic explanation of Black criminality (Lea & Young 1982).

There is no space here to detail either the political furores that have surrounded the Left Realist work or the academic exchanges that it has provoked (Gilroy 1982a,b, Gilroy & Bridges 1982, Bridges 1983a,b, Gutzmore 1983, Ryan & Ward 1986, 1987, Keith & Murji 1990). It is worth making just two points. The first is that, in the explicitly stated search for cultural generalizations to underscore an aetiology of crime (e.g. Young 1987: 353), a stereotypical *average young Black criminal* is constructed whose diagnostic features explain police/Black hostilities.

There is an elementary historical flaw in such a deterministically

16

CONCLUSION

phrased causal connection. This conflict quite clearly pre-dated any suggestion of Black over-representation among offenders. As early as 1972 the House of Commons Select Committee on Police/Immigrant Relations stated categorically that:

It was made clear by all witnesses . . . that relations between police and younger West Indians are fragile, sometimes *explosive* [my emphasis] . . . Of all the police forces from which we took evidence, not one had found that crime committed by coloured people was proportionately greater than that by the rest of the population. Indeed *in many places it was somewhat less.* [my emphasis]

The Left Realists do not so much revise history as forget it. Left Realist explanation can only incorporate processes which take place at no place, always in the present. As the following chapter will emphasize, the conflict between the British Police and British Black Communities possesses an historical and geographical depth which is misrepresented by a focus on problems of crime (e.g. Lea 1987 and 1986 on police racism). The focus on "the youth" is also disingenuous. As Part Two of this book demonstrates, conflict has often drawn in a wide cross-section of Black community life, not just a demographic fraction that equates with "the young".

The second point to make about Left Realist criminology is that it involves a rhetorical shift of analysis of major significance. This is a sort of mystification, the lens through which one problem is viewed dominates our understanding; a debate about the relations between one of the major institutions of social control and a subsection of British society becomes structured by a complex debate about race and crime. Later chapters of this book argue that such slippages are far from innocent.

Conclusion

Two points recur in most academic attempts to explain conflict between the police and British Black communities. The first is that both a focus on Black communities and a focus on the police themselves have too often shared a notion of theory that takes as a central goal the production of generalizations about, respectively, police behaviour or migrant culture. This notion of theory as generalization necessarily creates the raw material for insidious stereotypes, laying the ground for misleading representations of police culture and Black community life. It is a sad irony that such pathologies share a common academic fraudulence, but are used by opposite ends of the political spectrum to vindicate notions

17

of either a police force that can be understood as a crucible of a disease called racism or of Black community life as a hotbed of criminality.

It is of equal significance that there is something innately forgetful about certain approaches to explanation. Generalizations, by definition, exclude the significance of the historically and geographically specific; by suppressing memory, they become the vehicles through which time is lost and places forgotten.

The second point is that a focus on the issue of crime has too often created an analytical fog, which mystifies the conflict by setting it against a context structured by debates around criminality. There is no attempt here to deny the reality of crimes carried out by Black people, instead only an assertion that the manifest antagonism displayed on both sides of this social schism predates allegations of Black criminality and is about a lot more than the relative proportions of criminal behaviour carried out by different fractions of society.

The search for generalized truths lends itself to both the crude stereotypes of pathology sociology and the spurious scientism of many theories of police racism.

What is normally absent from the academic literature, if not from popular memory, is a detailed historical account of the confrontations between police and Black communities. Such periodization cannot on its own provide an explanation for such conflict, but without it any explanation will inevitably lack plausibility. In the following chapter there is an attempt to provide at least a partial corrective to this systematic amnesia by highlighting the depth of conflict in three particular "places" that reappear thematically later in the book. It is only out of such a history that theorization can tentatively begin.

CHAPTER 2

Contested fictions:
local histories and glimpses of the past

"Memory is the truly subversive weapon"
Christopher Hope in *White Boy Running* (1988)

when you fling me inna prison
I did warn yu
when you kill Oluwale
I did warn yu
when you beat Joshua Francis
I did warn yu
when you pick pan de Panthers
I did warn yu
when you jack me up gainst de wall
ha didn't bawl
but I did warn yu

now yu si fire burning in mi eye
smell badness pan mi breat
feel vialence, vialence,
burstin outta mi;
look out !

it too late now:
I did warn yu

From "Time Come" Linton Kwesi Johnson

Official accounts may forget, but people still remember. If the systematic amnesia of authoritative accounts of police/Black relations is to be subverted, there must be a place for these memories. In this context

CONTESTED FICTIONS

this chapter has two aims. The first is to highlight the provenance of some of the recurrent themes that have characterized the traumatic history of police/Black relations in three particular locations. The second is to offer not a definitive account but a geographically specific historical background to the incidence of major riots or rebellions in the 1980s.

The three vaguely defined "places" that are used here as emblematic are Brixton, Stoke Newington and Notting Hill. All are in London. This confers all the usual advantages and disadvantages on the work. Perhaps most significantly, the policy and practice of only one police force in one local economy is considered. Less beneficially, the situation in London might be cast as in some way atypical; there is certainly no intention here to play down the significance of events in Birmingham, Bristol, Liverpool, Leeds, Manchester, Wolverhampton and many other cities during this period.

More particular attention is paid to three specific roads in these locations, three roads that, in varying degrees, were to gain renown as "Front Lines" of confrontation between police and local community. A certain publicly acknowledged status was conferred upon these roads by the Commissioner of the Metropolitan Police, Sir Kenneth Newman, who claimed in 1987 that in the policing of multi-racial London ·

Railton Road in Brixton, All Saints Road in Notting Hill and Sandringham Road in Hackney . . . These are at the centre of areas where crime is at its worst, where drug dealing is intolerably overt, and where the racial ingredient is at its most potent. (K. Newman, 16 February 1987)

This was an authoritative policing geography of London. The sites at which the putatively combustible elements of race, crime and disorder come together. It is the interaction of these three elements in various arenas that lies at the source of the "lore and disorder" debates of the 1980s and it is precisely the analysis of this interaction that forms the central theme of this book. Paradoxically, the very naming of these roads by Newman both invokes a particular version of history and also confers on three specific places a novel status. It would be misleading to overestimate the importance of three specific roads in the evolution of conflicts between police and Black people in London – national confrontation did not grow out of the events on these roads – or to take Newman's statement literally; there is no attempt in this text to describe such a history. It is instead the interplay between the symbolism of particular locations and the reality of violent conflict that is explored.

There is no way that this work would ever pretend to offer a definitive history of the policing experiences of any of the places mentioned here. Each location could easily provide the subject matter of books in

20

LOCAL HISTORIES AND GLIMPSES OF THE PAST

their own right if such an assertion were plausibly made. Neither would it be either academically accurate or morally justifiable to pretend to speak definitively for the experiential history of policing in Black Britain. Nevertheless, having said this, there are certain themes and perspectives tied to particular locations at various periods of time that it would remain important and reasonable to highlight in even the most superficial analysis.

The attempt is here to highlight some of the themes that run through relations between police and Black people in particular places, without pretending to produce a single, authoritative, true history of any place at any time. Not only is there no definitive account of a place's past, there always remains a multiplicity of assorted histories, simultaneously present; everyone's story is part of history. Hence, the academic historical narrative and popular memory remain distinct, neither innately superior to the other.

Recording these histories is a significant task, if not always a purely literary one. For a sense of the past is itself constructed.

Academic history has a particular place in a much larger process. We will call this "the social production of memory". In this collective production everyone participates, though unequally. (Popular Memory Group, CCCS 1982: 207)

Neither academic history nor popular memory is produced here.

But it is intended to highlight some of the themes and perspectives in three places that provide much of the empirical material later in the book. It is important to contrast the inscription of experience in time and place with the placeless, timeless theories of Chapter 1. However, the stories told can be no more than this. The descriptions here at best aspire to the status of partial second-hand accounts.

The choice of locations inevitably excluded the specific influences that resulted in White youth and, to some extent, the Asian community becoming involved in violent disorder in 1981. This is not to understate the importance of these influences – this study is not exhaustive – only to suggest that, in the cultural representations of civil disorder in the 1980s generally and the reality of 1981 London specifically, they were not quite as significant as the characteristic police/Afro-Caribbean antagonism that underwrote almost all of the clashes in the "1981 riots in London".

All three locations are at times referred to as the "Front Line". All Saints Road and Railton Road are better known than Sandringham Road where, thanks to the co-operation of very many people, it was possible to gather a more complete social and historical description. Consequently, this Hackney location is dealt with throughout the book in greater detail. Conversely, All Saints Road is dealt with relatively briefly because the characters and the places of the local history are well known and much written about; emphasis there is thus placed on just a few events of lesser renown in Notting Hill.

Neither is the emphasis on the local intended to suggest the irrelevance of more general factors in the genesis of conflict. Black settlement is not reducible to the people who migrated to Britain from the former colonies in the post-war years but those who did shared experiences nationally. The operation of institutional racism throughout society, the economic marginalization of the depression years and the continued reproduction of negative images of the ethnic others, stereotypes of migrant ethnicities, exemplify these. Other research has highlighted and explored these three universal influences extensively and so they are taken mostly for granted here, touched on in passing.

Railton Road, Brixton

There is no way that this tangential account can do justice to the complexity, the diversity of opinion and the multitude of different histories that are simultaneously present in accounts of Brixton's past. The intention here is only to pick out some of the principal threads in this tapestry, suggesting that Railton Road and the surrounding few streets were the one place in Brixton where all the forces that brought police and Black people into conflict came together. A particular history was tied to this location, preconditioning the road for the events of 1981.

Background history
(a) Police/Black relations in Brixton In its historical context the rioting of 1981 in Brixton was unsurprising. Police/Black relations did not suddenly collapse at local level in the period just before the riots, as the Metropolitan Police submissions to Lord Scarman at times suggested. Nor can mutual hostility be traced to the incidence of crime within the marginalized Black population, or even to media distortion of this level of crime. The roots of this hostility go back much further.

Put simply, relations between the Black community and the police in Brixton have never been "good", partly because relations of this sort cannot be measured on a simple one-dimensional scale, principally because of the pervasive and persistent racism of White society as a whole, exemplified by the treatment of Black people by the Metropolitan Police Force.

It is the contention throughout this work that the police force as an institution and police officers as individuals are no worse and no better

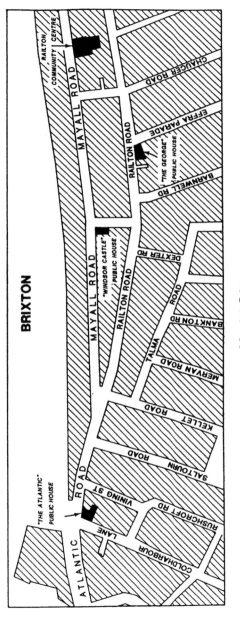

Map 2.1 Brixton.

CONTESTED FICTIONS

than the society from which they are drawn. The circumstances in which police/Black interaction has occurred structured the particular realizations of societal racism. Inevitable points of contact between police and Black people became the arenas in which racism was manifested and hostility flourished.

The evidence of this historical depth is well documented and clearly seen in the warnings of trouble in the late 1960s and early 1970s by local community workers such as Jeff Crawford, George Greaves and Courtney Laws (Keith 1986); in the submission to the Royal Commission on Criminal Procedure by the LVSC (1979); in the Report by the Council Working Party into Community/Police Relations in Lambeth (January 1981); and in the submissions to Lord Scarman by the Lambeth Youth Committee, the Brixton Neighbourhood Community Association, Concern, and the Runnymede Trust.

Yet, in hindsight, perhaps the most significant document was the work by Joseph Hunte titled *Nigger hunting in England?* (1966). This report states quite categorically that,

for the seven years that I have been residing in Brixton, I have been constantly besieged by members of the immigrant population with matters of conflict between them and the Police Force,

going on to cite the ready use of dogs against Black people, overtly racialist abuse and the allegation that

it has been confirmed from reliable sources that sergeants and constables do leave stations with the express purpose of going nigger hunting (1966: 12).

More recently (in 1966) he suggests that this victimization had taken the form of "trying innocent West Indians before the court for loitering with intent to commit a felony" (1966: 14). When asked in a private interview about the accuracy of this report, Commander Alex Marnoch, who worked in Brixton at the time of Hunte's work, commented,

It has to be said that although exaggerated the allegations in that report were basically true. When there had been some trouble, especially if a PC got hurt, it was not unusual for a group of police to pile off down to Somerleyton Road for a fight. It was very regrettable and it has to be seen in context. At that time everywhere you went in Brixton you could see signs saying "no coloureds" and lots of pubs wouldn't even serve Black people. Yes, racism was very common in the police force, but it has to be compared with everywhere else and in comparison with that the police record was a good one.

Crucially, the report alleges, and Marnoch confirmed, that not only had the hostility been established over a long period, dating back to the early 1960s, but it was also inscribed in the scenes in which confron-

RAILTON ROAD, BRIXTON

tations occurred; Hunte mentions several times the small area of Brixton around Coldharbour Lane and Somerleyton Road.

Relations between the police and large sections of the Black community have been "bad" for a very long time. This does not mean that they have been bad for the same reasons, or bad in the same way for all that time. The nature and form of this conflict has changed. Overt racism, institutional racism (stereotyping by SUS), and policing a divided society are disparate phenomena. Similarly, antagonism may be realized in resentment, passive subjection, open abuse, violent resistance or many other forms of behaviour. Rioting is merely one of several alternative expressions of this conflict.

(b) Locational background The central part of Brixton, which provided the private rental reception area for Caribbean migrants in the 1950s and early 1960s (Patterson 1963), gradually shrunk in size over the following two decades. One by one the dilapidated old housing districts were knocked down and replaced by new estates such as the Moorlands Estate on Somerleyton Road and the Stockwell Park Estate. In hindsight it is too easy to note that these local authority developments may not have been unqualified social successes.

It is also quite possible that the manner in which Lambeth Council used the police to enforce particularly unpopular aspects of housing policy in the 1960s and 1970s (e.g. squatter evictions) may have contributed to a particular local antagonism between police and community. But the new developments answered a pressing need and the problems they produced were new problems, rarely foreseen. As part of this process the areas of Railton Road and Mayall Road were scheduled for redevelopment, but this project was defeated in 1975 after a protracted period of protest, public inquiry and ministerial prevarication. By 1977 only 22 of the 400 properties in the Railton/Mayall Road Housing Action Area were considered by the Council to be, "satisfactory in terms of state of repair, housing conditions and general environmental quality". (Scarman 1981: 5) A vital element in the evolution of Railton Road as a Front Line was that by 1981, whereas the face of Brixton as a whole had been refashioned (often several times), the face of Railton Road was unchanged but for the progressive deterioration in the quality of its property. Nowhere else was the living history of the Black community in Brixton so clearly embodied in bricks and mortar. There was no need continually to remember the past because on Railton Road more than anywhere else the past was always present.

This is not to say that Railton Road was alone a site of confrontation with the police. In the years after 1981, as explained in Chapters 6 and 7, hostilities were evinced in several other parts of the area, and before

CONTESTED FICTIONS

the events of April 1981 Stockwell Park Estate had witnessed several violent incidents. In the early 1980s sustained efforts were made to reduce the number of derelict properties and squats. Many of the consequent evictions, most notably in November 1982, resulted in minor violent clashes. Indeed, by the middle of the decade the local commander of police was to take solace from the fact that very little happened on Railton Road itself in the later uprising in 1985. Instead the focus often shifted to some of the local estates (see Ch. 9).

Sometimes this took the form of high-profile police raids such as Operation Whispering Eagle in November 1987, which involved 150 police officers with full riot equipment and helicopter support. One of the significant features of the Whispering Eagle raid was that, in its coverage, the *South London Press* (13 November 1987) explicitly defended the scale of the operation as a successful attempt to prevent the development of another Front Line. Railton Road had implicitly assumed an iconic status; the term could be used by a popular press confident in the belief that the meaning "Front Line" needed no further elucidation.

Notwithstanding this, the road did continue to be a site of some trouble. In 1986 the massive raid on ACCE, the Afro-Caribbean Cultural Centre, Operation Condor, involving almost 2,000 police officers, produced little violent conflict principally because of its vast scale. There were also further confrontations over drug dealing, with more clashes in July 1989. Perhaps most notable of all, however, the terraced streets around Railton Road were, in varying degrees, ideal targets for the gentrification of the late 1980s property boom. Certainly, by the end of the decade the area in the centre of Brixton had changed considerably.

The Front Line before 1981

To some, whose knowledge of these streets came only with hindsight in the aftermath of the disorders, the "Front Line" may seem an apt description for an area where a mob battled with the police. But, almost certainly, the term is used to describe a place where people meet on the street to talk and relax. (Scarman 1981: 17)

One of the minor, but significant, debates that ran through the public hearings of the Scarman Inquiry concerned what the term "Front Line" actually meant. Courtney Laws (Brixton Neighbourhood Community Association) suggested that,

The historical fact of the Front Line, as I understand it – because I helped to name it – is where people from the Caribbean normally gather, meet and talk and often start up socializing groups and functions. It is very peaceful and quiet.

District Detective Chief Superintendent Plowman flatly contradicted this image:

the words "Front Line", as far as most people understand it, came about from . . . a film that was done by the BBC in 1965 when they said that Railton Road was the front line of confrontation between Black and White in the Brixton area and . . . that is why it is called the Front Line. There is only about 200 of that Black community that collect in the Front Line or Railton Road area. They are mostly Black people that are unemployed or Rastafarian type who display an anti-authority attitude . . .

He also suggested that the Front Line was used to "dispose stolen property". Plowman was candid; the "place" was stigmatized, explicitly labelled, as a "criminal area". In stark comparison, in 1976 *Race Today* (pp. 148–152) claimed that,

Railton Road is a heavily policed area. The Brixton end of the road is referred to among Blacks in military terms as "the Front Line". It is the front line of defence against the police.

In the political campaign for "Black resistance". *Race Today* in the mid-1970s were explicitly characterizing the Front Line as a source of potential Black political solidarity. From this perspective the "*riots*" were the logical outcome of this local mobilization. (see *Race Today*/Howe, "From Bobby to Babylon" 1981)

Similarly, although everyone accepted that the *Front Line* covered some part of the Railton Road, several different definitions of its precise boundaries were offered at the Inquiry, some confining it to a very small stretch of the road between Atlantic Road and Leeson Road, others including a larger section of Railton Road, yet others using the term more generally to describe a whole area.

The point Scarman missed was that the term Front Line may have been clearly defined for some individuals, but on closer inspection there are many different understandings of this "sense of place": a social centre, the epicentre of Black resistance, a location for trading stolen goods, a home, a drugs market place. There is no one meaning of Front Line. It was a variety of competing, frequently contradictory, perceptions held by individuals and institutions. At one time or another the Front Line has been, in part, most of these things. In a strictly geographical sense it is a term that serves in "the naming of parts", spatial parts. As shorthand definitions of places, based on subjectively defined salient characteristics of those places, they are near universal features of the way in which the lived world (the *umwelt*) is internally reconstructed in comprehensible form.

A name denotes a place and connotes a history. As ever, assorted histories are woven together and sieved by experience. Front Line did not mean the same for old and young, Black and White, police and policed. Yet, through all these histories a common theme is the conflict

CONTESTED FICTIONS

between Black people and the police (Lambeth Council 1981). This chapter attempts only to touch on this complexity, to illustrate that there are variations on this theme, not a simple phenomenon but a stage on which history has been played, each act linked to its predecessor, each act perceived from many different angles.

(a) Social and drinking clubs One of the oldest bones of contention between Black people and the police in Brixton stemmed from the existence of social clubs (shabeens) in which drinking and gambling were commonplace. Again, the history of these places is not straightforward; they symbolize neither simple cultural expression nor manifest criminal behaviour. It has often been suggested, not least by certain former "landlords" of Brixton shabeens, that the latent and overt rejection of Black customers in pubs in Brixton made the growth of these, technically illegal, facilities inevitable. As the Brixton Domino and Social Club (1981) stated,

> In the 1960s there were no recreation facilities for Blacks. We used to have lots of house parties. The pubs that existed in England then did not cater for West Indians and people from the Caribbean. Thus we created our own social gatherings and clubs.

Such euphemism hints at a cruel history. Racist hostility greeted those who would socialize with the majority, bureaucratic illegality conferred upon those who would replicate these same facilities within the minority. Certainly, drinks were sometimes sold at blues parties; certainly this was at times used as a pretext by some local police to raid any Black house where there was any sort of party (IRR 1979, 1988); certainly at least one individual who used to run a shabeen is now a respectable pub landlord in the Brixton area.

Many of the clubs were set up in the Coldharbour Lane / Atlantic Road / Railton Road area (Hunte 1966: 3). This pattern persisted throughout the 1960s and 1970s. Just before the riots of 1981 there were at least three well known clubs on Railton Road, so that in 1981 the Brixton Society commented,

> The past pattern of the police activity in the Brixton area has been to tolerate the clubs, etc. in the Front Line area of Railton Road for most of the time, but to stage the occasional raid in strength, apparently in connection with drugs offences.

Several long-serving Brixton police officers confirmed this pattern; in the nebulous divide between the illegal and the criminal, the raids on drinking clubs provided a forum for the rationalization and justification of racist police behaviour, taking on the respectability of official police actions. Some of these raids, professionally conducted and well organized, passed peacefully; others most certainly did not (e.g. the raids on

28

clubs in Kellet Road and Talma Road in 1975).

(b) Political groups A second longstanding element in the Railton Road scene was the high-profile presence of political and quasi-political groups. In 1968 a Black Panther group was set up in nearby Shakespeare Road, and campaigned for both Black rights in general and over specific issues such as the Joshua Francis case. In 1970 Francis was severely injured in his home and later charged with assaulting three police officers in what was widely believed at the time to be yet another instance of the "nigger hunting" that Hunte had drawn attention to. This group were regularly monitored by Special Branch.

Similarly, many groups who became incidentally involved in Black political mobilization of one sort or another were clustered in this area (Black Unity and Freedom Party 1985); the radical paper *Race Today* was based at 38 Shakespeare Road (and later in Railton Road), the Melting Pot Foundation and the Law Centre had offices in Atlantic Road, and Brixton Neighbourhood Community Association at 1 Mayall Road. That the White, predominantly middle-class, Anarchists' Centre and bookshop were set up in the mid-1970s at 121 Railton Road said a lot about this political symbolism, even if many would suggest that the shop itself was a near irrelevance for most of the Black community.

This author is not in a position to evaluate the significance of this pattern of clustering on the political consciousness, or the political attitudes, of Black residents of the area, but the various institutions were for a long time part of the identity of the Front Line, particularly when perceived by outsiders or by the police.

(c) "Shepherds" and other youth clubs The youth club may serve as a refuge from the hostility of the "outside world", a place in which dignity and self-respect are internally defined. The Railton Road Youth and Community Centre (RRYCC) of the Methodist Church, more commonly known as Shepherds, was such a place, and since the mid-1960s has been a major social focus for young Black people in the Railton Road area.

> Over the years the Centre has provided a home for many who have few roots in the community and some have found themselves welcome in the Centre who might well have found themselves rejected elsewhere. (RRYCC 1981)

The club was considered somewhere safe from police interference and as early as the late 1960s hostility against the police was such that there was physical resistance to attempts to search the club (normally when a young Black suspect was seen to run towards the club). In the late 1970s, as unemployment among young Black people in Lambeth

CONTESTED FICTIONS

grew rapidly, the average age of the clientele and the social importance of Shepherds grew alongside it. These changes prompted a struggle between those, often the older members of the club, who wanted to increase their participation in its control and organization, and the traditional youth worker system of the Methodist Church, a struggle *Race Today* described as "Brixton's Battle of Jericho". In 1979 the Methodist hierarchy tried to close the club, but this was successfully resisted through an occupation by the members. The Action Committee at the time stated,

> We cannot look for continuity in the workers because they come and go. Some are promoted, some get married, some get fired. We cannot look for continuity in the Minister/Warden. They too change from time to time. The membership on the other hand, has, in its older members, people who have been participating in the club since its inception.

At its heart this struggle would seem to touch upon two irreconcilable visions of the function of the youth club; one based on the paternalistic rôle of juvenile socialization, the other on the significance of particular "places" in local Black dignity, self-respect and mobilization. This struggle continued right up to the rioting of 1981, over such issues as the attempt to ban all members over 21 years of age from the premises.

At the time of the disorders the club remained untouched, "a haven of tranquillity in a sea of destruction" (RRYCC 1981). In this context, the contrast between the feeling of security inside the club and the violent clashes outside reveal much about the nature of the rioting in 1981:

> The other strong sense created by police presence and action is that of claustrophobia. The loss of open space to run and play is keenly felt. But this central Brixton area has become a home in which the community like to feel free to wander, congregate and stop and chat with friends. The sense of a heavy and pervasive police presence in this area is not a friendly and communal presence but a multiple and hostile one. (RRYCC 1981)

Also

> the Black community of Brixton is not a lawless community whose area has to be policed as though it were hostile territory requiring an army of occupation. (RRYCC 1981)

The sense of indignation at violations of this "home" was exacerbated in raids on Shepherds, first in 1974 and then at least ten times between 1974 and 1981:

> They have sometimes come in with dogs and once with guns . . . once inside their treatment of members has varied from moderation to provocation. Their sudden and sometimes violent entry into what is otherwise felt to be a secure Black community creates im-

RAILTON ROAD, BRIXTON

mediate tension and contributes to longer-term resentment. (RRYCC 1981)

Most often these raids were in pursuit of a suspect and in such circumstances it is notable how cynical or, perhaps more often, thoughtless police can be. This problem was clearly outlined in 1986 by a senior member of Brixton's Community Involvement Section, who was then on the managerial board of Shepherds:

> PCs just don't understand the damage they do. I mean I would defend what they do. I've even done it myself. The kids are all there and all of a sudden some prick with a blue hat on kicks the door in and comes charging in. Now I'm the youth worker; that place, those kids, are my responsibility. I walk over to the policeman and say, "Excuse me officer, can I help you?" and he just says, "Who are you?" and tells me to fuck off in front of everybody there. Now the kids there don't know that he was chasing his prisoner, he's angry with himself for losing a body, and he doesn't understand or doesn't care about the damage he is doing. And then if anyone in the club starts getting out of hand, the youth worker has been seen to lose his authority and if the place goes bang anything can happen. (private interview)

Tales abound of similar incidents that have occurred in Brixton and elsewhere (IRR 1979, 1987). Horrendous stories of District Support Units and Immediate Response Units charging in at the slightest sign of trouble, making large numbers of random and unnecessary arrests, are countered with the rational defence of the need for police officers to support their own at times of trouble. In such circumstances conflict reproduces itself, becomes cumulatively more entrenched. It was in such circumstances that a common belief on the Front Line in 1981 was that,

> the police were no longer protecting the people, or policing the area in a responsible manner. They were in fact a force of occupation within the Brixton area, and the people felt threatened by their presence in the area in such large numbers. (Brixton Rastafarian Collective 1981)

In this context the police rôle is crucial, but actual behaviour of individuals cannot be divorced from the institutional practice of "occupation of the ghetto", practice that is tied to the societal forces that have racialized space and created the ghetto in the first place.

(d) Crime on Railton Road Much of the debate in the Scarman Inquiry focused on the relative levels of crime, particularly "street crime", in Brixton and Lambeth compared with other divisions and Districts in London (e.g. Concern 1981). What was rarely disputed was the exist-

CONTESTED FICTIONS

ence of some criminal activity in Railton Road. In particular:

(i) Certain properties in the area were used for fencing stolen goods, particularly after street robberies.

(ii) Drugs were sold on the street and at certain properties there. The level of "hard" drugs as opposed to "ganja" (cannabis) and the alleged historical complicity of certain CID officers in this trade were both moot points in Brixton. In the immediate aftermath of the 1981 riots this trade grew dramatically as police, fearing public-order problems, were reluctant to take action against dealers operating openly on the street. In 1986 evidence mounted of some police involvement in recycling confiscated drugs, and Brixton police station was raided by Scotland Yard Drug Squad.

(iii) Because the people who used the Front Line frequently opposed any arrest, street robbers were known to make a run for Railton Road if caught, in order to seek protection from the crowd there.

Time and time again in the Scarman Inquiry police officers made it clear that they regarded all people who used the road as involved in at least one of these three categories. The whole road was stigmatized as a criminal area. District Chief Superintendent Plowman stated that,

the type of person that commits footpad robberies are the young fleet-footed youngsters between 12 and 17 that commit these offences [sic]. They do not get down the Front Line except to dispose of stolen property.

This statement was made in the full knowledge that on Front Line was a youth club (Shepherds) which on a busy night held almost two hundred people (RRYCC 1981). Implicitly, all people who used one of the few leisure facilities in the Brixton area were labelled as criminals and the charge of SUS was readily available to confirm this label in a perfect exercise in circular verification. The high incidence of SUS charges on Railton Road (cf. Demuth 1978) "proved" the road was a criminal area.

As Astel Parkinson, a youth worker in Brixton since the mid-1960s, explained in an interview: "Our kids just could not walk down the street without the risk of being picked up and charged." Those who looked suspicious were picked up, yet the criteria by which this suspicion was defined was rarely questioned. Crime was a problem on Railton Road, and a difficult problem for the police, but it was a problem perpetrated by a small minority, not a whole community.

A notable exception to the stereotypical view was expressed in the evidence given to Scarman by the Home Beat officer on the road, PC John Brown (in the police since 1963). Between 1971 and 1981 he had never been attacked in Railton Road and, although keen to point out the problems of criminal activity, painted for Scarman a much more subtle picture of the Front Line, going so far as to say that Black people

32

were friendlier towards the police locally than White. Once again the mythical Railton Road was perhaps not so readily susceptible to blanket classification as hindsight might suggest.

Sandringham Road, Hackney

Background history

The part of Hackney around Dalston and Stoke Newington may be less well known as a scene of confrontation between Black people and the police than either Brixton or Notting Hill, yet the story of Sandringham Road in particular appears remarkably similar to that in the two other areas. As early as 1970 the local Community Relations Council was demanding an inquiry into the poor state of police/Black relations. Again the worst confrontations occurred with groups of young Black people; again they occurred most often at youth clubs, dance halls and cafés. Local Black people working in such places in the early 1970s, and several local Black ministers, have given long accounts of many incidents of blatant police misconduct at that time, involving the same sorts of complaints about SUS, knock-on offences and provocation (Keith 1986). So, although the national renown of this part of Hackney may not have been so marked, the local history of conflict and antagonism, particularly concerning the reputation of Stoke Newington police station, was deep rooted, well remembered and commonly recorded (Hackney CRE 1983, Benn & Worpole 1987, Roach Family Support Committee 1989).

As in so many parts of London, local resentment tended to surface in one-off campaigns over particular cases. In 1970, Asetta Sims died in Stoke Newington police station. A copy of *Black Voice*, "Popular paper of the Black Unity and Freedom Party", led with the headline "WHO KILLED ASETTA SIMS?", adding in a smaller headline "She was murdered". Any substantive account of police/Black relations in Hackney would have to go back not only this far and further in time, but would also have to take into account the major watersheds of the death of Michael Fereira in Stoke Newington police station in 1978, the Knight case, the death of Colin Roach in Stoke Newington police station (1983), the death of Tunay Hassan in Dalston police station in 1987, the circumstances surrounding and following the arrest of Trevor Monerville in 1987, and the political mobilizations that drew their rationale from, while not focusing exclusively on, these incidents. The catalogue is a frightening one and it has bestowed on Stoke Newington police station in particular, a singular notoriety.

CONTESTED FICTIONS

The depth of feeling was long recognized both inside and outside the police force, and at both local and national level politically. In 1985 an internal police report in Stoke Newington commented on the fact that

Unfortunately, Stoke Newington has a notoriety relating to incidents occurring within the station. Despite great efforts it has been difficult to allay the misguided fears of certain sections of the community.

Similarly, in a letter to Council Leader Anthony Kendall in 1983, even a Conservative Party Home Secretary, Douglas Hurd, commented that

I recognize that there is a widespread feeling that the actions of police officers in Hackney over the last years have not always been above reproach.

Local police and Hackney council held similarly low opinions of each other throughout the early 1980s. In 1982 a Hackney Borough Council Police Committee had been set up, backed by a Police Committee Support Unit. Very much a phenomenon of its time, the Committee attempted to "persuade" police to report to the Committee, or at least be present at Police Committee meetings, a struggle that was closely tied to the debates over consultation and accountability that characterized the early 1980s politics of policing (see Ch. 9). In 1983 relations reached a nadir when in February the Council voted to withhold the police precept. It has to be said that such a stance reflected an important strain of local opinion, most readily evinced in the "break links" campaign of from 1983 onwards. The campaign, led by Hackney Community Action (a federation of 180 community organizations), aimed to persuade people to withdraw official links with police locally in schools, in council facilities and other institutions, until major reforms of policing were carried through. Similar stances were taken by groups such as Hackney Black Peoples' Association, Hackney Legal Defence Campaign, Hackney Legal Action Group, Hackney Black Peoples' Defence Association and, for a while, Hackney CRE, who in 1983 published a catalogue of grievances against the police locally. Several of these groups were closely involved with Hackney Community Action.

There is no attempt to describe any sort of exhaustive chronology here, but this should not be taken as an underestimation of the significance of such events as grounds for mobilization, in the racialization of policing politics and in the local history of Hackney in general, and the almost mythical notoriety of Stoke Newington and Dalston police stations in particular (see the *Policing in Hackney 1945–85* report (1988) for such a perspective).

In some arenas there has more recently been the suggestion, particularly amongst some older members of the Black community and church ministers, that the level of manifest misconduct and overt harassment

SANDRINGHAM ROAD, HACKNEY

has declined significantly since the late 1970s. During the same period Hackney was hit hard by economic decline, and by 1980 was the poorest borough in London (Harrison 1983), with high rates of unemployment generally and even higher levels of Black unemployment in particular. Again, within a widespread critical atmosphere, it is dangerous to make blanket generalizations about the attitudes or perception of *any* community. Hackney CRE began to talk formally again to local police in the late 1980s, although it should not be imagined that this was an uncontentious change in their position.

The area close to Dalston Lane and Sandringham Road became, in the late 1960s and early 1970s, one focus of young Black community social life in the borough. Johnston's café, which opened in 1972, served a purpose typical of many similar premises in London at the same time. Talking of the daily routine of "the young Black man" using such places, Stevenson & Wallis (1970) commented that, after spending two to six weeks in a fruitless search for a job,

he is likely to stop trying and to join a group of similarly discouraged friends at some common centre – often a café. There he will stay more or less permanently, only surfacing every so often to try for a few more jobs. If he does not succeed with the first few jobs he goes back to the café.

Obviously this sort of description sails perilously close to the stereotype, yet it is easy to imagine the common significance of such locales.

Much of the housing in Sandringham and the surrounding roads was in a derelict state and several itinerant shabeens would set up for a while before being shut down by the police. One local White resident who has kept meticulous records of the history of the road at this time, and who is overtly racist in his comments about young Black people, claimed that it was not unusual for over a hundred people to be milling about in a twenty- to thirty-yard area at the Johnston's end of the road (see Map 2.2) and "loud music" to go on through the night at shabeens and blues parties. Police would occasionally raid these premises and, by the mid-1970s, it was not unusual for fighting to break out as a result.

On 16 July 1975 in one such raid (with dogs) at the Four Aces Club on Dalston Lane, a few hundred metres from Sandringham Road, these clashes escalated into what was described at the time as "a battle" (*Race Today* 1975: 173) and several people were seriously injured. Later that summer similar fights occurred in Sandringham Road, as they did again several times over the next few years.

By the late 1970s Sandringham Road was already known as a Front Line. Over the same period of time groups of pickpockets (dippers) had begun to use Johnston's (JJ's) as a premises on which they could fence

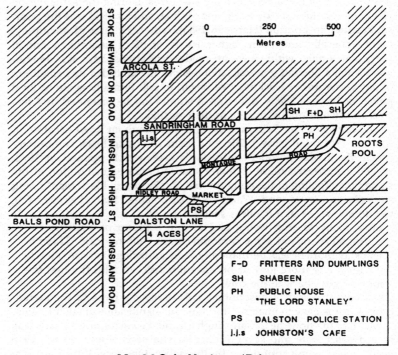

Map 2.2 Stoke Newington / Dalston.

stolen goods (particularly cheque books, cheque cards and cheap jewellery) and during the same period the area also became well known for the sale of cannabis. A level of "hustling" (see Hall et al. 1978, Pryce 1979) became a common, *if not a normal*, way of life. The road offered a series of, sometimes transient, locales for people to pass the time twenty-four hours a day: by the early 1980s JJ's, Fritters & Dumplings take away, the Lord Stanley pub and several shabeens, dance halls and youth clubs lay within a few hundred yards of one another. Subtle variations developed between locales (e.g. JJ's clientele tended to be older than those at Fritters), but together, particularly when perceived from outside, they formed an organic whole; "the Sandringham Road scene" that existed alongside residual, sometimes resentful, White residents who would at times lay claim to the title of being the true Sandringham Road "community".

It is impossible to assess accurately the attitude to Sandringham Road of the rest of the Black community in Hackney at this time (pre-1981),

SANDRINGHAM ROAD, HACKNEY

although it would clearly be an empirical, moral and logical error to assume that there was any single "Black perception". Many of the more politically active knew that the place was a site for clashes between police and local Black people, yet many of the older members of the Black community went on record as regarding the road and the clashes that occurred there with some ambivalence; having great sympathy with the plight of the younger generation, but talking of JJ's and some of the shabeens with great suspicion. Indeed, in a submission to the Scarman Inquiry, the Caribbean House Group, based in Hackney, suggested that

> The situation in Hackney is just as bad as in Brixton and it is certainly worse than in St Paul's, Bristol. The miracle is that in Hackney there have been so few incidents up to now.

With reference to the sort of social scene in Sandringham Road, there was the suggestion that

> Many parents cannot understand why the police refuse to do anything to stop these Black clubs preying on children and destroying them in this way. The police that refuse to withdraw their presence at times of disorder, are the same police that treat these clubs as "no-go areas".

Again there is only a suggestion that this sort of analysis was one perception of places such as Sandringham Road.

It was in this context that the summer of 1981 witnessed major clashes between police and a predominantly Black group of people in Sandringham Road (see Ch. 7 for greater detail). The riots of 1981 are best seen as one event in the evolution of this "place". The rioting became a watershed in the history of the road, but not an unexpected watershed. The confrontation was one "battle" among many, the most violent clash experienced but not surprising in its arrival.

In the wake of the disturbances, Sandringham Road received special police attention, including the controversial use of dogs to patrol the road, a policy that produced many complaints and a political furore. Similarly, when a young Black man, Colin Roach, shot himself in Stoke Newington police station, the police version of events was considered inadequate locally, reflecting and amplifying local hostility towards the police. The renown of Stoke Newington police station itself continued to grow with revelations concerning drug trading levelled against the station in the early 1990s.

Roots Pool

One of the many places on Sandringham Road that served as a community focus was Roots Pool. In 1982 several of the younger Black people who spent much of their time in the road squatted in number 144,

CONTESTED FICTIONS

about 100–150 yards down the road from JJ's, and close to two shabeens which were operating at the time. The borough council managed to persuade them to leave this council flat, in return allowing them to occupy three derelict shop premises at numbers 165, 167 and 169, farther down the road. Here they set up Dalston Community Centre, generally known as Roots Pool.

After the council repossessed numbers 165 and 167, 169 was gutted by a petrol bomb attack (10 July 1984). The council offered temporary use of an old synagogue in Montague Road, which was accepted, and the club remained there for several years in spite of an long-running dispute with the council and the possibility of a further move just up the road to Arcola Street. The difficulties faced by the community centre could be said to display in microcosm the history of what the Metropolitan Police have labelled a "symbolic location".

Even in the supposed anonymity of the twentieth-century city a neighbourhood can still exert a powerful formative influence on all communities. So perhaps it should have been no surprise to find in interviews that, for many people working at Roots Pool in 1986, knowledge of relations between Black people and the police remained structured much more by local lived experience than by higher-profile events which had received national media attention (Keith 1986).

There was surprisingly little knowledge of events in other parts of London, even when these events meant a great deal to the people using the centre. Broadwater Farm Estate was only a couple of miles up the road, yet at the time of research there was no contact at community worker level between the Youth Association there and Roots Pool. However, if local knowledge was spatially circumscribed, it was, in equal measure, temporally extensive. Without exception, all people interviewed, both formally and informally, told stories of first- and second-hand experiences with the police (Keith 1986). The various raids people had witnessed taking place on Sandringham Road, as far back as the early 1970s, particularly when dogs were used, were not forgotten. More obviously, the whole set of rationalizations and understandings that make up the "common sense" of any group was dominated by the bitter personal experience of Black Britain in the 1970s and 1980s, for some ordered by the Rastafarian faith. Rasta "reasoning", as with all belief systems, makes a "sense" out of "reality" and the two principal social workers at Roots Pool accounted for all local events in terms of Rasta cosmology. The police in particular were seen in conspiratorial alliance with the malevolent state.

The police attitude towards Roots Pool in the mid-1980s was characterized by a certain ambivalence. At one time in 1985 an official internal police memo commented on the police records that "their main pre-

SANDRINGHAM ROAD, HACKNEY

occupation was dealing in drugs".

However, the same analysis also distinguished the centre from JJ's, the Lord Stanley, Fritters & Dumplings and the shabeens, which were all rationalized as purely criminal enterprises. After their move to the synagogue, another report suggested that Roots Pool made efforts to restrict their membership and "without doubt have made efforts to obey the law and deny access to 'fugitives'." (1985, private correspondence).

By 1986 senior police tried to formulate a policy by which the centre was encouraged to act as the arena for the legitimate social functions of Front Line, while removing the other "locales" altogether. To this end, Sir Kenneth Newman was photographed handing over a cheque of police funds to "Sir" Collins, treasurer of Roots Pool.

The example is important because it raises so many of the perennial questions that recur in attempts to foster benevolent police–community relations. It also ultimately demonstrates how unanswerable some of these questions remain. Such a policy at one remove might readily be described as manifest co-optation. Yet ethically the policy was based on a pragmatic reaction to a particular belief in *the rule of law*. This may involve a notion of law that is not necessarily shared by this author. But it does not detract from the fact that, although acknowledging the major issues raised by such patronage, and acknowledging the potential invidious effects of such a policy, the pragmatism of two senior officers in particular contributed substantially to the transformation of the symbols connoted by Roots Pool and the creation of an arena in which minor confrontations might be defused before they escalated into major clashes. Moreover, it would be foolish to underestimate the significance of individual actions in such a policy by any suggestion that this strategy commanded the universal support of all local police. In the mid-1980s there were clear distinctions made between different officers from both Dalston and Stoke Newington police stations.

At this time many in the drug squad at Stoke Newington believed that "serious drugs" were sold on the premises and, maintaining a wholly negative view of Roots Pool, frequently put pressure on senior officers to mount major and regular raids on the club. At different times during the research described in Chapters 7 and 8, two PCs were later to try and persuade me that the people there, that I had spent time with, were no less than nascent mafiosi. Although there was a possibility that I was deceived by the Roots Pool staff in such matters, I believe that this was extremely unlikely. Nobody would question that "ganja" was smoked openly by many in the centre, including some of the staff. I never saw any evidence of harder drugs on the premises.

Two things were most striking about the relations between police and

CONTESTED FICTIONS

the people using the centre. The first stems from the relationship between "officials" and "clientele" there. At one time Michael Muirhead, then chair of the centre, explained:

White (then an Inspector at Dalston station) comes in here, turns around and says, "Look we've been good to you. Now you have got to go and stop them dealing in drugs out there" [the courtyard of the synagogue]. First he's got no right to come stamping in here like that. Second, he doesn't understand that if I go out there I can't just tell the brethren what to do. We sometimes have a hundred to two hundred people here at one time and there is only six staff. This is their centre, I'm not some sort of boss. I don't even know some of these people. (personal interview)

The idea that a "community leader" such as Michael Muirhead sits at the head of a pyramidally structured collection of people is obviously dangerously mistaken, just as is the idea that "only one type of person uses Roots Pool" (PC, personal interview). It is the failure to recognize this diversity and the naïvete in the assumptions of both police and council about the power of community leaders that led to a common, homogenized, stereotypical view of Sandringham Road. When such stereotypes are placed in the context of a raid on such a premises, the results have only to be imagined.

Linked to this problem was the standing of those involved at the centre who were prepared to talk to the police. Michael Muirhead at one time explained that, whenever there was any trouble with the police, he was subjected to extreme criticism by many of the young Black people at the centre. Yet he was also well aware that his actions in taking the side of some of the people at the centre against the police had made him, in the eyes of many PCs and other ranks, "a trouble-maker". As a result he found himself in a very precarious position, knowing full well that at a time of outright confrontation there would be no fence to sit on.

Yet the position of Roots Pool within the social fabric of the community locally continued to be a cause of controversy. By the late 1980s, negotiations with the police eventually led to the Club being used in a highly symbolic manner for meetings of the controversial Hackney Police Community Consultative Group, due in large part to the pragmatism of certain senior officers at Stoke Newington police station. Ironically, one of the principal sites of resistance in the early 1980s was by 1988 being picketed by those groups who resented the legitimacy conferred upon the process of consultation. It would take an arrogant commentator to pass judgement on these dramatic changes, but such a phenomenon certainly highlights the fact that notions of co-optation are sometimes more complicated in practice than they appear in prin-

OPERATION LUCY AND THE SCOTLAND YARDIES?

ciple. Equally significantly, the place of Roots Pool in the complex mosaic of the Front Line illustrates the complexity of functions the road served. Any suggestion that the whole of Sandringham Road was no more than what Kenneth Newman catalogued as a lawless frontier became risible in the light of the constructive work going on in Roots Pool.

Crime on Sandringham Road

By the mid-1980s there was undoubtedly a great deal of what is, strictly speaking, "criminal activity" on Sandringham Road, yet this generic term covers a multitude of different repertoires of behaviour. During research for this work it was obviously impossible to produce any kind of accurate picture. Certainly, cannabis is smoked openly, and frequently people come some distance to buy it; harder drugs were on offer, although not ostentatiously so. As early as 1985 it was alleged that organized crime groups (including early mentions of "the Yardies") had tried to "move in" on the drugs trade in the area. It is almost certain that in recent years one pub on the road has been used as a site for the sale of firearms, and that there have been extremely violent clashes between members of different gangs on the road (several stabbings and possibly one shooting). What was stressed by many of the local Black community was that this serious crime was very different from the fencing which was at one time also common (particularly at Johnston's), and that both serious and petty crime involved only a minority of the people who use the road as a social centre. There were several major raids on the road in the late 1980s, most notably in August 1987 when Roots Pool was forced to close down for a period of cooling off. If relations between Roots Pool staff and the police improved throughout the 1980s, the tension between the police and people using Sandringham Road barely dissipated.

Operation Lucy and the Scotland Yardies?

In early 1988 a series of sensationalist and malevolent tabloid press stories suggested the existence of an organized crime organization in Britain, known as the Yardies, run by people of Jamaican background. The alleged evolution of a Black mafia in Britain was described in the purple prose of Fleet Street, and the stories were commonly focused on one particular individual in Stoke Newington.

After press pressure, a special squad was set up in Scotland Yard (Operation Lucy) to investigate the prevalence and form of organized

CONTESTED FICTIONS

Black crime in Britain. Predictably, the press took this as a legitimation of the hyperbole of the headlines, and the popular imagery of Black mafiosi was firmly established on the popular media agenda of 1988. Yet beyond the manifest obscenity of press irresponsibility, there are certain features of this phenomenon that tie the local significance of events in Hackney to the interest of national media.

First, there was obviously a very real sense in which the racism of the popular press was instrumental in the creation of yet another invidious stereotype, another racist folk devil in the tradition of the pimp, the mugger and the rioter. The notion of a commonly held image of Black communities as hotbeds of organized villainy is quite clearly dangerous and a potential medium through which a whole generation of Black British people might be cast as criminals in the eyes of the majority. It may well transpire that the path of further criminalization of Black communities has been laid down by such stories.

Secondly, the relation between police and press was not always so clear cut as might be assumed. It would be wrong to assume that the police intentionally collaborated in purveying this melodramatic stereotype, however culpable they may have been for failing to tackle the distortions of press reportage. Significantly, Chief Superintendent Frank Wilkinson of Dalston chose, early in the panic, to hold a meeting at Roots Pool to try and reassure the local community.

To the credit of those involved in Operation Lucy, they were well aware and well briefed on the possibilities of creating a moral panic for the 1990s. Individual journalists from the *Daily Mail* and other tabloids, who had printed sensationalist stories, were given open briefings by the squad's senior officers and yet these served only to feed further the dramatic news coverage. This was compounded at a local level by the manner in which such stereotypes were rapidly taken on board as a means for some officers to rationalize particular police operations. During a visit to Dalston police station in August 1988, for a Radio 4 documentary based on Hackney, the team were briefed about a raid on a particular club where, the duty sergeant suggested, "There is probably a Yardie connection. We've been given a name". (Wilko's Weekly, BBC Radio 4, 8 August 1988)

The club concerned, the Four Aces, had long been a focus of conflict, as the 1975 incident alluded to illustrates. Operations against the club continued throughout the late 1980s, most notably Operation Full House in February 1988. The proprietor of the club, Newton Dunbar, was subsequently cleared of drugs charges. Even though Roy Ramm of Operation Lucy had briefed the *Daily Mail*, and by this stage was trying to play down the tabloid excesses, the paper chose to cite the club as one of the principal Yardie haunts, and the club was raided 13 times in

42

the next year.

Subsequently, police campaigned against renewal of the club's license. In the context of the deep-rooted antagonism a certain sense of scores being settled was certainly evidenced in interviews with some officers at this time. (Eventually the Four Aces closed down only to reappear as a haunt of White-dominated new wave music in the 1990s.)

So, in contrast, while at one public meeting a couple of months earlier the new Chief Superintendent of Stoke Newington police station, Peter Twist, was keen to stress the dangers of "the Yardies scare" being used as a justification for any police operation involving Black communities, his own junior officers were doing precisely this on national radio, lending credibility to the notion of "Yardies" and an apparently authorized rationalization for particular police actions.

Similarly, the co-ordination between a centralized squad and local management may not be quite the model of bureaucratic efficiency. In mid-1988 at a raid in Stoke Newington, in which the squad were involved, some of the most extreme front-page press coverage (e.g. *Sun*, *Daily Telegraph*, 15 April 1988) resulted from a local management insistence that press photographers should be present during the raid. Senior officers in Operation Lucy reasoned that they wanted to keep all operations low-key, but a local preference for "openness" allowed access to the raid to a press corps who, perhaps predictably, abused all privileges by creating a reportage in the next day's papers of imaginative and racist fiction.

Following on from this, a third lesson to be learnt might be taken from the justification offered for Operation Lucy by the senior officer involved in the squad. In a private interview he suggested that, *a priori*, all communities are involved in organized crime to some extent and, because so little was known about the sort of crime particular to Black communities, the squad served a key information gathering purpose. Put simply, he suggested, "We just don't know what goes on in Sandringham Road". Paradoxically, the police diagnosis of their own ignorance was, in another light, a candid reflection of the degree to which relations between police and Black communities generally were at such an abysmal level that there was a near absence of flow of reliable information. It is no more than a policing truism to suggest that a police force is only as good as the information it receives, and in this particular case a dangerous vacuum had developed in the place of communicative exchange, a vacuum which could readily be filled with the melodramatic imagery of pulp fiction.

The individual who was cast as a prime mafiosi both by the *Daily Mail* and by a subsequent, equally irresponsible, edition of the Cook Report on ITV, had operated primarily from Sandringham Road for a

CONTESTED FICTIONS

considerable period of time, and was rumoured to be involved in various forms of unpleasant activity, but was certainly no major figure in syndicated crime. Ignorant, or at least largely uninformed, about the reality of Sandringham Road, the police were in no position to answer the malevolence of racist tabloid journalism with anything other than vague assurances and *de jure* silences.

The reality of organized Black crime in Stoke Newington remained uncertain, although stories and rumour abounded and the police campaign achieved a high profile. In the ironic terms of a T-shirt logo popular on Ridley Road market at this time, everyone knew about the existence of "Scotland Yardies", even if the influence of their Jamaican namesakes was moot.

All Saints Road, Notting Hill

Background history

Possibly more than any other place in Britain, Notting Hill has witnessed in microcosm the full history of Caribbean settlement in Britain. Throughout this work, Notting Hill is not examined in anything like the same detail as the two other locations. The superficial analysis here appeared worthwhile because of the metaphoric linkages between all three sites. In the 1950s the area of cheap multi-rental property in North Kensington, close to Portobello Road, became a favoured settlement destination for West Indian migrants. The welcome they received ranged from the pernicious activity of the notorious landlord Rackman, who owned 147 properties in the area, to the steadily increasing number of racist attacks by the local Teddy Boys (Fryer 1984, Pilkington 1988), and the marches of Mosley's fascists in the streets.

By the summer of 1958 the attacks were so common that in one week more than 30 were noted by the local police in North Kensington alone. As "nigger hunting" reached a peak in the August of that year, a Jamaican was shot in the leg and there were several petrol-bomb arson attacks on West Indian homes. With racial clashes in Nottingham over the weekend of the 23/24 August, the tension spilled over into serious but isolated incidents of inter-racial fighting, much exaggerated by the press (Miles 1984b), but including a retaliatory petrol-bomb attack on a fascist club by West Indians trying to organize the defence of their own community. These Notting Hill "race riots" continued to bubble into occasional street clashes for the first half of September, and were echoed in other parts of London, but the incident that was to make a lasting impression locally occurred eight months later, when the situa-

44

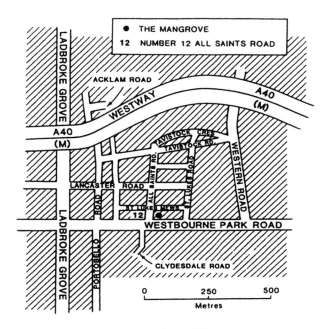

Map 2.3 Notting Hill.

tion had appeared to calm down. In May 1959 Kelso Cochrane, a West Indian carpenter, was stabbed to death in Notting Hill. No murderer was ever found and it would be a mistake to believe that the case is even now forgotten. The resentment at police treatment before and during the 1958 "riots" and the failure to find Cochrane's killer soured relations between the police and the West Indian community; the overt racism with which migrants were treated by both White public and White police made matters even worse. Pansey Jeffrey, working at the Citizen's Advice Bureau at this time, commented,

> From 1959 to 1961 we at the Citizen's Advice Bureau found it difficult to believe the behaviour of the police which appeared from stories told to us by callers who came to us for advice. Then it began to seem that there must be some substance to these stories. (Evidence submitted to the 1971 House of Commons Select Committee on Police Immigrant Relations, henceforth Evidence 1971).

The situation deteriorated rapidly throughout the 1960s. In 1969 Tony Leander, a local youth worker, took a survey of 130 young Black people in Notting Hill and found that out of this group 60 per cent felt that relationships between police and Black youth were "very bad" and almost 60 per cent had already been arrested; the most common char-

CONTESTED FICTIONS

ges were loitering and obstruction/assault, two of the more subjectively assessed forms of "criminal" behaviour. He concluded that, "the expectation of Black youths in the area is that they run a high risk of being arrested". George Clark of the West London Fair Housing Trust said of this period,

> The generality might be taken from the Portobello Road. Between the years 1966 and 1969 the youngsters were really exploring the area and finding their own territories . . . One remembers scarcely a day passed without a plea from the black youngsters, "We are being harassed. We are being moved on. We are being picked up." Indeed they were picked up, that was not say so, and they were being moved on and they were being harassed. (Evidence 1971)

Contact with the police came about in four arenas, all structured by the racist treatment of Caribbean migrants generally, all stemming from the group's position in White society. Overcrowded housing encouraged many young Black men to leave home when still young, and this shiftless, often jobless, population could rely only on shelters such as the one at 57 Acklam Road (North Kensington), which were often seen as crucibles of delinquency. Those who had nowhere to go were often in trouble for loitering; those who went somewhere were often in trouble at youth clubs such as the Sunspot or the High Street Wimpy bar. Lastly, there were the drinking clubs that similarly provided sites of confrontation. Each of these four arenas placed the police inevitably at odds with West Indian people, but also provided a forum for racist behaviour under the guise of law enforcement, an opportunity that too often was not missed.

Black Power and the Mangrove Restaurant

It was in this climate of increasing hostility, and in the wake of the contemporary American disorders, that the Black Power movement briefly flowered in London. Michael de Freitas (Michael Abdul-Malik, Michael X) established the RAAS (the Racial Adjustment Action Society); the Universal Black People's Improvement Association (including Darcus, then Radford, Howe) set up in Notting Hill and several cells of the Black Panthers were also founded (see Abdul-Malik 1967). The national press and the Metropolitan Police reacted to these associations with virtual paranoia, at what they saw as incipient subversion and revolution. The focus of this paranoia was the Mangrove Restaurant in All Saints Road (see *Police* magazine, January 1970). Set up in 1969 by Frank Critchlow, who had run several similar restaurants in London before, the place soon became well known for political discussion but was hardly a seedbed of "the revolution". Yet the police regularly raided the Mangrove from its opening, never arresting anyone or

ALL SAINTS ROAD, NOTTING HILL

pressing charges against the proprietor, but establishing a symbolic vendetta that has persisted to the present day. As Darcus Howe commented, the Mangrove

> opened as a meeting place for ourselves and others where we could discuss issues that we face . . . the Mangrove is quite different from what it was then. Today it has become a centre of resistance to police harassment, a black centre of resistance. We did not set out to make it like that, the police did. And that is not how we see ourselves, that is how black people see us. It is now a political fact that we are what we are because of certain experiences of black people in the area [Notting Hill]." (Evidence 1971)

Again, it would be wrong to equate the struggles of the Mangrove with the ubiquitous and dubious term "Black youth". In fact Ben Bousquet, one-time Labour Party candidate in the area, worked for Lambeth Police Support Unit but lives and grew up in Notting Hill and keeps a detailed local history of the area. He pointed out in a formal interview that the Mangrove was always known as the haunt of older, politically active people, not teenagers like himself at this time. Younger people tended to congregate instead at the youth clubs, another site of confrontation; a raid at the Metro Youth Club in Notting Hill led to serious clashes with the police in 1970. Following the repeated raids on the Mangrove (all with no charges pressed), an informal protest group banded together under the name "Action Group for the Defence of the Mangrove" and mounted a demonstration on 9 August 1970, demanding "an end to the persecution of the Mangrove restaurant", which also developed into a confrontation with the police. After the incident *Race Today* (1970: 456) commented:

> There is a tension hitherto unknown. The police, the Black community insist, are out to kill the Mangrove and other centres where Blacks get together."

Further marches followed the Black Defence Committee support of the Mangrove 9, the nine people arrested at the first demonstration, which culminated in 22 of the charges against the group (who included both Critchlow and Howe) being dismissed and only seven minor counts proven. The Mangrove was firmly established as the focus of police/Black conflict in All Saints Road, Notting Hill, the site on which control of the streets would be disputed.

Carnival

The salience of Notting Hill Carnival in the evolution of the conflict between police and British Black communities is hard to underestimate. There is no intention here of even beginning to describe the evolution of Carnival as a symbolic encapsulation of so much in Black British life

CONTESTED FICTIONS

(Cohen 1980, 1982, Edgar 1988, Gutzmore 1982, Jackson 1989, Pryce 1985) from celebration to quite explicit forms of resistance to oppression. However, some of the connections between perceptions of Carnival and notions of "disorder" are tackled in Chapter 6.

Drugs

Throughout the 1980s All Saints Road was known as a site for drug sales. How extensive such sales were, and how important this road was, as opposed to other well known locations where drugs were available, is more controversial. What was certainly the case was that the road was always very much more than an illicit market place. After a period of relative quiet in the mid-1980s a series of high-profile campaigns against drug dealing, such as Operation Trident in 1987 and Operation Mint in 1989, provoked further clashes on All Saints Road (Dorn et al. 1991). In the late 1980s and early 1990s, police in Notting Hill suffered a series of embarrassments as a number of cases initiated between 1984 and 1989 came to a head together and resulted in compensation of £100,000 (later reduced to £65,000) being paid to Robert Taylor (a teetotal lay preacher), in December 1989; an out-of-court settlement of £18,000 to Michael and Dennis Hayes; £3,500 to Vincent Lee for wrongful imprisonment and malicious prosecution in November 1989; and £20,000 in an out-of-court settlement with trainee accountant Hughie Wilson in March 1990. This was compounded by the high-profile arrest, trial and acquittal of Frank Critchlow on drugs charges. In 1992 Critchlow later received a five-figure sum as compensation in an out-of-court settlement. All cases were accompanied by allegations of planting of drugs.

Conclusion

In a comment in *Talking Blues*, already cited in Chapter 1, Roger Graef (1990: 76) describes the Handsworth uprising of 1985 as an event that was surprising in an area previously noted for good community relations. There is a semantic slippage here that is significant. The term "community relations" performs two rôles: ostensibly it is a comment on racial harmony, but "we", the reader, know that underneath it really means police/Black conflict. The slippage is invidious in that it excludes the possibility of the former existing alongside the latter. It is exemplary in the manner in which it captures a place through a single organizing trope: a place is defined by the meanings it connotes.

In order to avoid this tendency, it bears repeating that this work does

48

CONCLUSION

not attempt a definitive reconstruction of the complexity of British Black history that is so often unmentioned in social analysis. Rather, the intention is to pick up the historical dimension of just one theme that runs throughout this narrative; the manner in which the relationship between police and Black communities has been structured by social constructions of crime and civil unrest.

By a wholly incomplete selection of events, the suggestion is that the uprisings of the 1980s cannot be understood without causal reference to the portrayal of young Blacks as muggers, and Black communities as sources of resistance to the police prerogative in the 1970s, which cannot be understood without reference to the policing of Black political protest and social centres in the late 1960s, which cannot be understood without reference to the sordid details of "nigger hunting" and racial attacks in the early 1960s, which cannot be understood without reference to the social construction of Black communities as a pathological intrusion into British civilization in the 1950s and before. Only connect.

History is a continually reconstructed social product, a story through which the past is recounted in a way that renders the present comprehensible. Hence there are volumes to be written of all the perceptions and counter-memories at each of the three locations cited in this chapter. These unwritten histories might well disagree, possibly with each other, probably with the reading of events here. A single reality does not prohibit the existence of a multiplicity of valid but contradictory histories (and "herstories"). Consequently, the chapter has attempted only to set a scene in the most crude of senses, to stake a claim for the significance of the past in structuring the present, rather than provide an authoritative account of lost times.

These locations amounted to much more than any account here could offer. They had rich histories which were not in any way reducible to a reassuring narrative of police oppression. Yet in highlighting them as sites of confrontation, I am defining these parts of London as *places*. Such definition works as an act of closure which momentarily excludes alternative meaning. This moment of exclusion is as strategically essential as it is temporary. Alternative readings of the same parts of London were, and are, equally legitimate. The strategic point of the reading of the past used here is simple; to subvert the official memory resonant in Kenneth Newman's account of the same locations with which the chapter opened. An array of contentious issues, emblematic of the institutional racism of White society generally, were played out in these three locations. *All* of these events precipitated conflict and confrontation with the local police, *almost none* of them had anything to do with thieving or any form of serious criminal activity.

Conflict between the police and the local Black community is one of

CONTESTED FICTIONS

many organizing themes that help make sense of the past in these places. They were the stages on which the *danse macabre* of police/Black confrontation was to be played out over decades. These stages did not just bear witness to such events; they were defined by them and in turn gave them meaning. They were the sites in which confrontation became routinized.

Thus far the rhetorical intention is nothing more contentious than the suggestion that the history of a place becomes inscribed in the lives of people who live and work there. The closure that operates in Newman's statement draws its rhetorical power from the connotation of incipient anarchy, the latent image is that of riotous Britain. The provenance of this rhetorical power can be traced back to the disorders of the 1980s, and in Part Two of this book the source of this imagery is examined in greater detail before returning to these three same locations to analyze how the spatialized reproduction of conflict through time structured policing practice.

PART TWO

1981: THAT SUMMER *IN LONDON*

CHAPTER 3

Shaggy dog riots and copycat rioters: the "riots" in London as a moral panic

It is useful to begin in the summer of 1981, even if that is not where everything started. For the truth is that any historical starting point is in part arbitrary, some more senseless than others, but none the definitive moment at which the spool of history began to unravel.

Yet to state this is not to underestimate the difficulties that immediately appear when the riots of 1981 are examined as anything more than a rhetorical watershed. In a sense, it was the outbreak of civil disturbance in Bristol in April 1980 that marked the beginning of a new era of race relations in Britain. The events in the St Paul's area of the city were a shock to the national consciousness, but it was not immediately clear whether this was a single aberration or a harbinger of change. It was the burning and looting twelve months later in Brixton and the explosions of anger and violence in July, August and September 1981, when it seemed that every British city was expecting "a riot", that was to show that Bristol was not an isolated event.

Yet even at this distance the significance and the causes of the disorders are not clear. To some they were the revolt of the underclass and a precursor of the revolution. To some they were race riots, to others they were youth riots or anti-police affrays. To some they were universal events, to others they were highly differentiated outbursts. To some they were a continuation of the American Black ghetto revolts of the 1960s, to others they were a response to a uniquely British situation. To some they were the mindless hooliganism of the unemployables, to others they were a protest against unemployment. Some saw working class insurrection, others criminal vandals enjoying themselves.

Certainly, the events of that year have been endowed with a common provenance and a historical unity by the classification of the past; by placing the violence of the year into the single pigeon-hole – "The riots

THE "RIOTS" IN LONDON AS A MORAL PANIC

of 1981". Yet the easily won status of "rioter" endows a group of people with a shared identity of which they themselves may be unaware, and initiates a clichéd ontological spiral: impressionistic reportage creates a descriptive unity ("the crowd"), reproduced in the hard print and received wisdom of those rarely present. In turn, "the crowd" comes alive and the label assumes the status of an analytical structure which lays claim to the vocabulary of animus; a mood, an identity, a purpose. Similarly, the labels of "riot", "uprising", "disorder", "rioter", "youth" and "criminal" assume meanings historically generated as much by their use as by any descriptive correspondence with real events and real people. The very language that is used to describe history is at once problematic and contested in both popular idiom and the supposedly more objective field of academic discourse.

For emotive, value-laden collective nouns such as "the rioter" or "the crowd" do not necessarily create powerful, or even useful, behavioural classes. Yet, paradoxically, by simple and repeated usage of the terms involved they become actual analytical or cultural phenomena.

This is the substance of the modern myth which "transforms history into nature" (Barthes 1973: 129; 1979) and results in the "oppressive divorce of knowledge and mythology" (Barthes 1979: 37). In this way many passages of history or social movements assume a double life. The contemporary context and the temporally distanced states of mind of the participants or actors, which constitute causes of behaviour, lie tangled up in hindsight justification and selective amnesia, and are overshadowed by the manner in which events have "burgeoned forth" in time. The result is the divergence of the "private" and "public" lives of a "parcel of history", with social reality on the one hand and cultural mythology on the other. Identifying the former and exposing the latter are complementary analytical tasks.[1]

There is no suggestion here that any such cultural phenomenon is in any way an inferior or specious object of analysis. Indeed, history is littered with incidents whose "public life" caused events more significant than those produced by their "private life". British humiliation at Dunkirk was transformed into a national triumph. The Gettysburg address may have had very minor material effect on a war but major ramifications in the more nebulous world of political symbolism. So too with the British "riots".

As a curtain raiser to the decade, the events of 1981 were to provide the symbolic raw material and the social pretext for debates that covered issues as diverse as deprivation, policing, racism, alienation, the putative wisdom of Enoch Powell and the perennial law-and-order controversy. This profound influence in structuring the political agenda for years that followed is undisputed, yet the evolution of this particular piece of common-sense public knowledge was less clear in its production and much more complex in its deployment than hindsight perception of "that summer" might suggest.

Cartography

Even the seemingly straightforward task of mapping the riots is problematic, for even the most well intentioned cartographic exercise is never innocent. Assumptions, definitions and systematic exclusions are all built into any representation which pretends to provide an exhaustive list of collective disorders in the summer of 1981.

Many agencies drew up lists of "places" which had experienced rioting in 1981. Many authors, having referred to the widespread nature of disorder, produced catalogues of riots, rarely claiming to be exhaustive but never agreeing one with another. Such lists matter. Not only do they reflect particular conceptions of disorder and preconceptions about specific locations, they may also have serious material effects on the lives of people living in places listed. It is at maps such as those shown below (Maps 3.1–4) that the local state looks when making crucial decisions about service provision: it is to these maps that central government refers when allocating resources and it is such lists that are filed and remembered by the insurance companies, banks and retail chains that, in part, determine the life-chances of local communities.

It is in this context that the rioting in 1981 lives on in a set of cultural accounts of the past that underwrite our understanding of the present. Historical reality must sit beside this "public life" of a "parcel of history", the manner in which a series of events is coloured by contemporary insight, at times confusing understanding. The two are not the same.

Of course the distinction between reality and cultural reconstruction is never quite so neat; the uprisings were from the first understood through pre-existing frames of reference. This raises questions concerning the relationship between public perception of events and the immediate reactions of specific groups of people. Publicity stemming from a particular instance of a problem may focus attention on similar, related events, creating the false impression of a sudden increase in the increase in the incidence of such a problem. Typically, in late 1985 a series of gruesome court cases connected with the mistreatment or murder of infants in Britain resulted in an observable increase in press coverage of the apparent increase in child abuse. Whether such an alarming trend actually existed or whether, instead, the cases were co-

Map 3.1 Riots in London, July 1981 (by location and Metropolitan Police District). *Source: Home Office Statistical Bulletin,* October 1982.

Map 3.2 Metropolitan Police public-order operations, July 1981 (by location and Metropolitan Police District). ○ 8/9 July (Wood Green, Lewisham, Woolwich, Hounslow, Tooting); ● 10/11 July (Brixton, Paddington, Fulham, Chingford, Stoke Newington, West Ham (Newham), Peckham (Southwark), Wembley (Brent), Hampstead, Southall, Croydon). *Source: Annual Report of the Commissioner of the Metropolitan Police* for the year 1981.

Map 3.3 Nine riots in London with highest arrest totals (by location and Metropolitan Police District). *Source: Home Office Statistical Bulletin*, October 1982.

Map 3.4 London riots, 1981 (by date, location and Metropolitan Police District. ○ 3–5 July (Southall, Wood Green, Paddington); ● 16–19 July (Southall, Wood Green, Paddington, Fulham, Hackney, Newham, Brixton, Southwark, Lewisham, Brent, Woolwich, Hounslow, Tooting). *Source: Home Office Statistical Bulletin*, October 1992.

CARTOGRAPHY

incidental, or produced by changes in detecting child abuse, was rarely discussed. This "creation" of a new "social problem" is the phenomenon that Stan Cohen (1972), in a study of Mods and Rockers in 1960s Britain, described as a "moral panic". His work has since been taken as paradigmatic by a great many studies that incorporate widely differing political stances, varying from Marsh's social psychological study of football hooliganism (Marsh et al. 1978) to the CCCS structuralist sociology of the British mugging "problem" in the 1970s (Hall et al. 1978).

Crucially, the success of such work hinges on an ability to identify the manner in which public knowledge (common perception) is generated, which structures discussion of, and reaction to, the moral panic. This is a particularly problematic task because the concept of public knowledge is so nebulous (Keith 1984) and the links between belief and action in this context so intangible, the implicit public/private distinction as contentious here as in all other uses of this dichotomy.

The confusion of cultural product and historical reality arises in the case of the British rioting in 1981 because media portrayal was quite clearly instrumental both in the creation of a moral panic; similar to the phenomenon identified by Cohen, and in endowing the different disorders with a unity that was not necessarily present. There was certainly a replication of an American fascination of the 1960s in which

> The continued media use of the term ("riot") contributes to an emotionally charged climate in which the public tends to view every event as an "incident", every incident as a "disturbance" and every disturbance as "a riot"." (Knopf, cited in Cohen 1972)

There were demonstrable instances of this process occurring during the summer of 1981, and major differences in the severity of disorder subsumed within the "lists" of riots already alluded to. Whether or not it was possible to distinguish without difficulty between genuine riots and mere manifestations of copycat hooliganism, as was often claimed at the time, is a different matter, not to be confused with this process. Nor is it the purpose of this chapter to re-examine the ideological basis of the creation of the media images of rioting, only to recognize their significance.

Media portrayal of "the rioter" fits perfectly Cohen's definition of the folk-devil, a symbolic threat to establishment society. Crucially, the riot was always implicitly, and at times explicitly, classified as an expression of irrational behaviour, "A wave of horror" (*Daily Mail*, 9 July 1981). Events are classified by preconception, self-evidently anarchic. Nevertheless, our instinctive scorn at tabloid imagery should be tempered by the similarity between such barely hidden polemic and some of the more facile assumptions made in academic treatment of disorder (Keith

57

1987; Ch. 4 below).

More significantly, as part of such a bestial crowd, the rioter as irrational folk-devil was invariably the object of easy manipulation. The folk-devil lived in headlines such as, "SEARCH FOR MASKED MEN" (*Daily Mail*, 7 July 1981), "EXTREMISTS MASTER PLAN FOR CHAOS" (*Daily Mail*, 10 July 1981) and "PLAYGROUND RENT A RIOT" (*Sun*, 7 July 1981). Such images are, in their deployment, clearly metonymic – single items which represent a wider set of values, rationalizations and conceptions. This distorted mirror of media reportage provides an easy target for attack and these latent meanings have already been analyzed effectively elsewhere (CCCS 1982a, Murdock 1984, Burgess 1985). A moral panic clearly characterized many of the official reactions to civil disorder, yet a more interesting question remains – to what extent did this moral panic determine the actions of those involved at first hand with the novel possibility of rioting.

The most crude formulation of possible influences stemmed from the related debates on the effect of violence on television. Clutterbuck (1983) claimed that "the thirty-eight separate riots" which followed the news coverage of rioting in Liverpool and Southall on 3 July "can have no possible explanation other than the copycat phenomenon". The notion that the sight of violence prompts young people to "go forth and imitate" lacks a superficial credibility, the more so given Tumber's (1982) claim that most rioters did not even find out about rioting through television or press. Nevertheless, such an argument is as difficult to falsify as it is to substantiate, as the inconclusive, if substantial, literature on the subject would imply.

More convincing evidence is available to describe the effect of common conceptions of the rioting on the behaviour of other agencies and individuals. Most notable among these groups were the police. Murdock (1984) has suggested that news coverage of the early rioting may have

> primed them [the police] to expect trouble in major cities and strengthened their resolve to crack down on it early by stepping up their activities in inner-city areas.

Two factors compromise such generalization. One is that in 1981 there was no single police reaction, in London at least, to the initial rioting in Liverpool and Southall. Policy over the early period of July, in relation to possible "cracking down", was principally formulated at the level of Chief Superintendents in charge of individual stations and Commanders in charge of London's twenty-four police districts under the old administrative arrangements. There were clear variations in police reaction throughout London, although the meaning of the riots for streetline constables was not necessarily the same as that for senior police officers. Moreover, a second problem stems from the impossibility of quantifying the relative importance of public knowledge and private or professional experience in forming police interpretation of the "Toxteth" and Southall disorders.

A factor rarely acknowledged is that for any one event the significance of the reconstruction of the past as a public event is, *a priori*, in inverse proportion to the level of relevant experience (see Diagram 3.1). Fleet Street imagery is most likely to be taken literally on issues about which the reader knows nothing at all. In this sense, it would seem probable that Murdock exaggerates the influence of media reportage on the police.

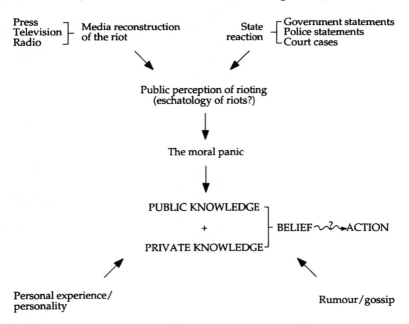

Diagram 3.1 The comparative performance of the reconstruction of the riot as a public event and introspection/personal experience will always remain impossible to assess. Similarly, beliefs are not always susceptible to generalization, particularly when they are beliefs of the past, as opposed to hindsight rationalizations. Only the actions that flow from this process can be *observed*; the link between belief and action is always contingent, and that between action and public knowledge is always crucial but nebulous.

SHAGGY DOG RIOTS AND COPYCAT RIOTERS

On closer inspection, what is apparent from police action is a series of implicit conceptions of conflict in London that can be more easily related to the local histories of the areas concerned than to public knowledge of rioting. The reality of "disorder" at several locations in London supports this point. In Lewisham in the 1970s there had been a rapid deterioration in relations between the police and the Black community which was closely related to the use of the SPG in the area on several occasions for operations of "saturation policing" (see Hain 1979, Scarman 1981) and apparent police "protection" of National Front marches. One march had resulted in serious disorder in 1977. Tension in the borough was particularly high in the spring of 1981 because of the local deaths of thirteen Black youngsters in the New Cross fire. The incident, widely believed to be the result of a racist attack, had assumed a symbolism of national significance.

According to several lists of the 1981 riots (see Appendix I), including those of the Home Office and the Commissioner of the Metropolitan Police, Lewisham was one of the places in London that experienced rioting in the summer of 1981. Yet although there were some isolated, minor clashes between very small groups of Black people and the police, with eighteen arrests made, there was no serious collapse of public order. Indeed, Asquith Gibbs, head of Lewisham Council for Community Relations, went so far as to make a public statement congratulating Commander J Smith of P District for the success of "community policing" by home beat officers in the borough at this time. There was no riot, but there had been anticipation of a riot by the local police and they had prepared their force accordingly, cancelling leave and drawing up contingency plans for disorder.

Local history and the contemporary context suggested particular patterns of possible trouble and the police frequently responded with a symbolic and ostentatious presence in a town centre. In parts of London, such as Dalston, Wood Green, Battersea and Fulham, many shopkeepers reported that they had been told by their local police constable that disorder was expected (Keith 1986). It was not always clear whether such warnings arose from personal initiative and individual interpretations of the phenomenon of rioting, or whether instead they were the result of instructions from senior police officers. Certainly there is evidence of the latter in Walthamstow where senior police asked Unigate Dairies not to deliver milk from the 10 to 12 July, and in Hackney where local shops were "advised" to shut early on the Saturday afternoon of the same weekend. It is not easy to evaluate such forward planning by the police. For the sympathetic, pre-emptive "heavy" policing was always justified. Either police presence was needed where there was disorder or accredited with preventing trouble

SHAGGY DOG RIOTS

if there was not. Several local papers, in areas of London that were "quiet", congratulated senior officers in this way.

Equally, for those less willing to give police the benefit of the doubt, the police were blamed for those disorders that did occur. Perhaps more significantly, police conceptions of disorder are revealed by the nature and geography of forward planning in the anticipation of violent clashes, anticipation that almost invariably highlighted the particular places renowned for confrontations between police and the local Black community.

One unavoidable effect of this process is that the Home Office list of "major incidents of public disorder" is, in part, as much a police index of London's trouble spots as a catalogue of locations of riots. This list in turn reproduces and reinforces common classification of parts of London; a form of criminalization by area that may act cumulatively as the "hot spot" is subjected to the sort of intensive policing that may itself result in a deterioration of police–community relations locally. Paradigmatically, beliefs cause action, regardless of their accuracy. This stigmatization of space was clearly manifested in the complaint of two shopkeepers in Lewisham who, in 1982, described how, after the alleged rioting in their area, their insurance had been doubled because they were now considered a particularly high risk (Keith 1986).

The neat categorizations of disorder in terms of simple presence/ absence was shadowed by a much more complex reality that can be readily seen in the experiences of just four of the places that were listed by the Home Office, all locations that allegedly experienced riots in the summer of 1981.

Shaggy dog riots

West Ham (10 and 11 July 1981)

Though featuring in the Home Office catalogue of places that experienced serious disorder in the summer of 1981, it is tendentious to describe the arrests connected with public-order offences in one London borough as occurring at a single "location". Even the Home Office classification is not quite sure of the name of this "place", sometimes referring to it as Newham (the borough), at other times as West Ham (Home Office Statistical Unit 1982). The disturbances that did occur at this one "location" were in reality scattered across the borough of Newham, in Forest Gate, in Upton Park and in East Ham, with West Ham proper remaining relatively peaceful. Symptomatic of this dispersed pattern, three different police stations were involved that weekend. The rioting that did occur was not greatly dissimilar from the trouble that follows a big match at Upton Park football ground. On

61

SHAGGY DOG RIOTS AND COPYCAT RIOTERS

Friday night (10 July) several incidents were closely related to crowds leaving pubs at closing time. One group in High Street North, East Ham, was broken up by the police; another group, estimated by the police to consist of about "twenty young men", began throwing some bottles at a police car outside the Queens pub in Upton Park. The latter group were moved on into Green Street where a dozen shop windows were smashed but no looting occurred. Similarly, the one incident in West Ham itself consisted of "a gang of about forty skinheads" (police statement) coming out of the Pigeons pub in Ranelagh Road and throwing a few bricks at two policemen. The crowd was broken up and four arrests were made. Later that night the crowd that remained in Green Street in Upton Park was involved in the most serious local incident of the weekend outside the Ace cinema.

One, or possibly two, petrol bombs were thrown at police (accounts differ) and five people were arrested and charged with Violence Against the Person (VAP). Perhaps significantly, four out of the five were Black and one was Asian. At this point the crowd was broken up and by 2.30am the streets were quiet.

On the Saturday there was further evidence of the rumour and anticipation of trouble so common throughout London, and again these expectations were not fulfilled. West Ham Park was shut down, shopkeepers spent part of their day boarding up their property and then reported a fall of between 40–60 per cent on normal Saturday trade, and the Newham Recorder (16 July 1981) felt moved to describe Forest Gate and West Ham as "ghost towns" on the Saturday afternoon. Dixons store in Queen's market did have a shop window broken and lost £300 worth of stereo equipment and at the local H. Samuels, jewellery worth £8,000 was stolen. One police constable commented that two such robberies did not constitute a particularly busy Saturday night (Keith 1986). Two small clashes with crowds did occur, one at Forest Gate, again outside a pub, involving a gang of about thirty White youths (police estimate), and another in Pier Parade, North Woolwich, where three shop windows were smashed by skinheads.

No looting occurred, although there were reports of the latter group being involved in a racist attack on a group of Bengalis later the same night. Again, such racial attacks were and are grimly commonplace in this area (see GLC 1985).

A crate of milk bottles was found on the waste ground behind the Queen's Market in Upton Park with an almost empty can of petrol nearby, although this possible manufacture of petrol bombs was not repeated anywhere else in the borough, and no more were thrown. In short, in West Ham in July 1981, if the location of "the riot" appears uncertain, its very existence is hardly manifest.

SHAGGY DOG RIOTS

Croydon (10 July 1981)

In the months before July 1981 the outer London Borough of Croydon had witnessed a dramatic increase in the incidence and seriousness of inter-racial violence which, after a series of assaults on both Afro-Caribbean and Asian individuals, had culminated in an attack by a gang of Black youths on a pub in Thornton Heath, allegedly a National Front meeting place, which resulted in the tragic murder of Terence May – White, disabled, and having nothing to do with any racist organization. The crude front page headlines the event prompted in the tabloid newspapers, especially in the context of the resounding media silence on racial attacks, did nothing to alleviate tension in the area. In late June a quasi-fascist group, the White Defence Force, had printed and distributed several hundred leaflets advocating racial violence. Asian shopkeepers had been attacked, two shop windows smashed and there was at least one attempted arson.

Under pressure from the local Community Relations Council the police revealed that there had been eight arrests between February and July 1981, "for such offences as daubing racialist slogans, and using abusive words with racialist connotations" (police statement). Chief Inspector Brian Turner of Z district went on record as suggesting that these figures demonstrated police awareness of the problems of ethnic minorities. Others thought differently, and as a result an assortment of local lawyers, social workers and Black activists, led by Fermi Adelaja (who later died in police custody while being held on remand in 1988) they formed the Croydon Black People's Action Committee. In August 1981, they attempted to set up "alternative protection" for the Black community in Croydon, in the face of opposition from senior police officers in Z Division. Exacerbating this tense situation, on Saturday 3 July, a group of youths had extensively vandalized Coldharbour School and Waylands Day Centre in Purley Way, Croydon, an incident promoted to the status of "an orgy of destruction" by a "mob" in the local press in the light of that weekend's violence in other parts of the country (*Croydon Advertiser*, 10 July 1981).

In the week following the disorders in Southall and Liverpool 8, "rioting" became the focus of local media attention, and rumours of imminent trouble abounded in Croydon. Replication of the incidents that were spreading throughout London appeared inevitable. Significantly, in both press coverage and the accounts given by local shopkeepers, "the riot" was described in the frequently mixed metaphors of combustion and medicine; the fire was spreading from central London, contagion (or perhaps diffusion) exemplified. In fact, nothing happened.

On the Friday night, as occurs on every division of the MPD on every

SHAGGY DOG RIOTS AND COPYCAT RIOTERS

Friday night, there was a fight outside a pub; 11 people were arrested. On the Saturday (11 July 1981), the police maintained a high profile throughout the centre of Croydon, using Alsatian dogs in a clear symbolic gesture. Groups of hopeful youths who had gathered on; the streets were quickly moved on, two speculative Black youngsters were apprehended on a bus coming into the town centre with milk bottles and petrol in plastic containers in their pockets. Saturday shopping crowds were smaller than normal; by 3.30pm Whitgift Shopping Centre was empty. Nevertheless, as the Home Office arrest data clearly show, there were 29 arrests on the Saturday (48 over the whole weekend) consisting principally of one group of young Whites who had travelled into the town centre "looking for trouble", and were arrested for trying, and failing, to smash a shop window. There were some scuffles between police officers and both Black and White gangs, but these resulted only in summary charges under the Public Order Act. Most of those arrested had come from outside Croydon (Keith 1986, 1987). This was not a local crowd, but one that had found it necessary to move some distance into the town centre: "all dressed up and nowhere to riot?"

Whether the events in Croydon over the weekend of 10 to 12 July 1981 are viewed as either a successful police operation or an example of mass hysteria is perhaps not as significant as the fact that they qualified as a major outbreak of public disorder in both the Report of the Commissioner of the Metropolitan Police for the year 1981 (Metropolitan Police 1982) and the Home Office classification. The Croydon "riot" is no more and no less than a product of public and police anticipation, and the binary format of bureaucratic and media recording (presence/absence of disorder). Reified by report, the incident sits as a dot on a map, the same size as that of Brixton or Southall, one on a confusing list. It is perhaps significant that of those arrested 89 per cent were White.

Walthamstow (11 July 1981)

One of the most horrific incidents of racist violence witnessed in the late 1970s and early 1980s occurred in Walthamstow in July 1981, when one of the many arson attacks on Asian homes in the area succeeded in burning down the house of the Khans in Belgrave Road, killing most of the members of the family (Hesse et al. 1992).

The funeral was scheduled to take place on Saturday 10 July and, in the light of disturbances in Southall and other parts of London at this time, it seemed to some inevitable that there would be major trouble in Walthamstow. Rumours of organized violence were endemic. Police asked Unigate Dairies to make double deliveries on the Friday and not

SHAGGY DOG RIOTS

deliver at all on the Saturday; several church and school fetes scheduled for the weekend were cancelled; buses were rerouted and/or cancelled on the Friday and Saturday, and doctors at St James's Health Centre refused to make house calls. As the general worry began to turn into a panic which almost bordered on hysteria, it was agreed not to open Walthamstow Market at all on the Saturday and very many shops, pubs and garages boarded up their premises and shut up shop early on Saturday morning.

The reaction of established Asian groups at this time was remarkably restrained, with the widower, Younis Khan, putting out a public appeal for peace rather than revenge to be the dominant theme of any protest, and the Joint Council of Asian Organizations (JCAO) announcing that there should be only a silent funeral procession on the Saturday. However, one section of the community, angered at the history of racial violence, demanded a more demonstrative protest and formed the Khan Massacre Action Committee, headed by Shabhaz Khan, which immediately announced a march from Leyton to Walthamstow, scheduled for the Saturday morning of the Khan funeral. A similar march in Coventry in May 1981, after the racist murder of two Asian men, had resulted in conflict between the marchers and skinheads who had stood along the route of the march, jeering.

With the announcement of the march in Walthamstow rumours of a National Front countermarch began to circulate, at which point the JCAO themselves asked for this march to be banned and cancelled their own silent procession. Sir David McNee, Commissioner of the Metropolitan Police, asked the Home Office for, and received, a banning order on all marches in London and police announced that groups would be breaking the law if they marched in crowds of more than ten people. On the night of Friday 10 July further rumours and unsubstantiated tales of petrol bomb manufacture were not realized in a tense but quiet night.

On the Saturday, the march from Leyton went ahead in spite of the banning order. Police did not try to break up the crowd, but lined the route in pairs deploying "dozens of mounted police" (*Waltham Forest Guardian*, 17 July 1981) and keeping several coach-loads of police in reserve. Abusive skinheads clashed with police on the march route, ten being arrested and charged with possession of offensive weapons (Stanley knives) and threatening behaviour. As the march approached the site of the funeral, behind Waltham Forest town hall, many of the marchers were diverted, which produced some clashes with the police. At the funeral itself there were some angry scenes involving clashes within the Asian community and afterwards with groups of Asian people, angry at what was seen as an extremely heavy and ostentatious

65

SHAGGY DOG RIOTS AND COPYCAT RIOTERS

police presence, as well as the sight of Walthamstow High Street looking "like something out of a Belfast newsreel" (*Waltham Forest Guardian*, 17 July 1981). Some were involved both in scuffles with the police and damage to some of the few shop windows that were not boarded up, although no looting occurred.

Although this group were generally construed as the younger half of an alleged generational split in the Asian community, reproducing the common-sense "between two cultures" metaphor, they were clearly not simply a youth or "juvenile" collection, as the arrest statistics from the time clearly show (Table 3.1). Of all "Asians" arrested, 71 per cent were over 21 and even when the average ages of the younger Whites arrested is included, Walthamstow still has the highest proportion of over 21s of those arrested in the whole of London.

Table 3.1 Walthamstow: arrests by ethnic appearance and age.

	White	Black	Asian	Other	Total
Under 14	–	–	–	–	–
14–16	–	1	1	–	2
17–20	4	–	4	–	8
Over 21	7	–	12	–	19
Total	11	1	17	–	28

Source: Home Office Statistical Unit.

The disorders were considered locally as negligible by shopkeepers, politicians, local press and local police and the "non-march" considered a success by the organizers. Shahbaz Khan suggested that

We were told that there would be a funeral march, then that it would be called off. Then they called for our march to be called off. It is only the Nazis that should get their marches called off. It is very sad that we are not allowed to make our protest known. We could not bury our dead without a protest. We have shown today that we could have had a peaceful march.

Yet, in spite of local opinion considering the day relatively peaceful, national television (e.g. BBC news, 11 July 1981) and national press (e.g. *Guardian*, *Times*, 13 July 1981; *Sunday Times*, *Observer*, 12 July 1981) painted a more melodramatic picture of events and in the historical annals of the Home Office, the Metropolitan Police and the GLC, Walthamstow had "a riot", even if the residents did not notice it. Equally significantly, the murderers of the Khan family have never been arrested.

SHAGGY DOG RIOTS

Penge (11 July 1981)

The danger of simplistic or exclusive reliance on the Home Office classification alone is never more clearly illustrated than in the case of "the rioting" in Penge which resulted in 42 arrests. As in so many other examples, the violence in other parts of London, and a particular conception of that violence, encouraged an expectation of trouble in Penge.

There is an almost surreal facet to the disorder in this case, which on the Friday night consisted of no more than a serious fight outside the White Swan pub on Anerley Hill, resulting in the premises closing early, and the unrelated smashing of some windows of the Salvation Army offices in Citadel Road. A milk bottle with some petrol in it was found outside. The expectation and rumours of trouble reached a peak on Saturday (11 July 1981), with rationalizations again phrased in the metaphors of combustion and diffusion – violence construed as contagious spreading through the capital.

In the Clockhouse Bridge precinct most shopkeepers boarded up their premises and shut at around 3.30pm. The predicted source of "trouble" was the "notorious" Blenheim council estate, and the newly-opened major branch of Bejams, part of the shopping precinct adjacent to the estate, was one of the many shops to shut early on the Saturday. On Saturday night a noisy party in Strood House, Eveline Road, on the estate, attracted the attention of police when the owners of Penge Angling Supplies in Croydon Road claimed that they had seen some youths outside Hood House (also on the estate) making petrol bombs. The party was raided, 41 arrested, 36 of whom were not charged, and no evidence of petrol bombs was found. However, an hour or so later, at around 12.45am, a small group of allegedly Black youths was seen to throw a "petrol bomb" at Rumbelows electrical store in Penge High Street, opposite to the entrance to the Blenheim estate. The "bomb" bounced back off the window and caught fire but caused no damage, at which point another youth tried a brick instead; this broke the window but did not leave a large enough hole for access and no looting followed.

A more serious incident occurred at about the same time when a petrol bomb was thrown at the window of Penge Angling Supplies, an action repeated to greater effect two hours later causing damage to the shop front. It would be foolish to trivialize such an attack, but it is perhaps no coincidence that the shop owned by those making a complaint to the police was attacked twice in two hours while only one other property in a retailing area was damaged.

The Blenheim estate may be a rough place but it certainly did not witness a riot in July 1981.

SHAGGY DOG RIOTS AND COPYCAT RIOTERS

Superficially similar, these four "non-riots" highlight two recurrent but separate themes of reportage. Failure even to address the possible rationality of rioting produces senseless and distorted versions of events. But underlying this nonsense is the clearly coded age-old racist caricature. British Black communities were potentially lawless outposts, sources of a dangerous insurrectionary contagion that might spread, if not contained, both to neighbouring districts and to the "hooligan" White peer group of "Black Youth". Although a geography of violent disorder is difficult to describe, the organizing themes of what Said (1979) might describe as the racist imagined geographies of Black London is much more clearly evident.

Copycat rioters?

According to Lord Scarman

> Indeed it seems likely that there was a substantial "copycat" element in many of the disorders which occurred during the summer." (Scarman 1981 2.30)

The reference to a contagious form of delinquency, reflecting contemporary debates, reinforces notions of collective violence as irrational and purely imitative. Yet, although the precise influence of "public knowledge" is again difficult to discern, the interpretation of rioting shared by many London residents is also implied by their actions in July 1981. Again the evidence is scarce but persuasive. The local press of every single London borough reported rumours of potential rioting in early July. Such rumours took on the gloss of prescience on those occasions when they were justified by ensuing disorder, yet had more tangible and consistent manifestations in the behaviour of shopkeepers across London.

In outer London boroughs such as Sutton and Merton, shop windows were boarded up as "the fire" appeared to spread outwards into suburbia. Testifying to the power of the explanatory frame of reference of metaphoric contagion (Murdock 1984), several areas of inner London which witnessed few, if any, disorders, prepared for the onslaught. The *East London Advertiser* described how, "The East End waited its turn for the riots which had swept the rest of London" (17 July 1981). Under a headline "READY FOR RIOTS – FACE OF EAST END IN 1981" the paper showed pictures of shopkeepers covering glass with wood, and described how, "the borough streets resembled a battle torn war zone as the boards went up on Friday" and "the word went around that Tower Hamlets was next on the rioters' target list." Notwithstanding the purple prose of the journalist, many shopkeepers confirmed that they had taken such preventative action, not only in Brick Lane, which has a history of racial violence, but also in other parts of the borough (Keith 1986). Likewise, in South London, Woolwich, Greenwich, Southwark and Wandsworth all reported a similar phenomenon. It was not only the shopkeepers who submitted to this wave of anticipation; most boroughs reported instances of fetes and fairs being postponed and a major jazz festival was later cancelled. It would seem reasonable to attribute such ubiquitous precautionary action at least partly to the imagery used in the reconstruction of the rioting as a public event: as part of public knowledge.

Moreover, it would be naïve to assume that such actions did not in turn have any effect on the behaviour of other residents in these areas. An opinion poll published in the *Sun* on 10 July 1981 was headlined, "SUN POLL SHOWS ALL BRITAIN FEARS RIOTS WILL SPREAD", claiming that 90 per cent of all people living in British city centres thought they would see rioting on their own streets. Whether press reportage created or reflected such expectation is in some ways not as important as the behaviour that may have resulted from it.

The events in Acton provide a case in point. Many shop windows in the area had been boarded up and, as elsewhere, rumours of possible trouble were rife and the shops had emptied early on the Friday night (10 July 1981). Interviewed five months later in December 1981, one individual claimed to have been involved in the events which the *Acton Gazette* (16 July 1981) was later to label, "A MOB's RIOT . . . A SAD DAY FOR THE TOWN." (Keith 1986) A celebration at Hutchies, a private taxi firm, was interrupted when, as the pubs were closing, a group of youths tried to "gatecrash" the party but were refused admission. Hutchies is near the busy junction of Churchfield Road and Acton High Street and this rumpus attracted other groups who were milling around the area at the time.

When one drunken youth smashed the window of Galleon Wines in Churchfield Road several others followed suit and 11 shops were looted, including a "hi-fi" store and a kebab house which had its till stolen. The whole "riot" took less than half an hour. It would be facetious to suggest that expectation can be considered the sole cause of disorder in Acton, but as the author was told (Keith 1986), in a High Street that was waiting for trouble, once one window was smashed, tearing down the boards and smashing a few others "seemed like the right thing to do at the time."

In fact the most complete plagiarists, the true "copycats" of 1981, were the shopkeepers in London who understandably, if unwittingly, fell for the common-sense conceptualization of rioting as fashion; an

SHAGGY DOG RIOTS AND COPYCAT RIOTERS

irrational and contagious excess of the young. In this context, the work of Erving Goffman (1971, 1972) is useful. Using the dramaturgical metaphor, Goffman has consistently shown how much social behaviour corresponds to a form of social protocol, conditioned by time and place. In this sense, when the pubs closed on the Friday and Saturday nights of 10/11 July 1981, the clientele in very many parts of London found themselves almost literally thrown onto streets that were like stage sets designed for disorder. Boarded up shop windows, deserted streets and a sense of expectation parodied the preliminaries to more tangible violent conflicts in other parts of the city. That putative riots sometimes developed from the usual late night weekend clashes cannot be entirely dissociated from such stage design, even if the actions of the designers were never causally sufficient to induce a major disturbance. Through examining, albeit briefly, the relationship between media portrayal, belief and action it is also possible to throw some light on a question that relates to classification of the London riots of 1981 as part of a moral panic; namely "To what extent were the summer riots of '81 a media creation?".

There is certainly an element of the shaggy dog story involved in enumeration of all the London disorders. As Appendix 1 illustrates, no two lists agree on how many riots there were or even where they occurred. Some press reported incidents of riot were exaggerated, others were more symptomatic of police anticipation of trouble than examples of conflict on the streets. Significantly, this anticipation always involved potential conflict with Black people. Both media exaggeration and police anticipation highlight problems of defining a riot as much as they detract from the validity of such lists. Although it is not easy to draw out reality from myth, the reconstruction of the rioting as a public event was more a systematic distortion than creation of a "new" social phenomenon.

The forms of collective behaviour that were seen in the summer of 1981 were not new to the streets of London, nor novel even in the recent past. Assorted violent confrontations had previously, and have subsequently, been under-reported in national media coverage. Nevertheless, the rioting represented both a qualitative and quantitative scale of seriousness of disorder that had not been seen in the preceding 20 years and, notwithstanding events of 1985 in Tottenham, Brixton and Handsworth, has not been seen since.

In spite of this qualitative change in the nature of disorder, the seriousness of the 1981 rioting was often exaggerated. As John Clare (1984) of the BBC pointed out, the worst rioting in London, that of Brixton in April 1981, was nowhere near as serious as many of the riots he had witnessed in Ulster throughout the 1970s. But the social signifi-

70

cance of popular violent conflict on the streets of London is not diminished by acknowledging that violent reality was not quite up to melodramatic insurrection. It is instead the case that adjectival exhaustion might blur the difference between the incidents of 1981 and 1985, and devalue the escalation of violence that these individual uprisings, in particular, later embodied.

In some instances what was seen on the streets of London and other cities in 1981 was no more than the normal weekend outbreaks of drunken aggression. In other locations the seeds of Saturday night trouble were placed on a stage, a stage with a quite explicitly communicative scene and a line of prompters in the wings. These were not the mythical conspirators, the Moscow agents, that *The Standard* and other newspapers talked of, but the local gossipmongers and rumourhawkers who constructed folk discussion in the metaphor of contagion, and to a man (and woman) "knew" that trouble was coming. That the response of assorted potential "trouble spots" was non-existent in the many parts of London that were so pump primed is, ironically, one of the most powerful arguments against the classification of collective violence as irrational.

There can be few more surreal images than that of the young Black man in Croydon "commuting to riot" with a milk bottle in one pocket and a Tupperware tub of petrol in the other, never reaching a destination where nothing happened, a destination that succumbed to the triumph of "common sense" over introspection. Yet such a scene was the echo of very real trauma. On its own, such a scene is piquant; beside the fire bombs of Brixton it is grotesque.

Notes

1. Epistemological problems prohibit such total exegesis but do not threaten the realist ontology implicit in such a dichotomy.

CHAPTER 4

Blame, guilt and "causes" of "riots"

"There are no stories in the riots, only the ghosts of other stories"
(Handsworth Songs 1986)

In the immediate aftermath of the events of July 1981 most political accounts or explanations of the riots were demonstrably, often openly, value-laden. For Margaret Thatcher and many of her then colleagues the disturbances were classified as a law-and-order matter and the issues that were raised were tied to related notions of national self-discipline, parenthood, juvenile delinquency and personal evil (see Lawrence 1982, Solomos 1986, 1988, Kettle & Hodges 1982). For the Labour opposition the causal process was explicitly attributed to the effects of government policy. Roy Hattersley, in particular, was keen to make the link between changes in levels of deprivation since 1979 and the incidence of public disorder.

Such behaviour was predictable in the initial reactions to rioting. Frequently it is the symbolic reading of events that is malleable, not the cognitive set into which they are fitted. Unsurprisingly, rioting as a political reality (Edelman 1971, 1985) came to reflect a series of preconceptions about the nature of disorder. In this way it was possible to sustain political differences about the causes of disorder within a political consensus, between government and opposition, about the need to suppress rigorously the symptoms of the same phenomenon ("violence and looting"). In policy terms this produced what Solomos (1986) has described as the interplay of reform and control; symbolic measures taken to counter deprivation, alongside a strengthening of the ability of the state to counter further uprisings in British cities.

Implicitly, in these circumstances, rioting was popularly classified as an aberrant or at least abnormal phenomenon, a reading of history which cast disorder as at worst a temporary dysfunction of the social system rather than a threat to the legitimacy of the prevailing social order as a whole (Solomos 1986). It is only one small step from such introspective reassurance to the polemical deployment of these reconstituted symbols to prove the validity of specific arguments about the nature of life in Britain in 1981.

In civil society this phenomenon was regularly seen in the competition for scarce resources. Given a felicitous causal relationship, a wide variety of interest groups could claim legitimacy for government or private funding in the name of preventing further public disorder. Police, educational, industrial, inner-city, employment and many other lobbies could all point to their own pressing need and base demands for resource input on the implicit, or even explicit, suggestion that without more money there would be more riots. Again, this was an understandable facet of the political process. In contrast, it was more disconcerting to see this practice of appropriation replicated in ostensibly academic explanations of British rioting.

Explanation

Given that the riots played such a major rôle in the shaping of popular perception of Britain in the early 1980s, it might seem reasonable to look to the academic social sciences to answer pressing and fundamental questions relating to the nature and causes of the events of 1981. Not only why disorders occurred, but also why they occurred in some places and not others, at some times but apparently not at other times.

It was in this vein that the *Times Higher Educational Supplement* (17 July 1981) bylined a story on rioting with the ironic caption

Peter David asks if social scientists will be able to command any greater respect for their work in the wake of recent rioting.

Indeed, if it is not possible to produce an objective or realistic account of these events then it would appear sanctimonious to condemn through deconstruction the rhetorical manipulation of the symbolic power of disorder in political and other discourses. Yet the attractive notion of the wisdom of academe contributing to the common good through contributions to the store of "knowledge" about the social world is at best a misleading vision of the manner in which "explanations" have been attached to the events commonly known as "the riots of 1981".

In this chapter, rather than provide an extensive bibliographic review of the academic literature that has attempted to explain civil disorder in contemporary Western societies, I want instead to highlight recurrent problems that arise in such attempts. Consequently, the focus is on the exercise of explanation as such rather than the content of competing analyses. I want to suggest that there are certain fallacies built into common-sense notions of what an explanation of a "riot" *ought* to look like which have been incorporated in much academic and quasi-academic treatment of violent unrest. In a similar but distinct manner from analyses of police racism this in turn has tended to highlight the ambiguous rôle of all social description that takes objectivity or naïve "realism" as a constitutive aim.

Riot commissions and the official inquiry

There are many reasons why "official inquiries" became a common feature on the political stage of so many nations in the twentieth century. A burning desire to seek the truth in any specific instant was not necessarily foremost among them. So it would be naïve or disingenuous to expect any commission of inquiry into riots to produce a definitive or balanced explanation of events.

The commissions themselves exist in a political environment and are implicated in political strategy from the moment at which they are appointed and their personnel selected to the moment in which they report, right on to the manner in which they are remembered. There were times in America in the 1960s when the weighting of a committee was quite blatant; the McCone Commission investigating the Watts riots of 1965 was chaired by a former head of the CIA and the emphasis on security issues prompted a major rift between the commission itself and its social science advisors (Fogelson 1969).

It was also this political rôle that led to Kenneth Clark's publicly voiced cynicism about the Kerner inquiry (the National Advisory Commission on Civil Disorders) and his renowned remark to the Commission that he found that the succession of twentieth-century official investigations into riots had about them an Alice in Wonderland quality, "with the same moving pictures re-shown over and over again, the same analysis, the same recommendations and the same inaction."

It is because of this dimension that Lipsky & Olsen (1969, 1977) have suggested that such investigations, by their very nature, create expectations that cannot be fulfilled. There are hidden tasks behind any ostensibly straightforward historical exploration, involving the purchase of political time in the lengthy process of investigation, the exoneration

RIOT COMMISSIONS AND THE OFFICIAL INQUIRY

of public officials as they are seen to be "doing something" about riots, and the provision of a comprehensive account to mediate between rioters and authorities that will not be totally alien to the vision of society held by those who commission the report in the first instance (Silver 1969, Feagin & Hahn 1973).

So it is with a considerable element of caution that the most well known of riot inquiries, the National Commission on Civil Disorders, better known as the Kerner Commission, should be considered. When Kerner's report was published, Johnson's presidency was coming to a close. From a British perspective Field (1982) has claimed that

as a political document, it is a public and unambiguous commitment to the plight of American Blacks, with the full weight of the American presidency behind it.

The reality was somewhat different. Johnson himself, after initial placatory statements and stirring calls for national unity, had become worried about the possible nature of the final report and had played an instrumental rôle in limiting the budget, scope and social science personnel of the Commission (Feagin & Hahn 1973). Lipsky & Olsen (1969) go so far as to suggest that Johnson himself tried to undermine "his own" Kerner Commission in his instruction to the (Milton) Eisenhower Commission on the Causes and Prevention of Violence to provide an alternative explanation of rioting. At the same time, on the public stage, the increasingly vocal George Wallace and, to a lesser extent, Richard Nixon as well, contributed to an incipient "white backlash".

It is always against this sort of background, forced to manoeuvre in the world of *realpolitik*, that the commission must be seen, at least in part, as just one pressure group in the ongoing struggle of American race relations, compelled to trade idealism for pragmatism in the art of what is possible.

Given these national political exigencies, it was perhaps inevitable that more radical criticisms of "the establishment" would be phased out of Kerner's final report, that moral statements on the evils of racism would not explicitly criticize the institutions in large part responsible for the perpetuation of that racism. This was most probably the cause of the splits that developed between some social science researchers working for Kerner and the Commission itself, a split that surfaced in public debate when a draft document entitled "The Harvest of American Racism", produced by this research group, was rejected by the Commission.

Similarly, tensions within the Committee itself surfaced in the final report. One of the more liberal members of the Committee, the Republican mayor of New York, John Lindsay, worried about the political

BLAME, GUILT AND "CAUSES" OF "RIOTS"

tone of leaks concerning the forthcoming report, drafted a short document that was much more strongly worded than the body of the report itself, presented it to the rest of the committee as a "summary" of the Commission's work and demanded that this be included in the final publication. Threatening to release the document independently if his demands were not met, Lindsay effectively presented other committee members with a *fait accompli*. It was this summary which included most of the well known "Kerner quotes", including the statement, subsequently cited by Lord Scarman, that the main conclusion of the Commission's work was that: "Our nation is moving towards two societies, one Black, one White, separate and unequal." (Kerner 1968: 1)

The slightly schizophrenic nature of the final draft that this produced, was complicated yet further when the report was published in a paperback edition, with an editorial introduction that was even more strongly in line with a liberal social science perspective than Lindsay's own document (Rossi 1970) of which over two million copies were sold. One consequence of this confusion was that public debate was often structured more by Lindsay's summary and this introduction than by the report itself. White racism, a term that is hardly ever used in the main report, appears more often in the summary, yet Nixon, in his public reaction to Kerner, complained that the problem with the report was that it spent too much time blaming the racism of White people and too little time blaming the rioters (Button 1978).

At its most strongly worded and most explicitly causal the main report exemplifies a mode of explanation that I shall refer to as *the recipe analysis*, a recurrent phenomenon in all accounts of rioting, easily identified by the regular recourse to the metaphors of combustion and cookery. The report states that, "we have attempted to identify the prime components of this explosive mixture". (Kerner 1968: 93).

Thus

the causes of recent racial disorders are imbedded in a massive tangle of issues and circumstances – social, economic, political and psychological . . . [a] list of factors [that] vary significantly in their effect from city to city and from year to year; and the consequences of one disorder generating new grievances and new demands, becomes the causes of the next. (Kerner 1968: 92)

The report then goes on to distinguish the different causal elements in this mixture, attributing to each an implicit proportion of the "blame" for disorder. At the primary level is White racism, "essentially responsible for the explosive mixture which has been accumulating in our cities since the end of World War II", creating the secondary forms of segregation, migration and "the ghetto". At the tertiary level frustration, powerlessness and the legitimation of violence, act as "powerful

76

RIOT COMMISSIONS AND THE OFFICIAL INQUIRY

ingredients to catalyze the mixture". The final constituents are identified as "incitement" and "police behaviour". Police behaviour is seen as "not merely *the spark*" (my emphasis) as "police have come to symbolize white power, white racism and white repression".

This notion of explanation as proportional guilt allocation, mediated by a recipe of "causes", constituted a consistent theme of explanation of the American disorders. Rival cooks proposed the superiority of their own particular recipe, varying principally in the causal significance attributed to each of a list of component ingredients.

It is worth dealing with Kerner at some length because the nearest British equivalent, the Scarman inquiry into the Brixton disorders of April 1981, reproduced not only much of the political controversy and agenda setting symbolism of Kerner but also, in large part, the explanatory framework on which explanations for popular violence were to be hung. Ironically, Scarman even concludes with a pious quote from President Johnson's address to the nation "supporting" the Kerner Inquiry (Scarman 1981 9.5).

Yet as the principal attempt to lend an official meaning to disorder, as the main determinant of Government pronouncements and a major influence on Government policy, the report by Lord Scarman on the Brixton disorders was the most important work published concerning the 1981 British riots. Rather than analyze the vast amount of material produced on both the substantive content and the political impact of the Scarman report (Benyon 1984, Gurnah 1987, Hall 1982, James 1981), it is intended here to suggest only that one of the many tasks that the Inquiry implicitly attempted to fulfil again reflects a demand for an *explanation* of disorder that effectively allocates blame. This process was highlighted by the courtroom setting of the Inquiry and in the final division of the report itself into sections on a series of social (pre)conditions, a chronology, and an examination of policing issues, followed by three chapters of policy and legal recommendations.

Similarly, the political context of several other investigations into disorder in British cities in the 1980s clearly structured the sort of explanation of unrest that they generated. Three liberal QCs chaired inquiries into uprisings in Handsworth, Birmingham and Broadwater Farm Estate, Tottenham, both in 1985, and earlier in Moss Side, Manchester in 1981 (Hytner 1981, Silverman 1985, Gifford et al. 1986); each allocating guilt as much as divining truth.[1]

Scarman divides his list of specific social conditions into the salient characteristics of a place (Brixton) and its people. In the former category the list includes location, environment, housing and leisure facilities; in the latter the family, education, unemployment and discrimination are the chosen themes for a discussion of the Black community in

BLAME, GUILT AND "CAUSES" OF "RIOTS"

Brixton, while the young are characterized as "A People of The Street". Together these elements are conducive to "a predisposition toward violence" (2.38), although they cannot "usefully be described as a cause of disorder" (ibid).

Regardless of any descriptive (in)accuracy, this act of placing a diagnostic sociological description of Black culture within a class of preconditioning factors for a riot implies a deterministic link, even though Scarman eschews crudely simplistic models of causality. For him, these preconditions are akin to a form of tinder, an unstable mix when combined with insensitive policing. Although less explicitly phrased than in Kerner, here again is the recipe for a grim flambé, just waiting for "the spark" of a single incident to light the fire (see Scarman 1981 8.9).

Essentially, Lord Scarman formalized the orthodox liberal view of the inner city, admittedly not a minor achievement in the social and administrative context that he was working in nationally. However, the rôle of counsels, pressure on individuals, and the difficulty of obtaining a full and fair spectrum of opinion, are just three of the more obvious shortcomings of any judicial inquiry. The inquiry reproduces in microcosm a competition over how "a riot" should be remembered and, most significantly, it is the corporate voice that will make more impression than the individual or aggregates of opinion. Of these corporate institutions the most articulate will, in all probability, appear most favourably of all. That Scarman's chronological reproduction of events from 10–12 April 1981 is almost exclusively based on police reports is just one facet of this imbalance (Scarman 1981, Part III).

As with Kerner, Scarman's report became an indictment of society in general. In the final conclusion he mentions the police, national and local government, racial disadvantage, institutional racism (a term he quite clearly does not understand), and even America, but never once Brixton, despite terms of reference which specifically cited these disturbances as the main object of the enquiry. "A riot" thus becomes a reified product of a particular situation, "the rioters" are faceless individuals in an animated "crowd".

In striving for the universal, Lord Scarman neglects the particular, and the social processes behind the Brixton riots remain, perhaps inevitably, uncertain even though a form of causal recipe analysis, so similar to that used in the Kerner report, is again deployed in order to ensure an equitable apportionment of historical responsibility. Causal significance and blame are implicitly equivalent, a generic flaw of the official inquiry.

I would suggest that this false equivalence between cause and blame lies at the heart of very many misapprehensions about the nature of urban unrest in 1980s Britain, and that it is an equivalence that can be

COLLECTIVE BEHAVIOUR THEORY AND "THE CROWD"

traced back from common-sense expressions and the judgements of the official inquiry through to the roots of behaviourist social science and a common failure to come to terms with the complexity of the ostensibly simple notion of causality.

Collective behaviour theory and "the crowd"

Collective behaviour theory assumes that there is such a thing as "collective behaviour", that "crowd psychology" is in some way different from "individual psychology". Possibly this creates a false dichotomy; the individual and society are mutually dependent; the one supposes the other. In spite of claims to the contrary (Taylor 1984), it is difficult to imagine a useful theory of collective behaviour or a theory of crowd psychology. Certainly, work in this tradition has tended to be speculative in the extreme; "theory" based on broad generalizations constrained by presupposition.

This is necessarily the case because "the crowd", although a recurrent analytical theme of history, is not necessarily a valid object of analysis. Value loaded invocations of "the mob" are not the most useful starting point for critical scrutiny, an analytical flaw most crudely seen in the pioneering work of LeBon (1898/1960) and Freud (1922). Nevertheless, the link between collective behaviour and irrationality persisted in the work of other theorists, notably Tarde, McDougall, and Blumer (Berk 1974, Moscovici 1985). It took the unique (as opposed to theoretical) work of historians such as Hobsbawm (1959) and Rude (1964), who have looked at the parallel developments of industrial change and popular unrest, to debunk this manic image of collective behaviour and recast disorder as social protest, restore faces to the faceless members of the crowd.

In contrast, those who have adopted a wider historical perspective have tended to be more ambitious, trying to produce theorizations at the national and even the international level about violent conflict, a historical project of enormous dimensions. Such a perspective is shared by Canetti (1962), the Tillys (1975, 1978, 1979), Moore (1978) and at times Gurr (1970), although the value of the sort of generalizations or "historical laws" that can be deduced at this level is questionable.

With the ascendancy of liberal social science in the USA, the influential and more sympathetic work of Turner & Killian (1957), Kornhauser (1959) and Smelser (1962) did little to restore rationality to the crowd because of a paradigmatic tendency to focus on a series of stimuli that preceded civil disorder in "mass societies" (Kornhauser) or in societies

BLAME, GUILT AND "CAUSES" OF "RIOTS"

suffering "structural strain" (Smelser).

This search for preconditioning factors, logically derived from the concepts of structural strain and riot proneness (Lieberson & Silverman 1965), also needed an underlying mechanism to account for the transformation of discontent and deprivation into violent action. The mechanism that answered this need, and provided the centrepiece for the vast majority of studies of collective behaviour throughout the 1960s, was drawn from the cluster of psychological and social-psychological ideas that can be loosely described as relative deprivation theory. At its most succinct (Runciman 1960), deprivation was reformulated in terms of perceived rather than absolute measures of wellbeing, comparative rather than absolute measures of economic status and, after de Tocqueville's explanation of the French revolution, unrest expected when relative rather than absolute deprivation increases most rapidly (Davies 1971, 1978).

In such models frustration was emphasized as the cause of aggression, a notion based on the work of the psychologists Dollard, Doob, Miller, Mowrer & Sears (1939). Gurr (1968) has gone so far as to say that relative deprivation and frustration/aggression theories were as fundamental to understanding civil strife as the law of gravity is to atmospheric physics. Conceptually and epistemologically this was nonsense. Conceptually, both central terms are ill defined, easily manipulated to fit any context. As Gurr himself repeatedly, if accidentally, reveals, the validity of the theory is based on the tautology that those who are frustrated display behavioural patterns that are defined as aggressive while those who display aggression must be in some way frustrated. The two terms are dependent; frustration is redefined as anything that causes violence. In the extremes of absurdity imminent assassination is classed as vexatious: "a threat to life is an anticipated frustration" (Gurr 1970: 36).

The epistemological flaws are similarly marked, relying on a long-since discredited stimulus–response psychology (Berkowitz 1982). So, in the realm of collective behaviour, frustration/aggression theory is at best a truism, an analytically impoverished device. At its worst it is a potentially powerful mode of definition by which the rationality of a collective can be kidnapped by social science and the personal project reclassified as *natural* response.

Although claims on behalf of crowd psychology, or the study of crowd behaviour, that continue to be made are fortunately rare (Reicher 1984, Reicher & Potter 1985, Benewick 1987, McClelland, 1989), they remain potentially dangerous sources of academic charlatanism. The social context in which such analysis is set potentially legitimizes the conflation of issues as diverse as football hooliganism, industrial strife and civil unrest under a heading of disorder. It may sometimes be possible to produce useful descriptive typologies, as with the "flashpoints model" developed in Britain in the 1980s (Waddington 1992, Waddington et al. 1987, 1989). But the reification of "disorder" is potentially so pernicious because, at best, it produces a conception of civil unrest which can never come to terms with the complexity of individual intentions and purposes and, at worst, lends credibility to explanations of disorder divorced from social context and devoid of political content (Keith 1988).

Given that stimulus–response psychology has largely been discredited, recognition of the failures of this paradigm adequately "to explain" riots is not particularly novel (Wanderer 1969, Berk 1974). Yet these failures remain seminal not simply for their historical interest. For the *political* function of blame allocation, so central to the workings of the official inquiry, exemplified by Scarman and Kerner, is not simply the product of their positions within the state apparatus; it is also the ideological heritage of a set of common-sense assumptions about the way in which particular events *occur*. These failures can be traced back to the Humean notion of causality that has underpinned much empirical social research, and forward, not only to academic responses to the long hot summers in 1960s America, but also to the manner in which violent unrest in 1980s Britain was in large part divorced from the historical and geographical context of the conflict between police and British Black communities in academic and popular discourse, in spite of an apparent move away from behaviourism in the social sciences more generally.

Guilt

The Greek *aitia*, from which the term aetiology is derived, covered both the concept of guilt and that of cause. This conflation of the moral and the theoretical, caught up in the language used to describe the social world, has persisted in common cultural understandings of the concept of causality.

The primacy of observation in the search for knowledge has regularly surfaced in Anglo-Saxon philosophy, from the experimental method of Bacon in the thirteenth century to the positivism of Ayer in the twentieth. Hence for Hume "we know nothing further of causation of any kind than merely the *constant conjunction* of objects" (1748, his emphasis). The Humean conception of causality stems from the proposition that no matter how many times A is followed by B the causal link

BLAME, GUILT AND "CAUSES" OF "RIOTS"

between the two can never be proved and so causal laws can only be considered as regularities of variable reliability. The foremost investigative task is to trace these regularities logically through induction; to identify "laws" that serve as the foundations of "theory". For Hume, it was only the principle of induction that allows us to assume that the sun will rise tomorrow and our food is not poisoned. There is a very high degree of reliability since both have been the case throughout most lives, although as Russell (1912) points out, it is the principle of induction that persuades the chicken to associate man with food until the day that man comes along and wrings the chicken's neck. The flaws of such a causal model have been pointed out in much twentieth century philosophy, but one point is of particular relevance here.

Investigation of "that which exists" cannot depend on simple empiricism. Verification or falsification of theory must relate to empirical evidence, but such evidence alone cannot possibly provide comprehensive explanation since it ignores process.

The Humean conception of causality is inadequate. A hypothesis generating mechanism must be central to any model of explanation; it was not 1700 years of autumnal apples that induced the theory of gravity but rather the matching of empirical evidence with Newton's provisional theory. One of the most serious flaws within the Humean model is the inability to incorporate intentional anticipation of the future (teleological causality) into an explanation. This effectively limits the rôle of purposive behaviour in the social world and makes the first step towards "black-boxing" humanity in a stimulus–response behaviourism.

From a Humean perspective an event, for instance a riot, can, once isolated, be rationalized in terms of a list of causes. These may be hierarchically ranked, or even tendentiously differentiated in terms of putative necessary and sufficient powers. Any theory derived in this way necessarily defines this list in terms of hypothetical regularities which would, if found together, lead to the regular repetition of the event. Enter the recipe analysis of civil disorder.

An alternative, *mechanistic*, notion of causality, often preferred to Hume's and which can be traced back as far as Aristotle, divides causality into material, efficient, formal and final elements. In Russell's (1946) example this is illustrated by the sculpting of a statue: the marble represents the material cause, the contact of chisel on marble the efficient cause, the essence of the statue (e.g. an armature) the formal cause, and the statue as envisioned by the sculptor is the final cause, teleologically defined. As argued in Chapter 6 and 7 of this book, the sort of conflict epitomized by violent unrest demands the more sophisticated understanding of different forms of causality precisely because we need to understand both the *processes* that underscore rioting and the *meaning* of such uprisings to the parties involved.

Unravelling the use of notions of causality is so important because the concept cannot be accepted as self-evident. The very notion of a "cause" is not consistent, since it can mean one thing at one moment and something completely different at another. Seemingly so self-evident, the term is in fact extremely problematic.

We can distinguish broadly between two explanatory conventions in the academic work on rioting. Both are flawed precisely because of their failure to understand the notions of causality that they deploy, implicitly or explicitly, in the explanation of disorder. One unintentionally mimics the conventional riot commission's rôle of guilt allocation by adopting the recipe model of analysis; the other prefers instead to cast uprisings as moments of insurrectionary solidarity. Both conventions have progressive and reactionary political formulations and both were commonly present in the attempts by academics and others to explain civil unrest in British cities in the 1980s and American cities in the 1960s.

An American precedent and an American import?

As Horowitz (1983) has pointed out, the long hot summers of ghetto rioting in the USA in the 1960s prompted a transformation in the scale and importance of the production of social science scholarship. For some, notably Field (1982), this massive literature is self-evidently relevant to studies of the British riots, both for the similarities between the events in America and in Britain in 1981 and because of the "advances" that were apparently made in collective behaviour theory. It is the contention here that this assumption cannot so readily be made.

Perhaps most obviously one insuperable problem underlying any comparison of British and American disorders is that, unlike two material objects, the two phenomena to be compared are indeterminate. As Killian (1981) points out, is it possible to say how alike the two experiences of rioting were when even the Americans themselves are still not sure of the causes or form of their own ghetto revolts, let alone how similar they were to someone else's? Furthermore, the level of generalization at which such comparison is made is inevitably on an unsatisfactory, grand, journalistic scale. While accepting that any two social contexts must always be historically unique, there are several facets to the situation of Black people in the two countries that particularly question the utility of jerry-built comparison. The whole heritage of an

BLAME, GUILT AND "CAUSES" OF "RIOTS"

explicitly colonial past compared to a rhetorical (if not real) commitment to racial equality arguably leads to significantly different ideologies of race and racism. In purely empirical terms the massive mobilization of the Black Civil Rights Movement, involving many millions of people, had no equivalent in the run-up to the British riots, nor was the national political climate of Democratic liberal reform mirrored in the British case. The economic experiences of Black people also differed on the two sides of the Atlantic. In America the riots followed a period of steadily improving economic status: in the United Kingdom the 1981 riots followed the onset of an economic depression in which Black people suffered disproportionately on racist, economic, structural and locational grounds (Scarman 1981, Cross 1986).

Building on the truism of frustration/aggression theory, the central terms of relative deprivation explanations can of course be twisted to fit any such distinction (see Field 1982), yet perhaps such casuistry says more about the value of this sort of theory than about any comparison between two sets of riots.

Nevertheless, some similarities do present themselves. There is an obvious difference between what is expected of one as a new arrival and what one expects as a citizen, and this difference between the willingness of first and second generation migrant groups to tolerate systematic discrimination and overt repression might find an analogy in the propensity to revolt among those who moved from the South of the USA and from the former colonies to major industrial cities. Consequently, the northern ghettos of the USA and the centre of British cities may have provided unemployed, discontented personnel and the locales in which such discontent could support itself; in a mundane, logistical sense providing the foci of Black resistance. Perhaps more significantly the politicized understandings of the uprisings undoubtedly did cross the Atlantic and resonate within diasporic Black identities, structuring the manner in which British Black communities rationalized the uprisings of the 1980s (Gilroy 1987).

It is also clear from simple historical research that the majority of American riots were also started by incidents involving police action, set against a background of poor relations between police and ghetto residents, which meant that the police did not simply act as a trigger to disorder (Kerner 1967), and that variations in the incidence and severity of rioting were related to variations in police behaviour (Wanderer 1969, Rossi et al. 1974). However, there was near unanimity in American scholarship that the police rôle was principally one of the vicarious target. They stood as the visible symbols of White society, racist White society. Making the police force more representative of the communities they police may or may not have had a substantial effect

AN AMERICAN PRECEDENT AND AN AMERICAN IMPORT?

on the apparent cooling of tension in American cities in the early 1970s. What is certain is that it was possible to make major advances in this field through campaigns of ethnic recruitment. From 1967 to 1982 the number of minority police rose from 10–48 per cent in Atlanta, from 5–10 per cent in New York and from 5–30 per cent in Detroit. Even in Chicago (17–19% in this period) and Philadelphia (19–17%) where the figures were less impressive, major campaigns in the late 1960s had succeeded in significantly boosting the proportion of Black police from single percentage figure lows in the late 1950s (Rossi et al. 1974, Sherman 1983). Even the most optimistic members of the Metropolitan Police Force and British race relations groups doubt that comparable improvements could be achieved in London or other major British cities. If London is typical and there is much greater resistance in Britain to joining the police, then quite possibly this difference might suggest that poor police/Black relations in the UK are not necessarily the same as poor police/Black relations in the USA.

In short, although comparisons may reveal occasionally useful insights, the differences between the two historical experiences prohibit any straightforward transportation of explanatory designs from one country to another, assuming that there are such valuable designs to transport. Yet there is major epistemological and methodological value in study of the historiography of the American disorders. There are important similarities between how people on both sides of the Atlantic investigated disorder, even if we remain unsure about any replication of the actual processes of rioting itself. Typologically, these can be divided into the two traditions already alluded to – on the one hand those who stress the unacknowledged conditions of action that precede a riot, searching for some consistent set of phenomena that underlie all riots, and on the other those that consider rioting as a form of social movement and so consequently emphasize the strategic nature and political significance of "a type of collective behaviour that is called rioting".

US Convention 1: "The recipe": behaviourism as knowledge

There is an intuitive logic in the pursuit of behaviourism. It is logical when confronted with a series of apparently similar events to seek out what they have in common, which factors recur in instances of riot. Such a search is not an end in itself, yet it is a search which has regularly proved endless in the analysis of disorder. Preconditions are so closely interlinked that it becomes virtually impossible to distinguish between them, given the relatively small set of the phenomenon "riot" that appear at any one time, a phenomenon that is so self-evident yet so vague and ill defined on closer inspection. Consequently, methodo-

BLAME, GUILT AND "CAUSES" OF "RIOTS"

logical difficulties lead to a debate revolving around rival recipes, the patterns of social conditions that serve as the material causes of the disorder. Inevitably, process is lost, or at best remains elusive or assumed, and as a result analysis falls back by default on tacit stimulus–response psychology: riots are relegated from social actions to social outcomes.

Two principal sources of information have been used in such analysis, both of them deeply flawed. In order to discern the salient characteristics of rioters, several studies used questionnaires in riot areas (e.g. Cohen's project in Los Angeles which led to the work of Tomlinson & Sears 1970, Sears & McConahay 1970, Raine 1970, Murphy & Watson 1970; see also Fogelson & Hill 1968, Caplan & Paige 1968, Rossi et al. 1974, Feagin & Hahn 1973). Such investigation generally tried to paint a portrait of the "average rioter on the streets", distinguishing between rioters and non-rioters in terms of personality traits and attitudinal measures. One major problem with such an approach is that it assumes that those willing or even keen to identify themselves as rioters in post-riot questionnaire surveys will represent a typical sample of those people who actually rioted. In reality there are *a priori* grounds for expecting those who have potentially more to lose from such identification, older people with family responsibilities and those in employment, to be under-represented. Conversely, those who have little to lose and the social kudos of the rebel to gain, particularly the unemployed and the young, are likely to be more willing to admit or even boast of their involvement in collective violence.

So although there are broad patterns that emerge from the American work; these should be treated with caution. Self-identified rioters did not come from the most deprived sections of the ghetto and were less likely to be first generation migrants to Northern cities and were younger than those who denied involvement in disorder (see Field 1982 for summary). This was generally taken as rejecting the notion that the "riff-raff" or "marginal men" in ghetto rebelled. However, the methodological difficulties are further compounded in such rioter/non-rioter comparisons by the stress on what are sometimes minor differences in relation to the distinct position of *the ghetto* itself. Unemployment among rioters is sometimes reported as higher than among non-rioters (as in the Watts study of Cohen et al. 1970) but unemployment rates for both are substantially higher than for other parts of the city and the nation. Similarly, educational differences between rioters and non-rioters (see Kerner 1968) pale into near insignificance when compared with the relative state of educational deprivation in the ghetto as a whole. Other socio-economic indices, such as family demographic characteristics (Bloombaum 1968), do not reveal any recurrent pattern.

AN AMERICAN PRECEDENT AND AN AMERICAN IMPORT?

Indeed McPhail (1971) has suggested that, although the majority of social, demographic and economic associations with riot participation are statistically significant, they are repeatedly of a low magnitude (see also McPhail & Miller 1973).

A second investigative formulation of recipe analysis attempted to distinguish between those areas that suffered rioting and other, ostensibly similar, locations that did not, although there is little agreement on any common characteristics (Adams 1972, Friedland 1982, Silver 1969, Spilerman 1970, 1971). Even the search for any diagnostic spatial pattern was at times rendered redundant, as in some cases the control areas where there had not been any disorders went up in flames while the researchers were still seeking the ecological criteria that sustained an absence of insurrection in previous years (Rossi et al. 1974).

Crucially, both those who stressed spatial variation and those who suggested that such variations were inconsequential worked quite explicitly within the frustration/aggression paradigm of collective behaviour theory, assuming that this natural causal link was given; the analytical task at hand rested in a definition of the distinctive features that contribute to a riot, distinguishing those elements which were causally salient from those which were merely coincidental.

US Convention 2: riots as mobilization

Some of the work which looked at the processes involved in rioting drew on collective behaviour models of dubious utility to suggest that the events could be understood as "defensive cultural adaptation" (Siegel 1979), "inarticulate protest" (Fogelson 1969), or, more normatively, "primitive and anomic" seeds of a political movement (Lang & Lang 1971), or even the product of "hysterical contagion" (Kerchkoff 1970).

More usually the uprisings were read as the continuation of the 1950s and 1960s Civil Rights movement by other means. The degree of self-consciousness attributed to this extension varies greatly from those who are keen to see rioting as a form of brief revolt (Gans 1969, Moore 1969, Rossi 1970; Smith 1969, Gurr 1978, Button 1978), to those who elevate insurrection to the status of considered and deliberate political strategy (Libman-Rubinstein 1972, 1979, Horowitz 1983).

In such work (see also Machiarola 1969, Piven & Cloward 1969), not only is the rationality of the rioters preserved but the rioting also is elevated to a form of mobilization equivalent to other social movements; for instance Piven & Cloward (1977) make a comparison with the organized labour movement. Yet a major problem that stems from such elevation concerns the viability and the validity of violent protest as a political tactic (cf. Piven & Cloward 1969, 1971, 1977, 1979, with Albritton 1978).

BLAME, GUILT AND "CAUSES" OF "RIOTS"

As Button (1978) suggests, an optimistic Whig myth of peaceful progress in capitalist democracies may be unsatisfactory, but there are obviously major pitfalls in replacing it with a myth of violent progress, pitfalls that are political and moral in their evaluation of behaviour and historical in the implication that violent disorder can be turned on and off like a tap in the service of a political strategy. This stretches back into the heart of so-called collective behaviour theory. If large numbers of people behave similarly at a certain time is this behaviour susceptible to generalization? Do these social movements possess an internal logic? Although such questions may appear divorced from the immediacy of violent conflict they recur regularly in sympathetic analyzes of movements of insurrection.

A stress on the strategic and controlled nature of the American riots is possibly best understood as, in part, a reaction to the behaviourist paradigm so clearly ascendant in American social science at the time of the ghetto revolts. In what is arguably the most impressive work on the American riots, Feagin & Hahn (1973) go so far as to suggest the development of a revolutionary ideology in the ghettos. They claim that riots followed logically from the increasing militancy of the Civil Rights Movement which had shifted from the legal action and freedom rides of the 1950s to the mass (peaceful) political mobilization of the early 1960s and increasing willingness to take defensive violent action against the many attacks on public demonstrations.

Clearly, recognizing the manner in which stimulus–response explanations deprived rioters of agency they were anxious to stress the rationality of those involved in disorder. Yet the analysis is flawed because, in an attempt to rescue the meaning of revolt, they accept the ontology of the crowd as supra-individual, replacing the de-individuated, primitive mob of behaviourism with a coldly calculating, politically conscious unit to be regarded as a lucid social actor on the stage of historical struggle.

Disorders in British cities

UK Convention 1: explanation as appropriation, behaviourism resurgent
If social explanation can neither transcend, nor expose, nor acknowledge, the ideological foundation of accounts it is worthless. Yet one characteristic common to much work in 1981 was to make the automatic step from coincidence to causality in using the rioting to justify otherwise powerful arguments. Gough (1982) was able to claim that the disorders represented "the chickens coming home to roost" for Thatch-

DISORDERS IN BRITISH CITIES

erite Policies toward the Welfare State, yet, after making this assertion, makes no further reference to rioting. Rex (1981, 1982, 1984) and Hamnett (1983) used similarly vague formulations as did Profitt (1984), who went so far as to support a demand for recognizing inner-city needs with the claim that, "Failing this action the message is clear; the uprisings will continue" (1984: 201). Such claims may not only be factually erroneous but also morally dangerous. For in this context the riot is employed as a cautionary symbol, even though there may be only a political, not a logical, need for so doing. Such a strategy may be two-edged, with the call for "welfare provision or else riots" in danger of backfiring if violence dies down. Levels of deprivation may remain as high as ever and the original case may be seen as discredited. Hence it was left to Prashar (1984) to suggest that the stark facts of racial disadvantage and inner-city deprivation stood on their own feet: there was no need to try and place them into a simplistic causal link with rioting in order to utilize that symbolic power. Even in heavy disguise the ecological fallacy is at best a clumsy vehicle for explanation. More detailed reportage of the events of 1981 (e.g. Waller 1981, Kettle & Hodges 1983, Clare 1984) suggested a complexity to the incidence of disorder that was belied by the simplistic notions of cause and effect manifested in the more clumsy sociological analyses.

There were attempts to replicate the American work, surveying areas where there had been disorder, although the results were hardly conclusive and even in one case – a Home Office Research Unit analysis in Handsworth (Southgate 1982) – was carried out when arguably the most striking feature about the events in Birmingham in 1981 was the absence of any large scale disorder, in spite of a local history of many past incidents of near uprising and the events that were to occur there four years later.

Other academic models of explanation were distinguished by their apparent determination to link the disorders to the authors' preferred interest. Notoriously, Cashmore & Troyna linked the genesis of unrest to their notion of "Black Youth in Crisis" and the alleged

> penchant for violence within the West Indian culture possibly stemming from the days of slavery when the only method of retaliation was doing physical damage to the overseer. (Cashmore & Troyna 1982)

This much criticized focus on Black communities was, in a slightly different manner, repeated by Lea & Young (1982) in their attempt to attribute the police/Black antagonism evinced in rioting to a putative over-representation of young Afro-Caribbeans in street crime, notwithstanding both the dubious evidence of such involvement and the clear evidence, already discussed in Chapter 1, that such antagonism clearly predated any allegations of possible over-representation.

UK *Convention 2: the riots as a social movement: disorders or uprisings?*
Memories attach themselves to uprisings. So too do explanations. Likewise, attributions of causality may mask a whole array of normative
characterizations of the phenomenon of riots. One of the central themes
behind which such classifications hide is the degree of organization
imputed to disorder.

Many who have written from a self-professed radical perspective
have been keen to stress the considered mobilization represented by
rioting. Joshua & Wallace explicitly suggest that they were united by "a
commonality of cause" (1983: 9) and can be placed as a benchmark in
the historical struggle of Black people in Britain. Similarly, Miles has
gone so far as to claim that among Marxist and radical authors, in spite
of other differences, there is an agreement

on a series of lower-level descriptions about, for example, the
institutionalization of racism and the origin of the riots of 1981 in
Britain. (Miles 1984: 217)

Such claims are fine in principle but it is worth asking whether they
mean very much. At any other than a superficial level such statements
may be no more than platitudes. Tying the signification "resistance" to
the signifier "riot" is vague enough to mean anything to anyone, particularly when no reference is made to actual events.

More pointedly, a problem arises when such interpretations are, on
close inspection, found to be contradictory, even when written from
similar and sympathetic political viewpoints. Once again it is the
explicandum that remains opaque. To take a case in point, Howe (1981)
was keen to emphasize the revolutionary nature of the disorders.
Verner (1981) suggests that in his various writings at the time Darcus
Howe saw the riots as "an organized guerilla uprising against the
police" (1981: 355). Paradoxically, Darcus Howe's description of the
uprisings was not dissimilar to many conspiracy theories proposed at
the time of the rioting by some senior police officers (e.g. Anderton
1981) and newspapers (*Sun; Daily Mail* July 1981 *passim*). Riots are cast
as wholly orchestrated protests: at times only approbation or oppro-
brium distinguishes Howe's from Chief Constable James Anderton's
conception of disorder. Yet for others (Rex 1981, Kettle & Hodges 1982)
the spontaneity of the uprisings is stressed and the rioting is seen as
essentially disorganized activity.

The one writer to acknowledge this apparent contradiction at the time
was Gilroy (1981), who suggested that

Understanding new political movements – new class struggles –
requires analytic concepts historically appropriate to the new forms

they take. These *spontaneous* struggles may sometimes become violent, but this does not render them irreconcilable with a strategic long-term war of position. (1981: 221; my emphasis)

Gilroy has gone on to develop precisely these same themes in analyzing the tension between social form and racial mobilization in *There ain't no Black in the Union Jack* (1987) and it is principally this tension around which many radical conceptions of disorder begin to flounder.

Frequently, in sympathetic analysis of civil disorder, violence is legitimated in the cause of Black resistance and rioting is seen as contiguous with other forms of racial mobilization and Black struggle. Such a position has profound implications that are not only moral but also relate to the sort of explanation appropriate to rioting. Specifically, "the crowd" is given the status of a conscious political actor and "the uprising" may become a tool of political strategy.

Yet the radical historical provenance of the riots of 1981 is also at times inconsistent. For some: "In the summer of 1981 the British state went on the attack against the people" (Bunyan 1981: 153)

The street conflicts were the inevitable product of a shift away from consensus politics produced by the late-twentieth-century crisis of British capitalism; the police are the iron fisted extremity of the authoritarian state and consequently the riots are not so much the property of any specific racial division, but belonged to the more general (and more abstract) unit "the people". Implicitly, Black people were caught in the front line of this conflict, almost by an accident of history. Explicitly, the ostensibly multi-racial nature of rioting is stressed and "a class dimension was added" (Bunyan 1981: 153). Conversely, the historical context for Fryer (1984) is the long history of repression suffered by Black people in Britain in general, and the repression of Black people in British cities by police over the past thirty years in particular. The difference in emphasis is crucial. The sense of ownership that underlies this contrast is an important and recurrent theme. Whether or not the proprietorial claims on the 1981 urban violence were age specific (the elusive notion of "youth"), gender-specific or class-specific are similarly moot points. As Martin Luther King said, riots are "the language of the unheard", but who speaks this tongue? Black people, young people, working people (who are not working), or is this merely the voice of the powerless? Many would bid for this powerful symbol and it is in the clamour of this historical auction that it is easy to concur with Rushdie's point that,

History is natural selection. Mutant versions of the past struggle for dominance, new species of fact arise, and old saurian truths go to the wall, blindfolded and smoking last cigarettes. Only the mutations of the strong survive. (1983)

BLAME, GUILT AND "CAUSES" OF "RIOTS"

In this sense the bid by the radical left to attach sympathetic meaning to riots, to define rioting as political action, may be pragmatically commendable, but on a purely academic level is no less tenuous an exercise than any other attempt to endow the disorders with meaning *post hoc*, particularly if it appears that there are contradictions within the meanings so offered.

The contrasts between spontaneity and organization, multi-racial rioting and Black rebellion, youth and people, are generally contrasts of stress rather than oppositions but are nevertheless significant and undermine Miles' claim of unity. The processes behind the genesis of disorder are lost in the competition to divine the political significance of rioting.

This is not to render the latter task illegitimate. A corollary of the distinction made between the way an event is remembered and the way an event actually occurred, that was so emphasized in Chapter 3, is the recognition of the validity of the symbolic power of particular passages of history. Alternative readings of this symbolism form an important field of analysis, just as the successful deployment of these symbols constitutes a crucial arena of political action.

In the statement of "What we believe" which appears regularly in the *Crossroads* Black Community newspaper the Black Liberation Front have made their approbatory classification of the events of 1981 explicit:

We strive to keep our community aware of the need to be vigilant and to promote activities whereby the ability to defend ourselves can be obtained. Within this context we consider the uprisings of the summer of 1981 as well as those since the 1970s as legitimate self-defence actions.

Historical events are subject to multiple readings of significance, questions of judgement rather than measures of truth, and in this particular context the Black Liberation Front's reading is likely to be more valid than most. But this notion of what an event *means* is not the same as what an event *was*. Again the difference between the "private" and the "public" lives of a "riot".

For this work, this distinction is important not so much in analysis which seeks to use the wisdom of hindsight – the past perceived from the present – as in the description or reconstruction of past events in their own historical context. This is one definitive distinction between political and academic discourse; both are authentic modes of analysis but they are different modes of analysis. All academic discourse is ideologically rooted but may still aspire to the status of realism, political discourse may legitimately refrain from doing so. Epistemology and ethics may always be simultaneously present in any account but they do raise slightly different sorts of questions.

92

DISORDERS IN BRITISH CITIES

The Institute of Race Relations and the Race Today Collective were in 1981 important and committed political institutions. A problem arose when writers such as Sivanandan and Howe purported to advance a historical account of events which was also a contemporary perspective on those same events. Realistic account and putative significance are woven together. This is not a criticism of the work of either author, only a suggestion that writing needs to be evaluated as operating on several levels rather than be taken superficially.

As we have already seen with the nature of the "official inquiry", the competition to attach meaning to a riot or an uprising is inevitably as much a moral and political exercise as it is a scientific one. Rushdie's notion of historical natural selection is realized similarly inside and outside the establishment, both in the alternative readings of the Handsworth disorders by three very different inquiries (Gaffney 1987) and in the attempts of progressive writers to rescue the political symbolism of disorder.

It should be possible, theoretically, to distinguish critical social theory based on the revelation of unacknowledged conditions of action (emancipatory knowledge) from rhetoric, albeit possibly laudable rhetoric, based on political campaigning. In practice it is often extremely difficult to do so, precisely because work that acknowledges the political ramifications of writing may be forced simultaneously to cast one eye to the past for accuracy, the other to the future to control the nature of its own dissemination. So perhaps much of the "committed" writing on the 1981 riots should be evaluated not solely on the grounds of accuracy alone, but also from an assessment of the function of the work – its intended effects.

Yet even this is problematic, particularly if the desire to place a proprietorial claim on the 1981 disorders as the uprisings of an oppressed Black community inadvertently amplifies the social processes which stigmatize all Black communities as potential sources of public disorder.

It is in this context that it is essential to find some alternative to *both* the cruel and illegitimate dismissal of "riot" as criminal subversion and the romantic portrayal of violent conflict as glorious revolution. It is important to discredit both the authoritarian paranoia of former Chief Constable James Anderton and also what Stuart Hall has described as the "essentialist logic" according to which, for the Black community,

in the absence of a credible alternative candidate, the white man's burden of keeping the flame of confrontation and the dream of the Winter Palace alive has descended on their shoulders, in addition to everything else. Black intransigence and street credibility are going to be pitted against the water canon and the plastic bullets in a pitiless confrontation. (Hall 1982: 66)

BLAME, GUILT AND "CAUSES" OF "RIOTS"

To place resistance in the historical context of social injustice and institutional racism is one thing, to elevate spontaneous anger to strategic violence is something else altogether.

Conclusion: towards a notion of rational spontaneity

In the most spontaneous movement it is simply the case that the elements of "conscious leadership" cannot be checked, have left no reliable document. It may be said that spontaneity is therefore characteristic of the "history of the subaltern classes", and indeed of their most marginal and peripheral elements . . . Antonio Gramsci (*Prison notebooks*: 198)

This chapter has attempted to highlight the common misrepresentation of the potential to produce knowledge about *rioting*, a common-sense frame of reference about what an explanation of disorder should look like that hinders understanding. What has been missing from so many accounts of the events of 1981, and for that matter from other studies of civil unrest, is a conception of *rioting* which captures the impromptu nature of events without reducing the actions of individuals to the behaviourist response to an array of environmental stimuli. Such a description demands a notion of *spontaneity* that does not devalue the rationality of individuals yet at the same time conveys a notion of the social context in which such actions are situated.

Regardless of the rhetoric of insurrection, people are reluctant to take to the streets in mass mobilization for the sane and self-evident reason that they are likely to be hurt, to be hit, to be arrested, to be incarcerated. To die. It is as well neither to trivialize nor to romanticize the real significance of violent disorder. For a challenge to police authority is not merely a political dispute on the legitimacy of a police force. It is also an explicit challenge to the power relation between the police and the policed that rests *ultimately* on the monopoly of legal violence held by the police as agents of the state. Nobody had to tell this to the people involved in major incidents of riot in mainland Britain precisely because they, more than the rest of the country, already knew this to be the case. Nobody had seen more of the short distance between the force implicit in the coercive facet of policing and the brutal realization of violent conflict on the streets.

Analytically, this problem is addressed by avoiding the pitfalls of common-sense models of causality as blame allocation – Hume's legacy. The structural context in which events occur provides the material causes of history, a *descriptive* logic. Formal, final and efficient causality

TOWARDS A NOTION OF RATIONAL SPONTANEITY

is distinct. Process and teleology do not provide "causes" of a different order, they are the source of "causes" of a different sort. This is essentially a call for the need to incorporate a notion of *contingency* into all explanations. Later chapters will stress that this necessarily involves an analysis of how social relations become inscribed in time and space.

None of this in any way detracts from the political imperative to take part in Rushdie's historical auction, to contest the manner in which uprisings are remembered. These memories are the "ghosts" of stories referred to at the opening of this chapter. Beyond this; ultimately,

"Some stories can't be told. They have to be lived."

(Frederic Raphael)

Notes

1. Although it has to said that the Gifford Inquiry on Broadwater Farm Estate at least followed up its recommendations at a later date (Gifford et al. 1987), unlike, for example, the Hytner Inquiry in Moss Side (Moss Side Defence Committee, 1981).

CHAPTER 5

The reality of insurrection? Empiricism and the search for the "average" rioter

> The bases for historical knowledge are not empirical facts but written texts, even if these texts masquerade in the guise of wars and revolutions. (Paul de Man, 1983. Essay on "Literary history and literary modernity")

In the more rational pieces of work written on the British riots of 1981 a common call was for the disturbances to be placed in "their overall historical context" (Rock 1981, Joshua & Wallace 1983, Clare 1984). Yet although there is self-evident sanity at the heart of such an approach, it is important to identify what is being placed before deciding where to put it.

The central tenet of this chapter is that the composition, actions and motivation of people on the streets cannot easily be taken for granted or subsumed under some consensual generic label "riot" if the charge of Lytton Strachey that "ignorance is the first requisite of the historian" (1918: 9) is to be rebutted. For a plausible account of the uprisings or riots of 1981 rests ultimately on the production of the most accurate possible description of the passage of history. Facts, facts and more facts are all-too elusive. Yet if accusations of systematic distortion are to be, at least in part, pre-empted, then a description of the events of that summer must be either provided explicitly, or else remain implicit in, inferred from, or connoted by, the context in which disorder is placed. After all, *something* happened.

In this chapter, I draw from a more extensive study of the events of 1981 (Keith 1987) to suggest that common fallacies have grown up around the popular memory of the uprisings that can be falsified by

EMPIRICISM AND THE SEARCH FOR THE "AVERAGE" RIOTER

careful analysis of the empirical evidence. This source is the Home Office Statistical Unit collection of data on those arrested in the riots of 1981; for all sorts of reasons a less than perfect source of material, but one that I have argued is superior to many other descriptive records of the 1981 rioting (Keith 1986, 1987).

Closer examination of this material clarifies one or two historical uncertainties. The disorders in London in the summer of 1981 did not involve a multi-racial alliance in insurrection and they were not attributable to any neatly defined demographic group that could be described as "Black youth". In fact the notion that it was possible to describe the average rioter who took part in the disturbances can be seen to be both empirically misleading and politically insidious.

Using state arrest data collected by the Home Office, this chapter attempts to provide such a description, accepting as a central premise that such a source may be useful but remains necessarily flawed. There are also many problems with the Home Office data which are used here.[1] But if this is not an ideal empirical source the material can supply powerful descriptions of the "faces in the crowd" at the scene of disorder. The contention here is that arrest records provide the most revealing empirical material *available* on a behavioural form such as rioting, certainly superior to information provided by the most commonly used alternative methodologies of either ecological analysis or post-riot questionnaires.

The highly empirical representation of events produced in this chapter is not equivalent to a causal explanation. This is not because of the limitations of the data used, but because of the necessary relationships between description and explanation, quantitative generalization and social action (Runciman 1983). Using material that is statistically coded and tested and derives from a computer file is not to subscribe to the fallacy that to measure all is to know all.

Neither does the attempt to provide a realistic description of the rioting crowd question the existence of a second phenomenon, "the riots" reconstructed as part of "public knowledge" (i.e. how riots are remembered). The nature of violent conflict and the cultural signification of that conflict are complementary, not competitive, descriptions of reality.

The Home Office data confirm the minimal value of notions of the average rioter. The search for a single explanation of a reified object of analysis (the riot) is an example of chaotic conceptualization (Sayer 1984). Rioting is a vague term that covers many repertoires of behaviour. Actors in the crowd played very different rôles and the Home Office data lend invaluable insights into the way in which these rôles were not distributed evenly across all groups present but were related

THE REALITY OF INSURRECTION?

to age, gender, residence and, most strongly of all, ethnicity.

Notwithstanding the profound ethical questions that are raised by using such a source, the most obvious flaw in this method is that the behaviour of many of this group will be misrepresented. Several people were found not guilty of any offence, several others were undoubtedly convicted of offences they never committed, having been picked out, almost at random, from the crowd. Similarly, there will be accusations that the chance of arrest in incidents of public disorder is disproportionately high for some groups victimized by the police – men and Black people in the case of the British riots and there is evidence of some discretionary and discriminatory charging patterns (Vogler 1982, 1990).

In this context, the value in study of arrest records rests on two basic assumptions. Neither in any way implies *any* approbatory or admonitory comment on specific actions at specific times. The *meanings* of actions are simply not touched upon by this sort of statistical description, even if the descriptions themselves were to be completely accurate. It is extremely important to note that the attempt to put faces to the crowd, while using "criminal" records, does not compromise an evaluation of civil disorder as a form of social protest.

The first assumption is that those arrested provide a sample of the sort of people "on the streets" during the violence, The second is that, however strong or weak the link, the actual offence charges against individuals will more often than not be indicative of an action or form of behaviour carried out by that individual during the disturbance. In a perfect legal system this connection would be explicit; in circumstances of occasionally arbitrary justice and institutionalized racism this is manifestly not the case. Nevertheless, given this link it should be possible to identify, with some degree of certainty, the sort of people who were carrying out certain activities in July 1981. These are loose generalizations at best but useful not least because they highlight the shortcomings of stereotypical portraits of rioters that abound.

Rioting is shown to be a complex behavioural form rather than a generic class of social action. Within this complexity specific descriptive classes are shown to be significant; stereotypical and dangerous caricatures of the average rioter are belied by statistical description.

Faces in the crowd or the average rioter?

Writing in 1964 about "The crowd in history", George Rudé forcefully suggests that the nature of civil disorders or disturbances could be divined from the composition of the crowd itself, remarking that, this is an aspect of the question that has been almost entirely neglected by historians and sociologists alike. Historians have, as we saw, been inclined to take refuge behind such omnibus and prejudicial or "value-oriented" labels as "mob" or "the people"; and adopting as their models Clarendon's "dirty people", they have appeared to assume that whether the crowd's activities were praiseworthy or reprehensible, the crowd must remain an abstract phenomenon without force or identity. And social scientists for all their serious concern with the crowd's behaviour have not done much better. (1964: 195).

Rudé's point was well made, and much of his work uses criminal records of various disorders at different times in history to identify "faces in the crowd" and to subvert the fears of the crowd, which we have already seen were commonly reproduced in early academic studies of crowd psychology. In humanizing the crowd Rudé restored its rationality, if at times he too simply attributed a collective purpose to its behaviour. At such times pejorative classification of "the crowd" is merely inverted, the flaws of romantic notions of popular mobilization discussed in Chapter 4 always incipient.

More significant for the purpose of this chapter, Rudé's work is of exemplary value for the manner in which, by humanizing the crowd, he attempts to describe the sorts of people who are involved in disorder, by capturing the diversity of those represented in scenes of unrest without ever trying to identify a caricature figure who is held up as "typical"; an individual whose actions can be explained by a list of salient social and economic characteristics.

In contrast, work in both Britain and the USA has used various methodologies to identify such an elusive individual. Almost by sleight of hand this fictional character then becomes the object of scrutiny, with a series of motivations and character traits imputed to him. The principal analytical task then becomes not to explain the individual riot, but to explain instead the generic rioter.

This point is most easily demonstrated by two examples from relevant literature. Caplan and Paige (1968), comparing the income of rioters and non-rioters in America, find that there is no significant difference between the two groups, and that

whereas there may be very many people with very low incomes who riot, a comparable percentage of people whose incomes that are just as low do not. (1968: 17)

From this trend they deduce that poverty was not a significant factor in producing riots. Quite simply there are no grounds for such inference from their data, precisely because generalized surrogate measures do not probe individual intentionality. Similarly, Cooper (1985), using

THE REALITY OF INSURRECTION?

the Home Office data to analyze the Liverpool 8 uprising of 1981, validly points out that those arrested, "included in significant proportions, persons who do not normally come into contact with the police" (p.64), and that the unemployed are not significantly over-represented in the figures. He then concludes that the rioting was, "an example of a community taking an opportunity to assert their right to equal concern and respect by means of violence." (p.68) Specifically, Cooper's explanation may well be correct. I certainly believe so. But the data do not, on their own, prove it as conclusively as he suggests. There is a danger, as can be seen from much of the American work on rioting, of the academic creating descriptive categories that may be related to riot participation at very high levels of statistical significance but which are causally meaningless. Identifying statistically significant vectors in a data matrix is not tantamount to the creation of comprehensible behavioural structures. Yet it is only such loose descriptive classifications that such analysis can aspire to. At best we pick "faces from the crowd".

Taken too far such descriptive classifications set into hard stereotypical categories which take on a life of their own. For this reason it is important to be cautious about identification of "the average rioter". In contrast the Kerner Commission in the United States suggested that,

the typical rioter in the summer of 1967 was a Negro, unmarried male between the ages of 15 and 24. He was in many ways very different from the stereotype. He was not a migrant. He was born in the State and was a lifelong resident in the city in which the riot took place. Economically his position was about the same as his Negro neighbours who did not actively participate in the riot. Although he had not, usually, graduated from high school, he was somewhat better educated than the average inner-city Negro, having at least attended high school for a time.

Nevertheless, he was more likely to be working in a menial or low status job as an unskilled labourer. If he was employed, he was not working full-time and his employment was frequently interrupted by periods of unemployment. He feels strongly that he deserved a better job and that he is barred from achieving it, not because of his lack of training, ability or ambition, but because of discrimination by employers.

He rejects the White bigot's stereotype of the Negro as ignorant and shiftless. He takes great pride in his race and believes that in some respects Negroes are superior to Whites. He is extremely hostile to Whites, but his hostility is more apt to be a product of social and economic class than of race; he is almost equally hostile to middle class Negroes." (1968: 64).

Similarly, for the British riots, Martin Kettle (1982) approvingly cites

FACES IN THE CROWD OR THE AVERAGE RIOTER?

The Times newspaper portrait of the "identikit" British rioter – "he or she was young, unemployed and living close to the rioting" (Kettle 1982: 180). Either explicitly described or implied by explanation (as with Left Realist criminology), the average rioter was a powerful and symbolic figure of the 1980s.

Whether such averages are useful or not will depend not simply on the statistical significance of a set of *average* personality variables, but rather on the explanatory power of the theoretical construct they represent.

In this sense it is important to justify the use of those personality attributes measured by state produced arrest records of the events of 1981, namely age, residence, employment, and the particularly contentious recording of ethnicity. *Use of such terms in this work does not imply agreement with either the use or the adequacy of the classifications but is justified on the grounds that variations in the data stemming from such descriptions can, if carefully used, provide one avenue for tentative description of the reality of disorder.*

Brixton: April 1981

The basic chronology and background to the Brixton riots has been described extensively elsewhere, the intention here is only to look, albeit briefly, at "faces in the crowd".

Although the events of 10–12 April might be validly considered as a single uprising, there were important differences between the violence of the different days. On Friday the 10th the rioting consisted entirely of a conflict between a group of young Blacks and the police and lasted for a few hours only. On the Saturday many more people were involved in disturbances that lasted from four o'clock in the afternoon until late at night and, significantly, looting and arson spread throughout the whole of the area. On the Sunday well over a thousand police officers were deployed in a high profile occupation of part of Brixton and, although there was both looting and attacks on the police, the disorders were not as serious as the night before.

One hundred and forty-five shop premises were damaged, 28 properties being damaged by fire. The targets within this group were not randomly chosen. (Keith 1986, 1987) Predictably, suppliers of consumer durables (particularly clothes, shoe and electrical equipment shops) and off-licenses proved favourites. However, shops owned by popular local figures in Railton Road escaped unscathed. Although it may appear a trite point to make, such rational actions must stand in contrast to the "mindless hooligans" that populated Fleet Street's rioting world. Similarly, the occasion was used by some to pay off old scores and a pub and a newsagent renowned locally for racism were burnt down (Keith

THE REALITY OF INSURRECTION?

1987). Even the *South London Press*, not noted for such local sensitivity, and which had taken an editorial line supporting the police actions at the time of the riots, remarked that one of these arsons was "undoubtedly an act of revenge for years of racial discrimination" (1981). Yet apart from a few notable exceptions, most of the damage to property occurred some two to three hundred metres away from the conflict with the police on the Saturday night (see Map 2.1). Lord Scarman even went so far as to say that,

> While the centre of the disorder was Leeson Road and the northern end of Railton Road, its effects were being felt over a wide area of central Brixton. In the commercial area of Brixton Road, the northern half of Atlantic Road, Electric Avenue and Coldharbour Lane, widespread looting had developed since about 6pm. Both Whites and Blacks – some of them very young – were involved. To several witnesses, the Whites appeared to be generally older and more systematic in their methods. It also appears that the looters were, in the main, quite different from the people who were attacking the police in Railton Road. Several witnesses had the impression that many of the looters came from outside Brixton, and were simply taking advantage of the disorders for their own criminal purposes. (Scarman 1981: 3.61)

Nevertheless, Scarman's suggestion is based on only a few eye-witness reports.

Records of many arrested during the disorders were gathered from local press, court records and personal research (Keith 1987).

There is a marked difference in the age distributions of those arrested for different offences. In Table 5.1 the data have been categorized to facilitate comparison with the Home Office data for the July riots. It can be seen that of the three major offence types (Violence Against the Person (VAP), Burglary/Theft and Threatening Behaviour) the VAP group has the highest average age. Of the 38, or almost 70 per cent, of this group who were older than 21, 13 were more than 30 years old. This compares with a figure of 60.4 per cent over 21 for the Threatening Behaviour group and the much lower figure of 37.3 per cent over 21 for the Burglary/Theft group. If figures are amalgamated to separate offences into those directed at the police, the rioters (VAP, Threatening Behaviour, Obstruction of a Police Officer), from those directed at property, the looters (Criminal Damage, Theft, Burglary), a clear difference in the age distributions of the two groups emerges. Of the rioters 66.1 per cent were over 21 compared with only 36.1 per cent of the looters. Such a disparity is, not surprisingly, statistically significant.

The addresses of this data set were mapped to compare distance travelled to offence for the two groups. The Railton Road/Mayall Road tri

FACES IN THE CROWD OR THE AVERAGE RIOTER?

Table 5.1 Brixton, April 1981: age distribution of arrested by offence.

Offence categories	Under 17		17–20		21 +		Total
	No.	%	No.	%	No.	%	
(a) Specific							
VAP	0	(0)	17	(30.91)	38	(69.09)	55
Burglary/theft	5	(7.47)	37	(55.22)	25	(37.31)	67
Criminal damage	1	(20)	3	(60)	1	(20)	5
Threatening behaviour	1	(1.89)	20	(37.74)	32	(60.37)	53
Obstruction	0	(0)	3	(23.08)	10	(76.92)	13
(b) Riot and looting							
Riot	1	(0.83)	40	(33.05)	80	(66.12)	121
Looting	6	(8.33)	40	(55.56)	26	(36.11)	72
(c) Idictable and summary offences							
Indictable	6	(4.72)	57	(44.88)	64	(50.40)	127
Summary	1	(1.52)	23	(34.85)	42	(63.63)	66

Sources: Keith (1986).

angle was taken as the epicentre of the rioting, the retail section of the Brixton Road for the looting. Concentric circles of 200 metres were then drawn around these two centres with residence pattern tabulated in terms of distribution across these concentric zones. Although most rioters and looters lived fairly close to the disturbances, the former are much more localized. Whereas 18.2 per cent of all rioters lived within 200 metres of the centre compared with only 1.4 per cent of the looters, 62.8 per cent of the rioters lived less than one thousand metres from the disturbances compared with only 36.1 per cent of the looters. Similarly, the median, upper and lower quartiles of the dispersions reveal the much higher concentration of the rioting group around the centre of the disorders. In short, there seems to be clear grounds for supporting Scarman's contention that there might be a difference between the distances the two groups had travelled to the disorders. This difference is important more in relative than absolute terms. At the time of the Brixton riots the Commissioner of the Metropolitan Police, David McNee, was quoted as saying that, "people from outside the area inspired Saturday night's riot" (*South London Press*, 14 April 1981).

THE REALITY OF INSURRECTION?

Given that chronologically the looting in Brixton did not start until two or three hours after the rioting, the extremely tightly clustered pattern of residence around Railton Road, the Front Line, would seem to belie any such suggestion, although it is obviously not possible to evaluate the significance of single instances in statistical generalization.

Police coded "ethnicity" also appears to be a crucial variable in differentiating between offence types (Table 5.2).[2] Again the most notable of the specific breakdowns occur in the VAP category. Every single one of the 30 arrests in this group stemmed from a physical conflict between police and the person charged, and of these 80 per cent were Black. In marked contrast to this, those arrested for burglary or theft were still mostly Black, but in this offence category 23 (41.1 per cent) were White. Hence, when the offence categories are amalgamated the White group, while constituting 26.8 per cent of those arrested for rioting, make up a much larger percentage (38.3 per cent) of the looters. Even those Whites who were arrested for rioting tended to be more often arrested for the less serious offence of threatening behaviour, a trend which is reflected in a comparison of the more serious indictable offences (45.5 per cent White).

The multi-racial composition of the arrest figures might masquerade as a cross-cultural conflict with the police, but when examined more closely this confrontation seems to be almost exclusively a Black preserve; only in the looting was there more general participation.[3]

If offence type is accepted as an approximate, if not completely reliable, indicator of behaviour then Rudé's call for empiricism is vindicated by an analysis of the arrest data. For those who would see riots as an expression of greed or criminality (Taylor 1984) the emergence of two valid analytical classes, the rioters on one hand the looters on the other, is difficult to explain. Suggestions of an influx of troublemakers into the area seem undermined by the fact that so many of those involved in the "uprising" lived so close to the scene of the disorders. Perhaps more importantly still, the crowd itself, so mythical, so bestial in rhetoric, begins to buckle under mundane scrutiny. In an earlier section of this work, Scarman was criticized for his portrayal of an almost regressive mob, in the worst traditions of the genre of crowd psychology and impressionistic melodrama:

In Brixton over that terrible weekend the (the police) stood between our society and a total collapse of law and order in the street of an important part of our capital. (4.98)

There is something slightly insidious in depriving a group of people of historical agency, reducing the considered to the instinctive or automatic and the human to the bestial. Scarman never rejected this sort of populist image of the crowd as animal and at times goes close to propa-

104

Table 5.2 Brixton: April 1981.

(a) Ethnicity by offence

Looting and rioting	Looting	%	Rioting	%	Total
Black	35	(58.33)	30	(73.17)	65
White	23	(38.33)	11	(26.83)	34
Asian	1	(1.67)	0	(0)	1
European	1	(1.67)	0	(0)	1
	60	(100)	41	(100)	101

Criminal offence

	VAP	%	Burglary/ theft	%	Criminal damage	%	Theft/ burglary	%	Obstruction	%	Total
Black	24	(80)	31	(55.36)	4	(100)	4	(44.44)	2	(100)	65
White	6	(20)	23	(41.07)	0		5	(55.56)	0		34
Asian	0	(0)	1	(1.79)	0		0		0		1
European	0	(0)	1	(1.79)	0		0		0		1
	30		56		4		9		2		101

Indictable vs summary

	Indictable		Summary		Total
Black	59	(65.56)	6	(54.55)	65
White	29	(32.22)	5	(45.45)	34
Asian	1	(1.11)	0		1
European	1	(1.11)	0		1
	90	(100)	11	(100)	101

(b) Ethnicity by offence by age (subset of (a))

	Under 17		17–20		21+		Total
White							
VAP	0		1	(9.09)	0		1
Theft/burglary	2	(100)	7	(63.64)	1	(50)	10
Threatening behaviour	0		3	(27.27)	1	(50)	4
	2	(100)	11	(100)	2	(100)	15
Black							
VAP	0		5	(38.46)	11	(78.57)	16
Theft/burglary	0		2	(15.39)	1	(7.14)	3
Threatening behaviour	4	(100)	6	(46.15)	2	(14.29)	12
	4	(100)	13	(100)	14	(100)	31

Source: Keith (1986).

gating such pictures himself. Such misunderstanding might be considered understandable in an old man talking about "the young", yet it took an even older man to put his finger on the tacit assumptions of the Scarman report. C. L. R. James pointed out that,

Lord Scarman is terrified by this power of young Blacks. If he understood the reasons for this power he would not exaggerate and *elevate their revolt into a force for the destruction of British society* (1981; my emphasis).

The kids on the streets?

The conventional criminological life-path passes from infantile conformity through a period of juvenile delinquency to a legalistic and moral, if not philosophical, assumed state of responsibility and stability in adulthood. As the limited notions of adult agency, implied by common usage of phrases such as "I could not help myself" or "I had to do it", and the very conformist, rule-following aspects of delinquency revealed by ethnomethodological studies (e.g. Goffman 1981, Marsh et al. 1978) demonstrate, this is a very simplistic model. Nevertheless, such trends are obviously relevant to a study of behaviour in riots, which involved, *inter alia*, a great deal of criminal activity.

Whatever the broader significance and deeper causes, there are some very straightforward similarities between incidents of public disorder in 1981 which cannot be overlooked. Most took place at night, most in cities and the majority at weekends. In any city on any weekend the majority of those people on the streets on foot late at night will be young. The central concern of the police during disturbances is inevitably more with public order than with law enforcement. In short, maximum opportunity for crime and large numbers of people from what are euphemistically referred to as "crime prone groups" are paired in time and space; almost a parody of a criminologist's combustion equation. To state this *is not* to impugn the motivation of rioters or to taint or criminalize those on the streets, but rather to suggest that given the context of disorder and the social reality of twentieth-century Britain, a large amount of criminal behaviour carried out by young males is to be expected. It follows that those people arrested aged 21 or older form a class which is, almost *a priori*, more "interesting", precisely because they differ from the criminal norm. This becomes doubly the case if the composition of this class, in terms of ethnicity and offence charged (taken as a rough guide to behaviour), can be distinguished from the younger group, thus making the division statistically, and quite possibly descriptively, significant.

Alternatively, in a search for the average rioter, it is always possible, given a full set of data, to produce a mean, median or modal age to slot

FACES IN THE CROWD OR THE AVERAGE RIOTER?

into our definition, in the manner of Kerner. But what do such creations mean? An average age means little or nothing if there is considerable variation about this average; it means much more if the age distribution is tightly clustered.

Unfortunately, the Home Office data was collected on a nominal rather than interval or ratio basis and so it is possible to calculate neither a mean, nor a median, nor standard deviation, nor many of the more rigorous statistical tests based on analysis of variance. The crime prone 17 to 20-year-old class regularly form a modal group of around 40 per cent of those arrested when the data is analyzed: 42.9 per cent of Whites, 42.2 per cent of Blacks and around 40–45 per cent of most offence groups fall into this category.

The two notable exceptions to this trend are the Asians (54.6 over 21) and the employed (64 over 21) modal groups (Table 5.3). Given the disproportionately high unemployment rates among those under 21 the latter figure is no more than a reflection of a national trend. The presence of such a high proportion of "mature, responsible" adults among those arrested on the streets is more important because it alone

Table 5.3 All London Metropolitan Police Districts.

Age	Under 17		17–20		21 +		Total	
Ethnicity		%		%		%		%
White	117	(23.35)	215	(49.91)	169	(33.74)	501	(100)
West Indian	118	(27.50)	181	(42.19)	130	(30.31)	429	(100)
Asian	13	(13.13)	32	(32.32)	54	(54.55)	99	(100)
	248	(24.1)	428	(41.59)	353	(34.31)	1029	(100)
Offence								
(a) VAP	30	(18.75)	73	(45.62)	57	(35.63)	160	(100)
Theft	74	(31.09)	100	(42.02)	64)	(26.89)	238	(100)
	104		173		121		398	
(b) Indictable	133	(27.76)	205	(42.80)	141	(29.44)	479	(100)
Summary	113	(22.69)	211	(42.37)	174	(34.94)	498	(100)
	246		41	6	31		977	
(c) Rioting	140	(22.08)	276	(43.53)	218	(34.39)	634	(100)
Looting	99	(32.04)	128	(41.43)	82	(26.53)	309	(100)
	239		404		300		943	
Employment (as percentages of economical active)								
Employed		(27.16)		(49.63)		(69.14)		
Unemployed		(72.84)		(50.37)		(30.86)		

Source: Home Office Statistical Unit

THE REALITY OF INSURRECTION?

is grounds enough for a rejection of an explanation of public disorder in terms of the delinquent or "riff-raff" groups in the Asian community. Yet even where the 17 to 20 group covers 40–45 per cent of those arrested, this still leaves 55–60 per cent of those arrested unaccounted for. The caricature image of "public-order problems" tied to endemic juvenile delinquency looks less plausible in this light.

The proportion of those arrested who were over 21 also varies significantly between the subdivisions of the data set. The total number of arrests of Asians is small in comparison to the other two principal ethnic groups but the age distribution would seem to suggest that those who were involved in the disorders came from a wide cross-section of the community. The difference between the age distribution of the Asian group and that of both the West Indian and White groups is statistically significant for very low levels of alpha (see Table 5.3).[4]

Rioters and looters

It has already been stressed that there is a marked difference in the behaviour implied by the different charges placed against those arrested in the riots. If such differences are not evenly distributed across all subdivisions of the data, this too would belie notions of the average rioter and suggest underlying patterns among those arrested. One of the more obvious distinctions here is between the offence category of Violence Against the Person (VAP), which almost invariably resulted from alleged confrontation with the police, and Theft/Burglary, which, presumably, more commonly reflected participation in looting.

Again there is a difference between the sorts of people who fall into these two classes. Of those over 21, 35.6 per cent were charged with VAP and only 26.9 per cent with Theft/Burglary. Of those under 17, 18.8 per cent were charged with VAP but 31.1 per cent with Theft/Burglary (Table 5.3). The fact that there is no significant difference between indictable and summary charge groups, and in view of both the potential and actual penalties for property crime already mentioned, any suggestion that the police might have been reluctant to make serious charges against young, and implicitly less responsible, offenders must be scotched. As in the case of Brixton in April 1981 those involved in conflict with the police (rioters) appear statistically distinct from those opportunistically seizing the chance to loot.

There is a strong case for considering any average age of those involved in uprisings a misleading figure. The age difference between those charged with VAP and those with Theft/Burglary is statistically significant at a rejection level of 5 per cent ($Chi^2 = 8.54$), and that between Asians and other groups invariably at 0.1 per cent. Put simply, Asian involvement in rioting was not a function of age, while large

THE INTENSITY OF CONFLICT

numbers of adult Whites and West Indians were also involved in the disturbances. The disorders cannot be considered only in terms of "the kids on the streets" (Rock 1981). However, age is a useful indicator for predicting the behaviour of the crowd. Those involved with theft and looting appear to have been much younger than those concerned in conflict with the police. This too is significant. Explanation cannot be couched purely in terms of police–youth relations if it is the elder group who seem most demonstrative in their withdrawal of the consent upon which all police operations hinge.

In short, the ubiquitous concept of the average rioter has been examined and found wanting. It is the central term of a set united by few similarities, a set with maximum extension, minimum intension. It was not, of itself, a meaningful concept; it became one after 1981 and has been one ever since. Images of the average rioter on the street provide a central organizing theme for all common-sense understandings of the incidence of civil disorder in 1980s Britain, but the relationship between representation and reality is not straightforward.

The intensity of conflict

Closer examination of the incidents packaged together by Home Office classification reinforce such systematic variation. Crucially, when the ephemeral, extraneous events that were tendentiously classified as "riots" are sieved from the Home Office data the level of White involvement in rioting is greatly reduced. In exactly the same way, the most violent clashes at the heart of rioting were between the police and a wide cross-section of the Black community, not between the police and the frequently posited mob of multi-racial youths.

The exploration of arrest statistics for the whole of London assumed that this data served as a sample of those people who were on the streets of the capital in July 1981. Although the April rioting in Brixton was discussed separately, the principal contingent premise was that these disorders together formed a whole, the 1981 London riots, and that those patterns that were discerned related to this essentially aspatial single phenomenon. Quite clearly, the putative generic activity rioting involved many different forms of behaviour and the analysis demonstrated that this variation was not randomly distributed across age, ethnic, residence and gender groups.

In order to summarize such variation a technique often used in American studies (e.g. Spilerman 1971, 1974, Wanderer 1969, Friedland 1981), was to differentiate between incidents in terms of their serious-

THE REALITY OF INSURRECTION?

ness, according to each a score based on the constituent events of each disorder, thus constructing slightly macabre rankings of the intensity of disorder by location.

The ostensible simplicity of this technique is belied by the problem of assessing the weight given to the different criteria involved in calculating such scores (are two arsons more or less serious than ten broken arms?). For the purposes of this work, a scale which is broadly based on that of Wanderer is used, although other indices would have served. "Seriousness" of a "riot" can be conceived theoretically in terms of "abstract distance" from an "abstractly normal condition of public order". Of course, this too is more complicated than it may at first seem, implicitly employing an undefined conception of public order. This must inevitably be tied to more general social theory, however hidden this connection may appear, a point that will be examined in greater detail in a later chapter.

The results of the index used here are shown in Table 5.4. They are crude and simplistic but useful in understanding some fairly general points. The index illustrates the diversity of behaviour that was subsumed under the label of serious "incidents of public order". The common fracas was commonly reclassified at this time, dressed up as disorder. The measure serves well in highlighting this process. At the same time it would be foolish to underestimate the importance of those occasions when large groups of people were involved in intensive, if short lived, looting in major retail areas of London (e.g. Tooting or Hounslow). The absence of any commitment to public order implicit in such actions is of major social significance, the "meaning" of such behaviour throwing a light on the nature of society as a whole.

Notwithstanding problems surrounding the derivation of this slightly bizarre index, two patterns in particular emerge from the London rioting when classified by severity. The ethnic breakdown of the crowds involved in the disorders is closely related to their seriousness. A positive correlation of $rs = 0.73$ between the proportion of those arrested that were non-White and "riot seriousness", and of 0.67 between the proportion of those arrested that were Afro-Caribbean and "riot seriousness", contradict notions of the rioting as a "multi-ethnic" form of behaviour.

There were very many White people arrested in London in the July disturbances (503, 48 per cent of the total) – they formed the largest single ethnic group in the Home Office data – but these people tended to be arrested in the most minor incidents. In those cases where the collapse of public order was most complete, in Brixton, in Hackney, in Wood Green and in Southall, the proportion of those arrested who were White is at its lowest and the involvement of White people at

110

THE INTENSITY OF CONFLICT

these locations is, with the major exception of Southall, peripheral to the main focus of the riot itself (see Table 5.5). In Brixton and in Hackney, White involvement, with some exceptions, was basically confined to looting. In Wood Green, White involvement tended to concentrate mostly on the second day of less violent, more voyeuristic disorder. Even in acknowledging the rôle played by White racists in their "invasion" of Southall when supporting the 4 Skins, a band renowned for its racist allegiances, the "riot" as a form of collective behaviour was an expression of the local Asian community.

Table 5.4 Riot intensity in all "serious incidents of public disorder" in London, July 1981.

(a) Key

Site (of disorder)

R	Residential
S	Retail
PH	Public house

Property: a quantitative measure of the type and extent of damage suffered by property at the scene of disorder.

D	Criminal damage
L	Looting
A	Attempted or successful arson

Conflict: a quantitative measure of the type and extent of violent conflict at the scene of disorder.

CF	Civilian fight
P	Violent confrontation with police
R	Racial violence

Petrol bombs: taking one particular element of the 'rioting armoury' as symptomatic of the escalation of violence.

A	Petrol bomb present or found at the scene of disorder
B	Petrol bombs used against property
C	Petrol bombs used against people

Each incident was assessed under these three criteria producing aggregate "scores" of riot severity in the manner of Wanderer (1969).

List of locations taken from Home Office records

(b) An index of riot severity.

	Dates in July	Site	Property			Conflict			Petrol bombs			Total	Rank
			D	L	A	CF	P	R	A	B	C		
Notting Hill	9	R+S	1	1	–	–	1	–	–	–	–	3	3=
	10	R+S											
	11	R	2	1	–	–	3	–	1	–	3	10	5=
	12	R											
	13	R											
Fulham	9, 10	S	1	–	–	1	1	–	1	–	–	4	13=
Hackney	9	R+S											
	10	R+S	3	3	1	–	4	–	1	2	5	19	3
	11	R+S											
Limehouse	10	S	–	–	–	1	–	–	–	–	–	1	27=
Chingford	10	PH	1	–	–	1	1	–	1	–	–	5	27=
Walthamstow	10, 11	R+S	2	–	–	2	1	3	1	–	–	9	8=
Chigwell	11	S+PH	–	–	–	1	–	–	–	–	–	1	27=
Dagenham	11	S+PH	–	–	–	1	–	–	–	–	–	1	27=
West Ham	10	PH	–	–	–	1	1	–	1	–	2	5	12=
	10	PH	2	–	–	–	1	–	–	–	–	3	16=
	11	S	2	1	–	–	–	–	–	–	–	3	16=
	11	R	–	–	–	–	–	2	–	–	–	2	21=
Brixton	10												
	11	R+S	3	3	2	–	3	–	1	3	5	20	2
	12												
	15	R	2	–	–	–	3	–	1	–	5	11	4
Southwark	10	R+S	1	–	–	–	2	–	1	–	–	4	13=
Penge	10	R+S	1	–	1	–	–	–	1	1	–	4	13=
Lewisham	10	PH+S	1	–	–	1	1	–	–	–	–	3	16=
Harlesden	11	S	–	–	–	–	2	–	–	–	–	2	21=
Bexley Heath	11	PH	1	–	–	1	–	–	–	–	–	2	21=
Woolwich	9	S	1	–	–	1	1	–	–	–	–	3	16=
Golders Green	11	S	–	–	–	–	1	–	–	–	–	1	27=
Chiswick	10	S	1	1	–	–	–	–	–	–	–	2	21=
	10	PH	–	–	–	1	1	–	–	–	–	2	21=
Hounslow	10	S	2	2	–	–	1	–	–	–	–	5	12=
Tooting	9	S	3	3	–	–	–	–	–	–	–	6	11
Battersea	9												
	10												
	11	R+S+PH	2	2	–	1	2	1	1	–	1	10	5=
	12												
	13												
Action	10	R+S	3	2	–	–	–	–	–	–	–	5	12=
Southall	3	R+S+PH	2	–	2	1	3	3	1	4	5	21	1
	10,15,16	R+S	1	–	–	–	3	3	–	–	–	7	10=
Wood Green	7,8	S	3	2	1	3	–	–	–	–	–	9	8
Croydon	10, 11	S+PH	–	–	–	–	–	–	1	–	–	1	27=
Sutton	11	S	1	1	–	–	–	–	–	–	–	2	21=

Source: M. Keith (1986), *The 1981 Riots in London.*

THE INTENSITY OF CONFLICT

Table 5.5 Involvement in conflict with the police in serious incidents of public disorder in London, July 1981.

	Arrests (total)	Black (no.)	Black (%)	Violence against people (total)	Black (no.)	Black (%)
Southall	61	4	7	21	2	10
Wood Green	71	42	59	5	4	80
Brixton	257	161	63	19	15	78
Hackney	107	75	70	23	18	78
Battersea	79	24	30	14	12	86
Tooting	41	10	24	6	2	33
West Ham	49	16	33	7	4	57
Croydon	45	4	9	2	0	0
Penge	42	22	52	1	0	0
Notting Hill	28	12	43	12	6	50
Walthamstow	29	1	3	9	0	0

Representation differs significantly at 0.10 level of significance using binomial test $z = 1.43$.
Source: Home Office Statistical Unit.

It is important to stress that no notions of either cause or allocation of guilt are implicit in such analysis. It is merely important to stress that the most serious rioting was the historical property of Afro-Caribbean and Asian communities.

Riot seriousness was also clearly related to the location of disorder. The stage which provided a platform for riot invariably consisted of permutations from three basic sets; residential areas, retail property and public houses. The most intense clashes often occurred in the residential areas, while the incidents that were exaggerated in media coverage seemed often connected with drunken behaviour and pubs.

The index of riot severity belies the clean cut certainty of those "lists of riots" so favoured by historians and sociologists alike. In places such as Sutton and Golders Green the small fights that were sometimes classified as serious disorder can be readily dismissed as fictitious insurrections. But even in other locations where the incidence of disorder is undisputed, no straightforward activity that can be labelled as "rioting" can be identified.

Because it highlights the imbroglious nature of disorder, the notion of riot seriousness is useful, but only in a very restricted analytical

THE REALITY OF INSURRECTION?

sense. The term is defined purely by a set of negative differences, "what it is not" as much as "what it is". It is meaningful only as a state of abnormality, a departure from the day-to-day routine of everyday life. It is clear from the varied reactions throughout London that there are very localized notions of what constitutes such a routine. The concept of riot seriousness embraces both the relative distance from a perceived normal order as well as an objective evaluation of social states. Any measure of riot seriousness can at best quantify the latter, and then only in a one dimensional format. Such a measure is again one important piece in the descriptive mosaic that serves as an image of the 1981 riots, and such a mosaic may be evocative, powerful, even emancipatory but never contains immanent truths.

Riot intensity and ethnicity

The crude measure of intensity of confrontation is also useful in analysis of the paradigmatic charges of VAP and Theft/Burglary. In 11 of the most serious incidents (The MPD 11) the Black component accounts for 56 per cent of all Theft arrest charges compared with 46 per cent of all arrests, matching the pattern for the whole of London (54 per cent and 41 per cent, respectively). However, when this relationship is examined for each location in the MPD 11, in no fewer than seven of the nine instances in which there were theft arrests the proportion of those arrests that were of Black people is smaller than the proportion of Black arrests in the total. If anything, rather than a simple over-representation of Blacks in this offence category, the reverse is the case. The trend for the whole of London is produced by a concentration of Blacks in those locations where most looting occurred.

Emphasizing once again the concept of riot seriousness as abstract distance from a state of public order, and the criminological conception of looting in terms of opportunity-based crime rates, these figures reinforce hypotheses already put forward. Black involvement and riot seriousness are closely related. Collapse of public order creates an ideal environment for opportunistic action. If looting is most often a secondary activity to violent conflict, determined principally by opportunity, peripheral to the central action, then those who take advantage of this environment will reflect the ethnic make up of the crowd at the scene of disorder (or adjacent to it). Yet this is only partly the case in the 11 cases here. The most serious disorders involved a disproportionate number of Black people and the looters were predominantly Black, reflecting this opportunistic advantage. Nevertheless, this predominance is not as great as expected. The fact that in seven of the nine locations where there were theft arrests, the Black component was, relative to each incident as a whole, under-represented, again supports the

THE INTENSITY OF CONFLICT

contention that Black involvement was more concerned with violent confrontation with the police than material accumulation of plunder. A much more emphatic and equally important pattern emerges when the offence category of VAP is examined in the same way. The Black component is over-represented in the VAP offence category in eight out of the eleven locations. This is the case even in locations such as Battersea, Tooting and West Ham where the Black group accounts for only a small proportion of total arrests. If the VAP offence is an effective indicator of the most serious physical conflict, and examination of magistrates' courts records and the disproportionate link with riot intensity would suggest that it is, then this over-representation again indicates that even where the crowd on the streets was predominantly White and not so violent, conflict with the police was dominated by Black groups. The Asian pattern of arrests – almost entirely absent from the theft category (only four Asian theft arrests in the whole of London), but accounting for 14 per cent of the VAP arrests – serves to highlight the under-representation of the White group in the latter category, accounting for only 30 per cent of VAP arrests compared with 41 per cent of all arrests in the MPD 11. Moreover, whereas almost all the Black and Asian charges for VAP were associated with conflict with the police (96 per cent of those traced for the former, 82 per cent for the latter), 41 per cent of the White VAP charges traced are associated with racist attacks on Asians in Walthamstow, Southall and West Ham.

In summary, it is possible to identify the offence categories of Theft and VAP as epitomizing two very different forms of riot activity. The latter is slightly ambiguous as it picks up those involved with all the most serious violent behaviour, although those VAP charges not related to conflict with the police arose only in Walthamstow, Southall and West Ham and came mostly from the IC1, White ethnic group. In almost all disorders, Black people are disproportionately involved in those activities that relate to violent clashes with the police and almost invariably the majority lived very close to the centre of the disturbance. Their involvement in looting tends to reflect the extent of the breakdown of public order generally, and although there is over-representation for London as a whole, this occurred because the most serious disturbances tended to be those in which most Black people were involved. Asian involvement was both highly localized and almost exclusively concerned with protest, both peaceful and violent.

Conclusions

The very task of using statistical description of state generated arrest records involves a process of generalization. If such description is to be morally defensible, let alone academically useful, it must avoid decaying into stereotypical portraits of "the average rioter". If groups of people become known solely for their propensity to riot we might say that the "articulating principle" which structures their identity becomes that of civil unrest; more straightforwardly that they are seen only in terms of potential disorder.

The arrest records provide some link between individuals and actions, no necessary connection exists between the data and mental states of the actors; intentionality is not probed and statements that are essentially semantic, relating to the meaning of behaviour, cannot be based on these records alone. Actions may be manifest, acts remain opaque.

However work here and elsewhere does demonstrate that patterns are present in the arrest statistics for the events of 1981 which reveal that there are marked differences in the behaviour of different groups in different locations (Keith 1986, 1987). In simple terms there are significant trends throughout all locations, between locations and within locations (e.g. Brixton).

The arrest data are scrappy and full of problems. They provide a vital source of material for both initiation and examination of particular notions of disorder, but these hypotheses must be regarded as provisional, since statistical testing, even when mathematically very rigorous, can provide no more than descriptive hints at explanation.

Some of the conceptions that underwrite the explanations of rioting examined in Chapter 4 can be dismissed outright. The notion that in 1981 Black and White regularly fought a united battle on the streets (e.g. Bauman 1982: 179) becomes virtually untenable in the light of the analysis. White involvement in rioting was consistently very different from that of Black people in terms of age, residence and, most significantly of all, actual behaviour. At times different ethnic groups may have shared the same streets but, leaving aside instances of multi-racial looting, a history of united ethnic insurrection can be rejected.

Similarly, the common-sense rationalization of trouble solely in terms of a "police/Black youth conflict" is equally spurious. Lawrence's (1982: 54) suggestion that the social category "youth" may hide rhetorical preconceptions or ideologies is nowhere more insidiously supported. In confining the ambit of the conflict to the young – those who remain immature and not quite agents of their own destiny, there is an impli-

CONCLUSIONS

cit, possibly accidental, relegation of the status of the rioting. The unspoken assumption behind such a move follows the conventional path of the modern myth (Barthes 1967). People on the streets, the rioters, are endowed with a new history. They epitomize the long, traditionally fractious, socialization of the adolescent (Corrigan 1979, Downes 1966, Robins & Cohen 1978). Potentially the riot is transformed into part of late-twentieth-century rites of passage. History is transformed into nature, the natural pains of growing up, albeit that these pains are exacerbated in the immiserated inner city. In benevolence condescension. For the data pattern shows consistently that violent conflict with the police, so common to disorder, was not the province of Black youth alone indeed the Black people who dominated this conflict tended to be older than those involved in other activities at times of riot.

The sort of generalizations that do emerge from the statistics have the status of competing descriptions of the shadows of reality. The "academic" descriptive classes may be modest but are not less invaluable for being so. Human behaviour does not fit into neat pigeon holes. Two that are consistently useful, in both analysis of London as a whole and in individual histories, are those which distinguish in the residence pattern between "travellers" and "locals", and in offence groups between "rioters" and "looters". Typically, the rioters were older and more involved with attacks on the police than the looters, and on almost all occasions, even when the majority of the crowd were White, were invariably Black people. The residential division is blurred by the Home Office classification process, but highlights the fact that on those occasions when a large proportion of those arrested were "travellers" the disturbances were generally less serious and involved relatively young crowds of people.

At one level, the events of "that summer" appear on closer inspection no more than a disparate collection of very different events. Yet at another level even the unity of individual incidents of disorder seems seriously questioned by the arrest data. If classifications suggest that different sorts of people were concerned with very different sorts of actions in Brixton or Hackney, and they do, then the terms "the Brixton riot" or "the Hackney riot" are, like "the London riots", descriptively meaningful but of restricted analytical use. It is simply not good enough to assume that individual disorders, which are by definition "abnormal" or "deviant" forms, must be united by a "commonality of cause" (Joshua & Wallace 1983). Themes of motivation will run through the crowd, never repeated identically for any two individuals, but by their relative strengths defining the nature of specific riots. Explanation must relate to these themes, not to a pathology of rioters, nor to a path-

THE REALITY OF INSURRECTION?

ology of any subset of these rioters. It is this thematic diversity that makes explanation so difficult, so contingent on this "character" of the disorders.

Combining the Home Office statistics with other background information highlights three common facets of behaviour. First, a conflict between the Black community as a whole and the Metropolitan Police. Secondly, there was a highly localized, predominantly Black, male crowd on the streets prepared to turn this conflict of interest into a conflict of arms. Thirdly, a series of processes related to commitment to public order evolved around these initial clashes and transformed the nascent riot into a highly complex behavioural form.

It is this complexity of the end product that prohibits easy rationalization of this type of popular mobilization and mocks theories of crowd psychology and collective behaviour. As the riot proceeds and is conjoined with repertoires of behaviour not directly related to the genesis of violent conflict, it becomes progressively more difficult to identify a generic form of activity that could be called rioting. Scenes of disorder appear to converge on one, almost identical, product, regardless of whether they are produced by a wrongful arrest in London or a power cut in New York. Rioting is more comprehensible as a state of disorder than a verb of action, one more reason why the rioter/non-rioter dichotomy is so problematic.

It is because the arrest data represent the empirical realization of these broad trends that they provide a powerful and indispensable source for description of the rioting in London in 1981. They salvage the complexity of civil disorder from crude common-sense classification and highlight the centrality of localized clashes between a particular social order and a broad cross-section of the local British Black community.

The image of the young Black man as the quintessential rioter in the events of 1981 is in so many ways a misleading stereotype. The significance of racial mobilization in the genesis of uprisings is one thing. The rôle which the political concept of "race" played in rationalizing riots, building a history and making a sense out of the chaos and putative anarchy of street disorder is a different *thing* altogether. Likewise the conflicts at their most serious were, in their most serious forms, both racialized and localized, themes that related to the evolution of conflict in particular places. Part Three of this book attempts to look at such locational specificity in greater detail, to see if it helps contextualize the timeless and placeless rationalizations of both police racism and civil unrest criticized in Chapters 1 and 4.

NOTES

Notes

1. For a fuller examination of these problems see Keith 1987, Vogler 1982.

2. Data sets that overlapped with those used in these tables facilitated both a general breakdown by ethnicity and age of the characteristics of 101 offenders and a 46-person subset of this group.

3. The breakdown of offence groups by both age and ethnicity is based on too small a sample size to endorse or produce any conclusive comment or statistical testing. However, the trend that does emerge to some extent is that the majority of both Blacks and Whites arrested for looting were in the 17–20 age range, contrary to Scarman's suggestion; again, only Black arrests for VAP emerge as a class notable for the large numbers in the Black 21+ group.

4. Given that there is also a marked difference between age and offence (see below) it was considered that this might be caused by a concentration of Asians in those offences with higher average age for offenders. Although to an extent this is the case, when standardized for offence an "unexpected" figure for Asians of 34% over twenty-one (cf. White 33%, West Indian 31%), slightly higher than for the other two ethnic groups, but accounting little for the over-representation of elder Asians. Nevertheless, this process does account for most of the small difference between the White and West Indian groups, which is already minor and statistically insignificant.

119

PART THREE

"GRIEF"

CHAPTER 6

Front Line policing in the 1980s

The events of 1981 irrevocably changed the nature of policing in mainland Britain. Serious civil disorder, once only the stuff of pipedreams and strategic planning was now to be incorporated as a significant factor in the managerial organization of particular forces. Clashes that could have escalated into major incidents of riot, but did not quite do so, littered the decade, as the annual reports of the Chief Constables of the major cities and the Commissioner of the Metropolitan Police readily confessed. Particular places were identified, rightly or wrongly, as potential scenes of confrontation. Civil disorder was written onto the political agenda of the 1980s as a social problem in British cities (Keith 1988). The context in which such clashes were placed drew together the three contentious subject areas with which this book is concerned: notions of race, criminality and civil order. Kenneth Newman, in his time as Commissioner of the Metropolitan Police, was quite prepared to go on record publicly with his own analysis as already cited in Chapter 2. To repeat Newman's diagnosis, these three elements in the recipe for violent conflict were said to come together at various symbolic locations, listed specifically:

Railton Road in Brixton, All Saints Road in Notting Hill and Sandringham Road in Hackney and so on. These are at the centre of areas where crime is at its worst, where drug dealing is intolerably overt, and where the racial ingredient is at its most potent. K. Newman (16 February 1987)

In truth, there *were* particular local realizations of the national conflict between police and British Black communities. The *local* is important, although not necessarily in the sense that Newman implied. This chapter attempts to examine the significance of specific local histories on the basis of participant observation work and interviews with serving police officers from 1986–8 in precisely the places that Newman lists as symbolic locations. Again, as in Chapter 2, constraints of space have produced necessarily abbreviated accounts of these places and, as in Chapter 2, greatest attention is paid to the events in Stoke Newington and least to the events in Notting Hill.

Any piece of work which attempts to take on board the perspectives of a particular professional group leaves itself vulnerable to criticisms of partiality, exceptionalism and a tendency either to oversympathize or to be parasitic upon the group that is being studied. Undoubtedly, all these criticisms contain significant degrees of validity; they are the internal shortcomings of all ethnography, and there is no attempt here to speak on behalf of the police institution or make sweeping generalizations about police behaviour. As with the local histories in Chapter 2, the intention is only to provide glimpses of the past in three places, this time from a police perspective.

By its very nature, ethnographic work demands a basic level of empathy and the author was regularly surprised by the enormous variations in police attitudes and behaviour, from the very impressive to the less than admirable. Yet the nature of the police organization and the particular antagonisms and real hatreds that are the day-to-day reality of violent confrontation raise many questions about such work. Ethnography demands that the individual researcher position her-/himself as "member", yet at the same time sustain critical distance: the oxymoron at the heart of the term "participant-observation" (Pile 1991), and the context of police/Black antagonism, may question the very notion of engaging in such work (Keith 1992). Such questions can be answered only in terms of the sort of end product that results and the expression of that research product in particular contexts.

In terms of the overall structure of this volume, the concern here is with establishing the manner in which policing practices evolved in the 1980s and, in particular, were structured by the riots of 1980 and 1981. In doing this, the intention is both to look backwards to render an understanding of locationally specific protest more comprehensible (Ch. 7) and forwards to understand how a form of policing, that both Kenneth Newman and his successor Peter Imbert have subsequently described as paramilitary, became unexceptional in much of London.

Notting Hill

The Carnival clashes 1975/76

The long running tensions in Notting Hill burst into large-scale violent disorder at the Carnivals of both 1975 and, in a much more dramatic fashion, 1976. This confrontation between police and community has been described in detail on many occasions (Gutzmore 1978, *Race Today passim* 1975-9, Howe 1980, Rollo 1980, IRR 1979, Fryer 1984, Jackson 1988, Pryce 1987) but two accounts, those of Cohen and Gutzmore,

FRONT LINE POLICING IN THE 1980s

stand out above all others. Abner Cohen (1980, 1982) has described how the Carnival became the classic example of "resistance through rituals", a cultural expression subsuming political protest. Cohen's study of "how symbolic performances reproduce or modify power relations" highlights how, throughout the early 1970s, in the face of societal repression, Carnival epitomized a form of cultural politics, political action and aesthetic expression that were inseparable.

Bound up in the Carnival was a statement about an oppressive White society. The police responded by actively campaigning to prohibit the Carnival, co-ordinating and publicizing a petition demanding that the event be banned. When this tactic failed, police chose instead to station more than fifteen hundred men at Carnival in what was later conceded by some officers as "oppressive formations". Typically, forty police were placed as an "escort" on each steel band. The violence that ensued was almost inevitable, but the crudity of the conflict was perhaps only truly captured in Gutzmore's description (1978) in which he stated that the Black community had taken on the British bobby – and won. In his words,

> the police were almost unarmed. They just had their sticks and their numbers. But numbers were absolutely no use, in effect, against those weapons. They were roundly beaten. Hundreds of them were injured. Absolutely justifiably – because what they were attempting to do seemed to us in the community to be totally unnecessary. We had warned about what would happen. They might just have got away with it, if they had attempted to do it with a little less brashness and a little bit less brutality. But, in fact, they did it both brashly and brutally, and *they were confronted and defeated on that terrain*, in the second most important single battle fought by the Black Masses in the UK – the first being of course the Black Resistance in 1958. (1978: 24; my emphasis)

By 1976 the conflict in Notting Hill was almost that simple. Blue versus Black. Crucially, at the heart of these clashes almost invariably was the Mangrove and All Saints Road. On the Sunday night of the 1976 Carnival the police cordoned off the road at the height of the festivities and raided the Mangrove in strength. On the Monday the retaliation – the open fighting and what was seen by both police and Black community as a "defeat" for the police – made banner headlines in the national press.

The development of All Saints Road as a symbolic location

Clashes in All Saints Road grew in ferocity throughout the 1970s. In 1977, although there was less trouble at the Carnival as a whole, there was again a major raid on the Mangrove. Two police informants, both

NOTTING HILL

working at this time in Notting Hill, who asked to remain anonymous, described the events of the late 1970s from the opposite perspective. For them the All Saints Road had become both a dangerous place to patrol and hub of illicit activity. The Apollo pub, a hundred yards up the road from the Mangrove, was a well known site of drugs sales and there were "four or five" illegal drinking clubs on the road as well. The explicit suggestion of one informant was that in this situation the police were unable to enforce the law in this part of their division and occasional raids *en masse*, particularly on the Mangrove – seen as the source of greatest hostility toward the police – were quite clear demonstrative gestures of police power.

In the summer of 1981, against the turbulent backdrop, the police decided not to attempt to remove the crowds who gathered, or the barricades that were put up, on All Saints Road. The chronology and the significance of what happened that year is examined in greater detail in the following chapter, but on one level, the reason for this was quite simply that, by 1981, in the on-going confrontation the All Saints Road and the Mangrove had won a form of *de facto* "privileged status". Any police action, sensitive or senseless, was likely to be opposed, a state of affairs widely resented at PC level, reluctantly acknowledged at managerial level, but recognized by all actors involved in the life of the area Black and White. It was a situation Chief Superintendent Whitfield (Notting Hill, 1982–4) described as: "a stand off and a virtual no-go area for a while both before 1981 and at times since" (personal interview).

Revenge

On 24 December 1981 the Mangrove was raided. In April 1982, one of the first operations involving deployment of the newly formed public-order units of the Metropolitan Police (the Immediate Response Units) was another raid on the Mangrove, after a suspected thief was seen "entering the premises". There was no doubt in the minds of most local Black commentators and most of the police in Notting Hill that these two raids partly compensated for the loss of face suffered by the police in the preceding summer. Again the fearful symmetry of views. Shortly after this raid, Chief Superintendent Whitfield assumed command at Notting Hill. He described the atmosphere in the station at the time as "euphoric" because of this "triumph".

Transforming All Saints Road

During his three years at Notting Hill, Whitfield was involved in a conscious attempt to "take away the symbolism of All Saints Road". This project was to be achieved by completely changing the style of policing in the area. The first step Whitfield took was to prevent all cars patrol-

125

FRONT LINE POLICING IN THE 1980s

ling All Saints Road and have instructions placed at Scotland Yard that no car from any other division was allowed in "hot pursuit" into the road either. This was not popular with either junior officers or several sceptical superiors at Scotland Yard itself. The reasons that Whitfield first gave for this order was straightforward: he could not afford all the wrecked police cars on his budget. But underlying this problem, he admitted, was his desire to prevent incidents where officers drove into the road, jumped out of the car and piled a "prisoner" into the back seat before driving off at high speed.

Mass raids in All Saints Road were also dramatically curtailed. Again the ostensible reason was down to earth: "in the main it was to stop visiting PCs in hospital". Again there was an obvious secondary purpose; again the new policy was unpopular with many of the PCs in the division. Similarly, police from adjacent divisions were given the message to keep out of Notting Hill. Replacing the raids on All Saints Road, Whitfield introduced to the area high technology targeting and surveillance of the road.

At this time anyone walking down the road who looked a potential customer would be offered drugs for sale. The location of dealing became more subtle as people caught on to the presence of cameras and used truanting children of twelve and under to "front" for sales; once paid they would dart into basements with the cash and emerge minutes later with a suitably weighed bag. However, it would be a grave mistake to suggest that the long history of All Saints Road was reducible to this trade, or that more than a small minority of these "dealers" traded in anything other than cannabis, for which the road had become a market place well known across London.

The third step Whitfield took, which was to win him respect both inside and outside the police force, was to make two arrests on All Saints Road in May 1982 at considerable personal risk. He also embarked on an extensive PR campaign, making himself available to all community leaders twenty-four hours a day, a move that won him grudging respect from some of the most hostile local people. For much of his time he was one of the very few Chief Superintendents on speaking terms with Frank Critchlow, veteran of the 1960s campaigns, who ran the Mangrove. Along with his deputy, Superintendent Aitcheson, he set up a series of informal police–community consultative meetings, prefiguring the initiatives that later became standard across London (see Ch. 8), which included one-off special meetings on All Saints Road itself at times of greatest tension.

A fourth strategy was an attempt to involve other agencies in "policing" the area. A story was leaked to a Sunday tabloid on the "festering sore" (police interview) of the Apollo pub and by Monday

126

NOTTING HILL

morning the brewery had shut it down. This property and several others on the road were bought up and administered by local Housing Associations.

However, the most profound change that Whitfield introduced was the All Saints Road special patrol. A squad of 24 PCs, picked from all officers on the division, was set up with the express purpose of "recovering" All Saints Road. From the end of the Carnival in 1982 the idea was to keep six officers stationed in the road twenty-four hours a day. The initial local reaction to this move was one of fury. On several occasions pairs of policemen were bundled off the road by large crowds of people who resented what they saw as an "army of occupation". In spite of this, the patrol was maintained for several years and certainly the police goal of reducing the number of "frequenters" on the road was, in broad terms, achieved. With increased participation by the Housing Associations and the co-operation of other agencies, the face of All Saints Road began to change. Indeed, with what eventually proved to be mistaken optimism, Whitfield claimed in 1986 that with the Mangrove receiving a lump-sum grant for refurbishment, "When the Mangrove re-opens as a decent West Indian restaurant that will be the end of the symbolism."

A successful solution?

There were two major flaws in the logic of Whitfield's claim. The first became increasingly evident throughout the last months of his time in charge at Notting Hill. The problem was that among very many of his junior officers his new reforms were extremely unpopular. Through a snowball interview technique in-depth formal interviews were completed with seven PCs working on Notting Hill Division at this time. All gave extremely critical reports of the changes in policing methods and greatly resented the restrictions placed on police discretion on All Saints Road. Whitfield was not unaware of this feeling and after he had left the area remarked, "We are not in business to be popular . . . I know that in many ways I am not popular at the Hill", and "I have got no illusions about policemen and the fact that they are human."

Several incidents occurred in both 1983 and 1984 where the special restrictions were effectively subverted. One PC admitted to deliberately flouting the regulations about car patrols; another caustically remarked when I defended Whitfield's approach, "Well obviously he should have told us more about what was going on." It is against this background that some of the *causes célèbres* of the latter 1980s, already alluded to in Chapter 2, involving massive compensation payouts by the Metropolitan Police must be set.

The second flaw stems from an assessment of the achievements on

FRONT LINE POLICING IN THE 1980s

All Saints Road in the early 1980s. Although the number of people using the road as a social centre greatly diminished, there remained three "official" clubs at Number 12, the Sunlight and the Paradise, as well as occasional "unofficial" clubs in other parts of the road. The drugs trade continued to be a source of police attention in the area, particularly in the late 1980s, during which time Frank Crichlow was charged and cleared of drug offences, and Chief Superintendent Pearman won notoriety for himself by trying to place pressure on the local council to alter their funding policy for community groups. In a singularly clumsy move Pearman, in the wake of Operation Trident – a major drugs crackdown in 1987 (Dorn et al. 1991) – made his own comment on Whitfield's legacy;

I am concerned that organizations which create divisiveness in the community are not encouraged by receiving public funding. The success which has been achieved in bringing the community closer together is still quite fragile. . . . This can be easily threatened if highly emotive and, arguably, politically extremist organizations are given a public-funding platform. It is unlikely that this form of appeasement will ever lead to the integration of such groups within the community. I think the recent past is adequate testimony of that failure. (Letter to Nicholas Freeman, Leader of Kensington and Chelsea Council, 16 December 1988)

It was such interventions that prompted much scepticism about the meaning of multi-agency policing. It was after all routine for money to be paid out from the Police Property Act Fund to community groups (over 600 in 1985).

In spite of the permanent police presence, the drugs trade continued. Because of their own manifest ineffectiveness in combating this trade and a reluctance to stand for eight hours at a time on one road, the All Saints Road patrol became an increasingly unpopular tour of duty, until in 1985 it was effectively separated from the rest of the station, to become within months notoriously referred to as the "Black Watch". The level of antagonism between the two parties remained as high as ever, only the numbers involved decreased. This numerical decrease was not due solely to police action. The elegant but dilapidated rental properties of the 1950s and 1960s have to a great extent been lost to "the reclaiming of the inner city", the wholesale gentrification of much of the area. In 1985 the Residents' Association of newly refurbished St Luke's Mews threatened to sue the police for their failure to enforce the law in the area (particularly drug trafficking). Nevertheless the road remained a social centre in which bars and clubs at times thrived. However the constant raids on All Saints Road in the 1987–90 period made the road less popular again and the old Black community area of

Notting Hill has been significantly eroded, as people are displaced by the forces of gentrification. If there is no serious disorder in Notting Hill in the immediate future it might be as much due to gentrification as to successful policing strategy. The closure of the Mangrove in 1991 was perhaps the logical conclusion of this trend.

The lessons of All Saints Road

The post-1981 experience of Notting Hill is significant because it confirms the rôle of one particular place in the symbolic vocabulary of the language of conflict. Prior to 1981, during the summer of 1981 itself, and subsequent to 1981, there existed a remarkable consensus about the importance of this symbolism, "Who controlled All Saints Road?" The question could be couched in either of the mutually exclusive idioms of *community resistance* or *policing strategies*. This question was the spatial realization of a deeply rooted historical struggle. The uneasy peace that has mostly prevailed from 1981 onwards is no more than a compromise answer to this question – it is not an authentic resolution of the conflict.

Brixton

"The Job"

Spending time in participant observation work on patrol with police in Brixton in the late 1980s, it was not difficult to appreciate the variable calibre of personnel, the major problems involved in "the job", the entrenched nature of the mistrust between police and much of the community or the low morale of police officers in Brixton division of the Metropolitan Police.

Perhaps one experience encapsulated many of the incidents witnessed. At 12.30 am we answered a call from a council estate, which said that two IC3 (Black) youths had been seen trying to break into a flat; we arrived to find two people "answering to the description" walking away from the block where the call had originated. The car stopped (abruptly) and one of the two ran off. One PC in the car, after a chase on foot, managed to catch this individual while the other "suspect" was detained. The noise of the siren, the speed of the car and the ensuing chase had drawn a large crowd of onlookers. The crowd grew rapidly as the names of the two suspects were checked by radio for criminal records. Angry at being made to chase a suspect, angry at the realization that there was no proof that the two had done anything, one PC in particular made little effort to hide his contempt for

FRONT LINE POLICING IN THE 1980s

the Black youths, yet his questioning remained technically correct in every other respect and violence was never threatened. After ten minutes of waiting it was discovered that one of the youths had a criminal record. A friend of his, who had appeared subsequently, protested the innocence of the two, and was nearly arrested for assault when his verbal abuse of the two police began to get out of hand. These secondary offences, known as "knock-on offences", are common in this sort of situation. They are partly the product of the rift between the police and the Black community, and are a major element in amplifying the process of criminalization already described. Just as the two PCs decided there was nothing more they could do, a couple of bottles were thrown from the back of the crowd.

As we drove away both were convinced that the two suspects were guilty, both had acted correctly (in spite of the poor manners of one) and both had been "bottled" for their pains. Similar incidents, all involving objects being thrown, occurred four times on this one shift (relief). One of the police in the car repeatedly "explained" these experiences in explicitly racist characterizations of Black people.

It is the sense of hopelessness in the face of the outright collapse of "policing by consent" that made one PC suggest to me, "this nick must have the lowest morale in the whole of London".

This morale problem also dates back a long way and forms part of the day-to-day reality of policing Brixton. Another PC, who had been in Brixton since the mid-1970s, said,

> before 1981 everyone knew that Brixton was a place where you got a lot of hassle. Nobody wanted to come here. As a result, it became a sort of punishment centre. I personally know PCs who turned up on a Monday morning after annual leave at their station in – say Croydon – only to be told, "No you're not here any more, you've been transferred to Brixton." Senior officers used it all as an excuse to get rid of the men they didn't want.

As a managerial strategy this was not verifiable; as a perceived notion of rank and file police officers it was frequently manifest. Consequently, mistrust reproduces itself within the police service, poor expectations confirmed by experience. As PC Peter Lawrence commented,

> In my time here I have seen the most liberal and left wing people come down here and within months completely change their attitudes. The hatred on the streets is so awful that you have to conform to the views of the rest of the group to survive.

Antagonism has become built in to the job itself. To say that the police are hated by large sections of the Black population in Brixton is no exaggeration. The reactions of police officers vary enormously between individuals, but this extreme hostility is reciprocated by many members

BRIXTON

of the police force working in the division. But for most of the people I spent time with, the reasons for this mutual hostility were rarely considered; only occasionally were rationalizations offered and these were often openly and explicitly racist. For the majority the hostility appeared to be phlegmatically accepted as just "a fact of life", part of the daily routine.

When this level of antagonism is placed alongside the high degree of discretion of the PC, the frequently scant respect for senior management that is common among junior officers and the well documented difficulties involved in supervising police work, some of the better known events of the past on Railton Road become more comprehensible.

Tit for tat: "front line deviancy"

As part of the informal code that underscores all police actions it is very often taken for granted that violence against fellow police officers is settled in kind. I was told several times by the police themselves that this was no more than self-defence. By definition, police work can be violent work. Increasing regulation of what happens to prisoners in police stations has undoubtedly had a significant effect, but as one very senior officer stated,

I have no doubt that such incidents [violence against prisoners] almost never happen at police stations any more but I am equally sure that they do sometimes occur *en route* to the police station. (personal interview)

Scores which build up can be settled at future dates. In Brixton repeated clashes stemming from arrests have for a long time led to many police injuries. On Railton Road, where, since the early 1970s, these clashes were always at their most serious, there were a lot of scores.

It was the awareness of these incidents in the Metropolitan Police, particularly in Brixton and Notting Hill, that led senior management to coin the term *"front line deviancy"* to describe how junior officers could subvert official goals to ensure that scores were settled in this way.

One of the most notorious incidents of front line deviancy occurred in the wake of the 1981 disorders, when, on the 15 July 1981 at 2 am, 176 police were deployed to search 11 houses on Railton Road, in an attempt to find petrol bomb stores. The houses were torn apart. A later report of the Police Complaints Board commented on these raids,

it was difficult not to come to the conclusion that every senior officer in possession of a warrant regarded it as a license to enter the premises and, once having gained entry, to search for evidence of any crime. The board find it difficult to believe that this can be attributed entirely to ignorance of the law. (*Guardian* 24 September 1983).

FRONT LINE POLICING IN THE 1980s

More to the point, as both Commander Alex Marnoch (i/c L District [Lambeth] 1983–5) and several PCs I spoke to who were involved in this operation acknowledged, the raids had been used by some police to "avenge" the "defeats" of the riots earlier in the year.

Similarly, in November 1982, when several of the derelict properties in Railton Road that were being used for squats and shabeens were demolished, as in All Saints Road, the new Immediate Response Units were deployed to quell any public-order problems. A PC involved at the time stated categorically that the police had shown "who controlled Railton Road". A police presence was functionally necessary to aid the demolition but this function was reinterpreted and reconstructed by those carrying out the policy.

Marnoch also described instances of "fishing raids" on Railton Road drinking clubs, which had been made for similarly demonstrative reasons, and which totally contradicted his own instructions.

In such a climate a major problem for senior officers is to maintain simultaneously both discipline and morale. It is this context that reveals a secondary function of Operation SWAMP, the stop and search operation that preceded the April 1981 rioting in Brixton. When asked about the success of the operation at the Scarman Inquiry public hearings Detective Chief Superintendent Plowman did not mention catching criminals (in these terms it was a manifest failure) but said instead, "Yes I thought it was successful. It motivated officers."

Railton Road patrols

On taking charge of L District in 1983, Commander Alex Marnoch was given a free hand to attempt to "pacify" Brixton. A central part of his strategy involved the introduction of a form of policing in the Railton Road area that would defuse the symbolic power of the Front Line. Marnoch's policy was in these terms, perhaps in these terms alone, remarkably successful.

There were three main elements to this strategy. First, there was the introduction of a form of "multi-agency" policing into Brixton. Achievements in this field were in no small part due to Marnoch's personal relationship with the then Labour leader of Lambeth Council, Ted Knight, long before notions of multi-agency policing came into vogue. Rather than repeatedly raid the squats and drinking clubs on Railton Road, the Council repossessed and redeveloped several premises. Other developments in Railton Road included the building of an Afro-Caribbean centre, the reconstruction of a pub and the extensive redevelopment of the most derelict housing, and the refurbishing of an adventure playground. The physical and, hypothetically, the social environment as well were transformed.

Secondly, targeting and surveillance operations were introduced, as in other symbolic locations in London. A tower block of flats to the south of Railton Road was used to monitor all activity on the road with the aid of high magnification camera equipment. There were several major successes in combating drug dealing.

Thirdly, a special patrol of a sergeant and three pairs of PCs from each relief was introduced to guarantee a permanent police presence in the Railton Road area. For Marnoch, this patrol obviated the need for high profile raids in the road by "showing the flag": "Raids get you nothing – drugs on the floor and down lavatories, etc."

Similarly, Marnoch felt that he needed to "recondition the minds of the police officers" on the patrol. Arrests for "a few cannabis cigarettes" were strongly discouraged; any arrest at all on the Front Line itself was to be avoided if possible; suspects were to be arrested once they had left Railton Road. One aim of the patrols was to prevent the use of the Front Line as a safe haven for escaped prisoners and drugs dealers. This goal was to a notable extent achieved, not least because of Marnoch's personal commitment to the scheme. He described to me how many of the PCs had been scared to work on Railton Road "for the good reason that so many police had been injured there".

On other occasions, both members of the local community and his own junior officers described examples of the personal courage of Marnoch who was regularly present on the streets himself, both in and out of uniform. Moreover, when tension broke out into "a mini-riot" in June 1983, Marnoch held an open meeting at Shepherds, where the public were able to vent their feelings to the Commander in person. This meeting, in particular, won him much respect locally.

Yet there were drawbacks to this policy. The high profile patrols were still seen by many as a "force of occupation", and although in an interview Chief Superintendent Webber (i/c Brixton division in the mid-1980s) suggested that the Railton Road patrols could serve as "community patrols", it was quite clear to me, having spent time with one such patrol, that most people on the Front Line regarded the omnipresent sight of several police in a very small area with the same, if not greater, hostility as before. Webber also claimed that,

My men on Railton Road are there to police positively. It is made clear to them the sense of purpose in what they are doing. It is made clear that they are there to arrest people if there is cause to do so.

Perhaps inevitably, much of the drinking club/drugs trade was displaced to other parts of Brixton rather than removed. The main new sites were Acre Lane (where in early 1986 there was a shooting and several stabbings) and Landau Road. In later years policies were struc-

FRONT LINE POLICING IN THE 1980s

tured in part by the spectre of Broadwater Farm and some of the focus of attention also shifted onto the big local estates. Similar patrols were formed for all of these areas. However the public-order sensitivity of the new sites was never equivalent to other parts of Brixton, even if, as several people commented in interviews in 1989, "Railton Road is not the place it was".

Hackney

With the full co-operation of local police (Stoke Newington Division), it was possible to gather a much more comprehensive picture of the policing in Sandringham Road than in either of the other two case study locations.

Senior management

For some time Sandringham Road had been recognized by the police as a symbolic location with a high potential risk of public-order problems. In the mid-1980s Special Branch monitored the level of tension in such places and took a keen interest in all operations in the road. Although a registered special file on Sandringham Road as a whole was only "officially opened" in July 1982, a series of unregistered dockets concerned with specific properties there was in existence for several years before that.

However, rather than reflect the end product of a consistent and considered strategy, this official status subsumed a set of very different conceptualizations of the problems and history of Sandringham Road, a set that has underwritten police actions in the area. Preferred policy has varied both through time (before and since 1981) and, more markedly, between individual officers, whose "policing prescriptions" have often differed; sometimes only by implication, sometimes in outright contradiction and rancour.

Such differences can best be illustrated by comparing the opinions of three senior officers involved in the policing of Hackney. Commander W. Taylor was in charge of policing G District, whose boundaries coincided with the borough of Hackney, from 1981 to 1984. In the period of time following the riots of 1981, several minor local incidents threatened to escalate into conflict on a much larger scale. In the light of this potential for trouble, Commander Taylor became a keen supporter of Sir Kenneth Newman's new policing strategies developed for use in sensitive areas, which emphasized the priority of maintaining public order over law enforcement. A concentration on intelligence and surveillance in crime fighting was expected to minimize the abrasive street contacts brought about by random stop and search operations. Police officers were encouraged to make arrests away from symbolic locations through the targeting of known offenders; repeated raids on premises being used as bases for petty crime were discouraged; patrolling officers were reminded that in such locations they must consciously balance law enforcement with the danger of public disorder.

In the context of these commitments a major disagreement arose between Commander Taylor and Chief Superintendent Barr, who was in charge of Stoke Newington division (which covers Sandringham Road). On several occasions throughout 1983 and 1984 requests for permission to raid Johnston's in particular, and other places in Sandringham Road in general, were turned down by Taylor. At one time, Commander Taylor sent his Chief Superintendents a copy of a paper given by the Commissioner at a conference, outlining Newman's new strategy, and drawing attention to the policy on minimizing the number of such raids, pointedly remarking in a covering note, "This speech has been reproduced in whole or in part in a number of publications. Hackney Borough Council will have a copy."

With the reorganization of the Met by Newman in the mid-1980s the District officially disappeared as an administrative unit and the executive rôle of the District Commanders diminished. Chief Superintendents now reported more directly to the Deputy Assistant Commissioners (DACs) in charge of the new Areas. Within this hierarchy, DAC G. W. Jones was appointed to head Number 2 Area, which included the old G District. Jones's view on the necessary policy for Sandringham Road differed from Taylor's in several key respects. In an interview, when answering a question on the value of raids on Johnston's, he commented:

You seem to be a believer in symbolism. We have to show the whole community that we will not tolerate indefinitely petty crime in any area of London. We have to demonstrate that there are no places we will not go.

He went on to state that in such raids the total number of arrests was not, for him, the sole criterion by which success should be judged. One implicit meaning is straightforward; where police power was challenged, the police must not only respond to that challenge but must also be seen to respond.

For Chief Superintendent Barr the problem was bitterly clear; by refraining from taking strong action against illegal practices, because of the fear of public-order problems, criminal activity on Sandringham Road had dramatically increased. On top of fencing stolen goods and selling cannabis at JJ's, there was by 1984 clear evidence of harder

FRONT LINE POLICING IN THE 1980s

drugs, notably cocaine, coming into that "secure market place". In addition one pub on the road was establishing itself as a suspected major centre for the arrangement and equipping of armed robbery. Significantly, such activities would not necessarily "show" on crime statistics for the division.

With the departure of Taylor to the City Police Force there was an almost immediate change in policy. Although openly sceptical about the value of targeting and surveillance operations, principally because of the high manpower investment per arrest and the feasibility of such work in Sandringham Road, Barr had initially persevered with a special patrol (see below) and intelligence gathering on Sandringham Road, but by early 1985 was allowed to supplement this policy with a series of raids on both ends of the road. JJ's was raided on 16 February, 28 February, 19 March and 3 June (1985) and "five or six" operations were also carried out at the other end of the road. There was no single purpose to these raids; again the success of operations was judged by a complex set of criteria:

First I would seek results, secondly the calibre of prisoner, thirdly the morale boost to avoid front line deviancy and then finally add no complaints. (Barr, private interview.)

By June 1985 Barr felt able to report in an internal memo that JJ's was, "not the place it was in the numbers it attracts and that is without doubt due to raids on the premises". Two further aspects of police management in Hackney are noteworthy. One concerns the frequently voiced notion that because of the power of the police force, senior officers are able to control the "passage of events". The police have often been accused of seeking confrontation in order to justify increases in police powers (e.g. Bernie Grant, then leader of Harringey Council, speaking in the wake of the Broadwater Farm riot in 1985, Haine 1980) and/or orchestrating public opinion to stigmatize all Black people (Hall et al. 1978, Joshua & Wallace 1983). Yet again, while the effects of police actions may well be those alleged, the picture that emerges from any causal analysis of policing policy in Hackney is much more confused, belying this conspiratorial vision. Time and again during the research for this work instances occurred and occasions were recalled of decisions that were based either on pragmatic reaction or political/personal expediency. In the context of this book it needs to be said explicitly that Barr was an officer whose integrity was repeatedly demonstrated during this research, over and above the imperatives of any personal interest on his part.

After, and in no small part because of, the political row that followed the deployment of dogs on Sandringham Road, Chief Superintendent Young, Barr's predecessor, committed himself to avoiding such tactics

HACKNEY

in future. The miners' strike in 1983-4, the prison officers' dispute and the Wapping Print Works dispute in 1986, all made sudden and drastic alterations to the manpower available to police at a local level. A scheme of Inter District Transfers to encourage individual PCs to serve in different parts of London every five years had similar, if less precipitate, effect on Stoke Newington division. Although the number of officers applying to leave was less than the London average, almost nobody would voluntarily go there on transfer. Relations with the Council and other politicians were also a major focus of management attention. In such circumstances practical exigencies ensure that management is most often defensive and reactionary, more concerned with justifying practices and rationalizing operations than with long-term policies. Moreover a prevailing feeling among most senior officers at divisional level was that trouble, in any newsworthy sense, was to be avoided in order to maximize promotion chances. Conspiracies require premeditation and institutional co-ordination; few inside the police force would suggest that Metropolitan Police management practice is notable for either.

Related to this essentially bureaucratic characteristic is the remarkably limited "local knowledge" often possessed by senior officers. Normally serving only three years in any one post inevitably prohibits any one individual from gathering full background information about the policing history of his/her own division. When Barr first moved to Hackney in August 1983 it was in the wake of the protests over the death of Colin Roach, and it was this issue that appears to have featured principally in what (informal) briefing he received on arrival. He had never served before in Hackney and knew "little to nothing" about the development of Sandringham Road as a symbolic location. Hence, in a letter to the Commander of G District in mid-1985 he comments, "With regard to JJ's café; this has been in operation for some six years and featured in the 1981 riots." (In fact JJ's opened in 1972). As a result Sandringham Road was seen by Chief Superintendent Barr principally in terms of crime, as being first and foremost a criminal area and only secondly as a sensitive location. The pressures of management mean that these two salient characteristics almost inevitably become consciously or subconsciously linked. History was neither suppressed nor forgotten, but simply not learnt; any rioting in Sandringham Road can only be the activity of "criminals" resenting police interference in their own professional activity.

In this context, Barr's understanding of the events of July 1981 was revealing. His predecessor, an unpopular officer notorious for going on leave at the times of the Colin Roach protest marches, on the orders of his superior officer, Commander Howlett, had given instructions for

137

FRONT LINE POLICING IN THE 1980s

truncheons to be drawn and the crowd on Sandringham Road charged. That was basically all Barr knew of the disorders; he had been told that this action was considered extremely effective; he appeared unaware of the extensive looting that had occurred or the deep resentment felt by so many of those present who had been caught up in this charge. This is not a criticism of Barr himself, only an example of the problem, cited by senior officers themselves (Males 1988), of the manner in which police management turnover militates against an in-depth knowledge of local history.

The internal rows and the corporate politics are important not so much in themselves as for what they represent. The distinctive characteristics of bureaucratic organization are once again present. The chain of command is neither cybernetic nor conspiratorial but is mediated by personality. Disparate aims shape managerial behaviour. Ambition and promotion-seeking would dictate a strict conformity to rules and norms which may not be related to functional policing. Being a "popular governor" sets different problems again.

Chief Superintendent Barr suggested that his position was at least clear and with candour he suggested in 1986,

The worst they can do is turn around and say "Barr, we're going to do the worst thing possible to you" and send me back to Stoke Newington for another three years.

For Barr, this had the advantage of allowing him a free hand in the policing of the division, and whatever this author's thoughts about some of Barr's analyses the genuine commitment and the industry that lay behind them was unassailable.

Two strategies in particular seemed to distinguish Barr's approach. One was his determination to take action against criminal activity in Sandringham Road, already described. More revealing was the awareness of the discontent that existed among junior officers about the policing of the road. In this context he was quite candid about the sensitive issue of front line deviancy. This impression was reinforced when, on one night duty, a dedicated but less than sharp PC whom I had come to know reasonably well, put to me quite openly the following proposition:

If you raid somewhere and there is this bloke, who you know pushes, standing in there and there's drugs all around him on the floor that he got rid of as you arrive, you've got a choice. Either you let him go away to spoil more lives or you say you saw him drop the bags on the floor or "find" one of them in his pocket. That's not framing somebody. That sort of thing used to go on all the time but Roger (Barr) is particularly tough on it . . . It's not worth risking my money and my career for some little shit who we will catch later anyway.

How common this sort of practice ever really was it is not possible to say, but the very attempt to curb it might be considered significant, perhaps particularly in the light of revelations about drugs and Stoke Newington, which reached the public domain in the early 1990s but were common currency locally many years before. Rightly or wrongly I personally believed, from the nature of the explicit defence offered by the PC, that he had either witnessed or perpetrated such behaviour and that he genuinely saw such acts not as cynical malpractice but more simply in terms of naïve ideals of "summary justice".

It was this thin borderline between discretion and deviancy that lay behind a comment by Barr that he knew that "low profile policing" on Sandringham Road was considered degrading by many in the junior ranks, and he considered it a real danger that if he insisted on a police style there that was completely alien to the "crime fighting" definition of "the Job" held by many officers, then PCs would take their own steps to defeat that policy.

In realization of police strategy, maintaining the morale of junior officers was seen as a key goal for Barr. At one level this is obviously no more than a facet of good management, yet at another it may become dangerous if the standard of morale hinges on the settling of old scores in the guise of "victories" on Sandringham Road.

Institutional complexity

At any one time only a minority of personnel at Stoke Newington are involved in relief-based patrols of the division, although it is this aspect of police work that has received greatest sociological attention. Yet the different perceptions of Sandringham Road within Stoke Newington division of the Met often reflect the institutional complexity of any police station.

Space prohibits a detailed account of some of the more impressive community relations projects I witnessed. Citing just one individual, PC Steve Longhorn served as a Community Involvement Officer (CIO) at Stoke and has worked in Hackney for almost twenty years; his connections with the "outside" community were excellent, at times perhaps better than with the "inside" community of his own police station. He was on speaking terms with several of the staff at Roots Pool and he sometimes, although not often, dropped in there. Similarly, other police in the Youth and Community section were involved in trying to persuade local teachers to allow the police back into schools after the "break links" campaign (see Ch. 2), and in work with several youth clubs and in liaison with several tenants' associations. However, there was a marked difference between the attitudes of those involved in this

FRONT LINE POLICING IN THE 1980s

sort of work and many other police in the division. Overgeneralization must be avoided, but certainly Longhorn's awareness of the bitterness and the problems of young people in Hackney was not typical of many at the station, who tended to view such community work with either scepticism or scorn. Jobs such as CIO were seen as soft options, a license to go drinking. This hostility came from both junior and senior officers, with the notable exceptions of the then Superintendent and Chief Superintendent. The bureaucratic compartmentalization of "community relations" seemed to be functionally independent of other sorts of policing.

This attitude was dramatically reinforced one day in mid-June 1986, when, in my presence, a call came through to community involvement from Special Branch demanding to know why a raid was planned on Sandringham Road the following Saturday, given Newman's policy (see above), the road's quasi-official status as a symbolic location, and the hot weather at the time. Although even I knew from other interviews that the raid was due, nobody on the community relations side knew anything about it. They had not been informed.

A different voice was heard from the plain clothes officers on special squads (e.g. robbery squad, vice squad, drug squad, all overlapping with CID). Two examples were particularly telling. One was the public announcement of a campaign to combat street crime, particularly "dipping", in the Ridley Road market. The Detective Inspector in charge announced at several public meetings that although the operation was to concentrate on surveillance and arrest rather than random stop and search, some "public-order problems" were to be expected and catered for. In a private conversation he explained that, for him, such announcements were based on experiences of resistance to arrest in the Ridley Road/Sandringham Road area. At one level such experience vindicates announcements of this kind, but at another level, and this was confirmed by the DI, such notions highlight a conception of public-order problems as synonymous with criminal activity.

At another meeting, I was present when a Detective Sergeant from the drugs squad was pressing Chief Superintendent Barr to raid Roots Pool. In a private conversation the DS explicitly defended a set of professional goals which placed the detention and arrest of drugs dealers on a much higher priority than the risk of public-order problems. The suggestion that such raids should bear in mind community relations ramifications on Sandringham Road was considered laughable. As Barr later pointed out, similar demands were presented to him almost daily.

Junior officers: policing without consent
One way you could stop most of the crime round here would be by

HACKNEY

closing down Sandringham Road. The crime rate would almost disappear overnight. (PC at Dalston station.)

(a) The reputation of Sandringham Road Two caveats must be entered with respect to comments on the attitudes and behaviour of streetline constables in the Stoke Newington division. The first is, that any opinion voiced here is based on both limited participant observation and prolonged exposure to the sociological literature on policing. The second is, that in the 27 formal and informal interviews of police constables in the division any generalization that could be made was always contradicted by individuals. Notwithstanding this, the one issue on which there was most consensus at Dalston station (a subdivision of Stoke Newington) was Sandringham Road. Hostility towards the Black people who frequented the road was, with one notable exception, unanimous. Most officers were keen to differentiate between this "location-specific" hostility and "racism". The explanations of this hostility were much more varied.

For some, the knowledge that several police from the division had been seriously injured when making arrests there, and the regular abuse they received on the Front Line, were enough to generate reciprocal animosity. For others, the road was deemed a "criminal area": "They are all villains down there", one WPC claimed when suggesting that without exception anybody who walked down Sandringham Road deserved to be stopped and searched. I spent some time with two probationer PCs who had only been in the division a couple of months. Their graphic descriptions of Sandringham Road, given independently, gave the impression of a den of evil, a criminal community prepared to "declare war to protect their interests" (probationer PC, personal interview). Some other PCs gave less lurid descriptions, suggesting that the problem is principally one of,

> too many kids on the streets being a nuisance. If we could just get them off the streets and inside the place wouldn't be such a big thing to everybody. (PC, personal interview)

This point is an important one. Throughout the 1980s Sandringham Road signified "Trouble" for almost every single police officer on the division, but the rationalizations and explanations of this problem differed from one individual to another, there is no single "subcultural account". In linguistic terms the place (Sandringham Road) became a sign that was easily read – explicit communication. Yet the signification process, the genesis of this image of Front Line, remains opaque.

It is not easy to pinpoint a date at which Sandringham Road assumed this status for local police officers. Again it was striking how little local history was known or understood by most PCs. (One extreme

141

FRONT LINE POLICING IN THE 1980s

case was the PC who told me that he knew that, by 1986, the local Black community had completely forgotten about Colin Roach).

Promotions, transfers and departures ensured that by 1986 the majority of PCs at Dalston station had not been present before 1981. However, I did speak to several of those who had. One suggested that within a few months of Johnston's opening in the early 1970s Sandringham Road was already a site for clashes between police and Black people, since by that stage there was also trouble from blues parties and shabeens. Another claimed that the violent confrontations had started when young Black people began selling drugs there in the late 1970s. What is certain is that even before 1981 it was not unusual for crowds to gather and resist arrest or attempt to snatch back prisoners. Before 1981 "Trouble" was always anticipated when policing Sandringham Road; when the rest of London was seen to burn in the summer of that year the police of G District already knew where to expect confrontation.

(b) The Sandringham Road patrol: challenge and response In 1982, for the summer months, Chief Superintendent Young set up a special patrol on Sandringham Road of one sergeant and eight men, operating off two reliefs, similar to the patrols already described in Notting Hill and Brixton. His successor, Roger Barr, was not keen on such patrols, because he worried that PCs would become obsessed with the problems of Sandringham Road. Partly for this reason and partly because of manpower shortages the patrol was not reintroduced in the early summer of 1986 (officially this was only a temporary measure). Officially, the pre-emption of public-order problems was considered a major justification for the patrol, yet it appeared in discussion with PCs who had been involved in this group that such potential was not considered particularly important for them in comparison with the "crime problem" in the area.

Service in the group was not a popular duty. People tended to be "volunteered" in their absence; several expressed concern about both personal safety and the high element of tedium involved in spending eight hours at a time in such a confined area. It was suggested that some on the patrol had expressed their feelings by finding excuses to leave the road when on duty and also that some officers were reluctant to make arrests there, and would make them elsewhere out of personal fear rather than diplomacy. The patrol operated only in the daytime and early evening.

One of the central contradictions of the special patrol was summed up in a comment by one PC:

I used to stand there outside Roots Pool for hours on end with my

142

arms crossed, just staring into that place. That used to really wind them up . . . they used to call me Hitler; when you next go in there ask them about Hitler.

Two points are clear. To have four policemen standing around one street for eight hours at a time could easily be seen by innocent people using the area as provocative. The very collapse of policing by consent that leads to these special patrols could be said to guarantee "institutionalized harassment" and the criminalization of a whole area. The second point is that the behaviour of the individual PC cannot be so easily faulted because his actions are no more than taking the rôle of such patrols to their logical conclusion. The policemen – only men were allowed on the patrol – were there to establish control of the road. This task highlights the flaw in Webber's (Brixton) claim, that similar patrols can prepare the ground for improved community relations. These patrols may at times be functionally essential, defensible by certain criteria of police management, but on the street they drive the conflict between streetline police officers and the *habitués* of the symbolic location deeper into the consciousness of both parties.

Instead of resolving conflict it is possible to manage it, contain it and prevent escalation. In the jargon of social psychology the outcome is one of "agonistic resolution" not liberal reconciliation, hostility is sustained or even intensified but major violent clashes are averted.

There is a fundamental paradox built into the rôle of the PC in such situations. Because he is instructed not to make "inflammatory arrests", because he is expected to ignore "petty crimes" (notably car and cannabis offences), because he must always be ready to defend himself, his renowned discretion is strictly circumscribed. Never does he more explicitly symbolize state power on the streets yet never is his discretion in exercising that power more emasculated. It is this contradiction that made the Sandringham Road patrol so absurd and unpopular in the eyes of so many of those officers who had served on that patrol, an absurdity that caused much friction between senior officers advocating this policy and those who had to enforce it. It is this contradiction that reveals the fallacy of policing by consent and exposes the harsh reality of policing without consent.

(c) Cowboy policing? Two incidents summed up the essential problems of policing without consent. Holly Street estate was in the mid-1980s officially designated as one of twenty London housing estates which "Have a similar potential for disorder as exhibited on Broadwater Farm Estate, Tottenham." These are "graded in their likelihood of spontaneous public disorder occurring" (1986, Scotland Yard, internal).

The Holly Street Estate was classified as "Medium Risk". Late one

FRONT LINE POLICING IN THE 1980s

Friday night (10.00 pm), when I was in Dalston just as the reliefs were changing over, a call for "urgent assistance" came through from a PC on the estate. Immediately, everyone in the station jumped into the nearest available car and we all made for the estate at high speed with sirens blazing and lights flashing; nobody knew at this stage how serious the incident was. Within minutes between thirty and forty police were at the scene, cars coming from all directions, drawing groups of spectators with them. I was with the Home Beat Officer for the estate at the time, and he was livid when it transpired that a fairly young PC had panicked when called to the scene of a stabbing and one of the victim's family had lost his temper and struck out. "This is just what I don't want happening on my beat", the Home Beat Officer commented, as some of the gathered crowd began to get agitated and criticize what was by now, with the wisdom of hindsight, a clear case of police over-reaction.

Yet at no time was it simple to allocate blame for the incident. I talked to members of the crowd who had gathered: "They behave like fucking cowboys round here", one middle-aged white man said to me, "A small fight and they send in the cavalry to beat up anyone who moves." But the PC who had put out the call had previously been seriously injured in a similar incident on the same estate. When they heard the call for assistance all the other police were aware of was that a friend's life was in danger, so by the very nature of the job there was no way they would hold back from a rapid and collective response to the call. The number who responded was increased by the overlapping of two shifts. The impression of the police action for the watching, and unknowing, public was wholly negative. As the Home Beat Officer suggested, "there goes a few months work down the drain," although he seemed relieved that in the tension and confusion which surrounded the incident nobody had been thumped.

On returning to the station the change-over of reliefs continued for a few minutes until a second call for "urgent assistance" came through from the same housing estate. The same deployment, the same over-reaction occurred, but this time one of the abusive crowd was thumped. The incident was a secondary fight related to the first. I did not see the whole confrontation between the young Black man who was arrested and the PC, but it later became obvious that he had nothing to do with the fighting parties. Possibly the PC had lost his temper in the face of more abuse, more likely, in this particular case, the young Black man (who had been drinking heavily) threw a punch first. Certainly he now felt aggrieved; certainly he was about to be processed (criminalized) by the legal system, definitely; he had just drifted into disorder.

144

There has never (yet) been a riot on Holly Street Estate. However, resistance to arrest is not unusual there and police have several times lost prisoners to crowds of, mostly Black, youths. To understand why this occurs it is obviously necessary to go back in time to explain why the police are not readily allowed to "do their job" on that particular estate; why "consent" was lost. Yet the past is lost to people trying to cope in the present.

The issue of levels, or rates, of crime that occur on an estate such as Holly Street is only a secondary, complicating issue. In one sense it matters little what the rates of crime actually are, if, in reality it has become almost impossible to take even limited police action against such problems. In these circumstances, policing with heavy support becomes the only alternative to the complete withdrawal of police from the estate (a pattern that may creep in as individual junior officers become afraid to patrol an area and individual senior officers become afraid of public disorder potential). The result is the sort of "cowboy policing" outlined, which drives conflict and confrontation into the routine of both the young Black community on the estate and the police.

In this sort of situation bystanders are easily drawn in; police behaviour may get out of hand; as the Home Beat Officer stated, "PCs tend to thump whoever's standing nearest"; "knock-on" offences may proliferate. Experience of such incidents prompts police officers to stereotype a whole estate as a potential source of trouble, and residents (particularly Black residents), as all criminals. For many residents of the estate, old and young, Black and White, such incidents confirm the impression of a police force "out of control". Thus "places" are made. Once consent is lost, the antagonism between police and community reinforces itself as confrontation becomes routine; a facet of institutional practice, tied to sites of resistance, rather than individual proclivity.

(d) Front line deviancy The obvious interpretation of the term "front line deviancy" is in terms of malicious breaches of police discipline in sensitive areas. The phenomenon is in reality much more complicated, best understood by illustration.

On one occasion, one of the more intelligent and dedicated members of the Sandringham Road patrol saw a Black man in the road ostentatiously put a bag of cannabis resin in his pocket. Challenging him, the PC suggested (as was the norm in this part of the division) that he empty the bag on the street and then no further action would be taken. The man refused and when arrested tried to eat the resin. The PC grabbed hold of the man, forced his jaws open and recovered the cannabis, by which time the onlooking crowd had grown rapidly and were claim-

FRONT LINE POLICING IN THE 1980s

ing retribution for this apparent act of police brutality. As a result of the ensuing melée, which involved the District Support Unit, the PC was informally disciplined by senior officers and warned that if he were to become involved in a similar incident again stronger action would be taken against him. His bitterness, in part directed at senior officers, had quite obviously shaped his attitude towards the whole road; I was left in no doubt that the incident had not been forgotten.

In a similar vein, scores were undoubtedly payed off in the wake of the disorders of 1981. I spoke at length to one PC about the pursuit of several of the rioters into JJ's. This was by now several years later and there was quite possibly some exaggeration in his dramatic account, but again it was explained to me in detail that little effort was made to avoid damaging the premises in this pursuit; "summary justice" was done.

Location is a vital element in understanding conflict. The "right of the police to police" Sandringham Road had been challenged regularly for a long time; front line deviancy was primarily the lower ranks' occasional response to that challenge. Rioting in 1981 was in this sense both a symptom and a realization of this conflict as well as a mechanism by which this hostility became yet further entrenched.

CHAPTER 7

Building stages for confrontation: power relations and policing

Time present and time past
Are both perhaps present in time future,
And time future contained in time past.
If all time is eternally present
All time is unredeemable.
What might have been is an abstraction
Remaining a perpetual possibility
Only in a world of speculation.
What might have been and what has been
Points to one end, which is always present.

From T. S. Eliot, *Burnt Norton*

Space is political. Space is not a scientific object removed from ideology or politics; it has always been political and strategic . . . Space, which seems homogeneous, which seems to be completely objective in its pure form such as we ascertain it, is a social product. The production of space can be likened to the production of any particular type of merchandise. (Henri Lefebvre 1977)

Disorder and rebellion: three of the 1981 riots?

It is worth going back again to 1981, to look at the manner in which violent confrontation did, or did not, evolve in the three locations that provided the case studies for this work. The harsh reality of violent conflict becomes desiccated and dehumanized in prose and it is not easy to attempt to look dispassionately at such a phenomenon. However, in the context of the glimpses of local history in Chapter 2, and the reality of policing described in the last chapter, it is possible to view civil disorder in a different light. It is this perception that might be of value.

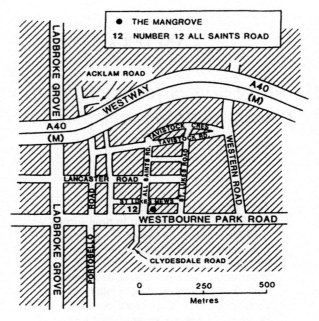

Map 7.1 Notting Hill.

Notting Hill (10-13 July 1981)

The chronic state of relations between police and the local Black community in Ladbroke Grove has already been documented in Chapter 2. Precedents of violent confrontation had already been set in the disorders that followed the 1969 raid on the Mangrove restaurant; in the clashes with the police that engulfed the Notting Hill Carnivals of 1975 and 1976; in the violence that occurred at times of SPG activity in the division, and following another raid on the Mangrove in 1979 (North Kensington Law Centre 1982).

It was because of this catalogue of violent conflict that the *Kensington News and Post* felt moved to comment on the 17 July 1981, after a week in which London appeared ablaze, that although there had been some trouble in Notting Hill, "the scale of violence was less than expected", and only 28 people were arrested. In a sense, Notting Hill was the major riot that was expected, but failed to manifest itself. In reality, the expectation was very nearly fulfilled, the pattern of events so close to cliché, only the result so dramatically different.

On the nights of the 9-12 July 1981 a series of confrontations around the local area was less significant than the barricades put up on All

DISORDER AND REBELLION: THREE OF THE 1981 RIOTS?

Saints Road. For the first three nights no attempt was made by the police to remove them or disperse the crowd that gathered behind them.

On Sunday 12 July the crowd that gathered in the evening, again in All Saints Road, was much smaller than during the previous two days. Two fire engines, called out to Saint Luke's Road, were attacked by members of this group and by about 11.30pm a compressor and an overturned car had again been made into barricades at the lower end of All Saints Road. Once again the police did not immediately try and disperse the crowd, instead waiting until almost midnight when numbers were greatly diminished. Fifty police then marched in phalanx down along All Saints Road and cleared the street, leaving plenty of opportunity for people to disperse along Lancaster and Tavistock Roads in order to to avoid giving any impression of trapping people. Sixteen people were arrested in the clashes that followed this manoeuvre and one police constable was injured. However, many eyewitness accounts describe this movement as well conceived but poorly executed, with little control by senior officers over the behaviour of the group of police marching down All Saints Road. One police officer present reported confidentially (Keith 1987), that there was a general resentment of the strategy adopted, which Chief Superintendent Moore was later to describe as "softly-softly" policing in the area throughout the attacks of the preceding three nights. The return of the police to the area around the Mangrove was achieved by what one journalist described as "unusual 'Zulu' style tactics", with truncheons used to beat a rhythm on riot shields while all the police constables "chanted" (*Kensington News and Post*, 17 July 1981). Others described an exchange of verbal abuse more ferocious than any violent conflict, with racist catcalls returned with interest by the crowd. By about 1.15am the area was again quiet.

The events of early July in Notting Hill represented, in at least one sense, the most successful strategic policing operation in the Metropolitan Police District in 1981. In an area where police/Black relations were traditionally amongst the most antagonistic in London, there was only limited violence. There is sufficient evidence to suggest that this was because of police tactics between the 9th and 13th of the month. Significantly, the disorder that did occur was relegated to the nebulous status of "copycat hooliganism" in both local and national press, the conflict placed in the realm of metaphorical contagion. Clearly, the ample evidence of considerable potential for collective violence belies such categorization.

Against the apparent public-order success of Notting Hill, anecdotal evidence suggested that the policy of refusal both to respond to the attacks on police officers in the area to attempt to disperse the hostile All Saints Road crowd, was unpopular at the junior level of the local

POWER RELATIONS AND POLICING

police (Keith 1986). This resentment at what was seen as surrendering control of the streets to the local Black community was vented in two police actions on the Sunday night; one the vociferous return to police "control" of All Saints Road, the other a police search that, by its own criteria and official report, succeeded only in causing a lot of damage to the Unity Association in Lancaster Road.

Hackney (10 July 1981)

In May 1981 a crowd in Kingsland High Street looted a jeweller's store. On the night of Tuesday 23/Wednesday 24 June, only a couple of weeks before the July riots, many of the four hundred or so people leaving Cubies dance hall at closing time again ran amok in Kingsland High Street and in Stoke Newington Road (see Map 7.2). In the latter incident several individuals were "mugged" and the till was stolen from the local Kentucky Fried Chicken shop. Neither disorder reached the national press, although a similar incident in Finsbury Park over the spring bank holiday in 1981 did receive splash headlines in several of the tabloids (*Daily Mirror, Sun, Daily Mail*, 21 April 1981), being firmly placed in the context of the Brixton riots rather than in that of the traditional expressions of (White) British cultural juvenile delinquency as as at Weston-super-Mare the same weekend (cf. Greene 1938). In the days following the disturbances in Southall, there was a gradual build-up of tension within the Stoke Newington area and an expectation of "trouble", particularly in the wake of the mid-week disturbances in Wood Green less than two miles from Dalston Junction station along Green Lane (A105). On both Wednesday 8 and Thursday 9 July there were incidents of police cars being stoned, and on the Friday the shop-keepers in Kingsland Road, Kingsland High Street and Stoke Newington Road were warned by the local police of the possibility, or even probability, of disorder over the weekend. Several shops went so far as to close early.

The initial sign of trouble on the Friday (10 July 1981) was another jewellery robbery in Kingsland High Street, this time at 5 pm. This was subsequently described by police officers as the trigger to disorder. However it was an isolated incident and did not precipitate immediate escalation of violence. At this point the police closed down Johnson's café (JJ's) in Sandringham Road (see map), a social focus of the surrounding few streets of mainly privately rented, terraced housing in poor condition, occupied principally by Black families. Johnson's had been raided several times in the preceding six to twelve months and might be compared with the Black and White in St Paul's, Bristol that had been at the heart of the disturbances there in 1980. In Stoke Newington (Dalston) the move to shut the café down was resented by

150

DISORDER AND REBELLION: THREE OF THE 1981 RIOTS?

the people gathered there. A large group of people would normally have been expected on a Friday night, and there was much talk of proposed "action". Some time between 7.30 pm and 8 pm a petrol bomb was thrown into the Argos showroom, 15 metres away from Johnson's near to the junction of Sandringham Road and Kingsland High Street, and the shop window was looted. Over the next few hours there was certainly a running battle between the predominantly Black crowd gathered around Johnson's and the police, but accounts of the specific details of the exchange differ.

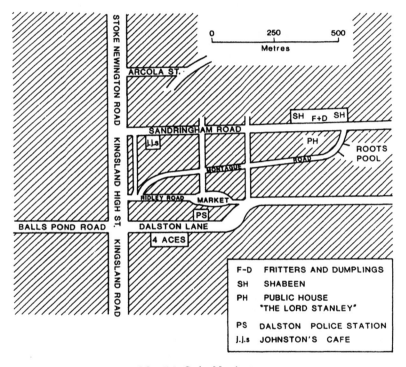

Map 7.2 Stoke Newington.

In general terms, after several attempts, police "successfully dispersed the crowd" but only after they drew truncheons and passed through a hail of cans, bottles, petrol bombs and any other detritus that came readily to hand. Thirty-one police were injured. Injuries were also suffered by the crowd, the most serious being that of a girl whose head wound needed immediate hospital treatment. More pointedly, many of

POWER RELATIONS AND POLICING

those present claimed that there had been extensive use of truncheons on heads and several claimed to have been "beaten up" after being arrested (Keith 1986). In his account of the Stoke Newington riot Paul Harrison, too, suggests that "some officers lost their cool" (1983, 349). Speaking for the Hackney Legal Defence Committee

In Hackney on 10–11 July 1981 the uprising of Black youth led to over a hundred arrests. We witnessed a military type operation by the police, who were drafted in hundreds. The SPG led the baton charges and snatch operations which caused numerous bloody injuries. (Hackney Legal Defence Committee 1981)

It was while this confrontation was at full pitch that groups of people who were on the streets seized the chance to loot and extensively damage 58 shops on the Stoke Newington Road and Kingsland High Street. Harrison, who arrived on the scene shortly after midnight, describes an incident where the window of Mr H, a menswear shop, was smashed and then looted by "five or ten youths, Black and White" (1983: 349) while three Whites in their late twenties stood by as lookouts.

Brixton (10 and 15 July 1981)

A central tenet of police policy in Brixton, in the period between April and July 1981, was to maintain a highly visible police presence on all parts of the division, including Railton Road. It was possibly inconceivable that the area could ever "return to normal" after the rioting in April and probably a return to the antagonism that had passed as normality was not desirable. Certainly tension persisted throughout the months of May and June. More importantly, Brixton had achieved mythical status, central symbol in a host of very different political rhetorics at all levels of society. Whereas in other parts of London, in the general climate of rumour and anticipation of the summer, people feared further trouble, in Brixton many claimed that they resigned themselves to it.

After a week of disorder in the rest of London, on Friday 10 July, during the evening rush hour, a police car was overturned and set alight in the centre of Brixton. However this did not incite an immediate reaction, although tension in the area was raised even higher. Later in the evening disturbances did develop, and the weekend saw widespread looting and confrontation on the streets. There is evidence to suggest this disorder partly involved a repetition of the pattern already described in the earlier April uprising – differences being the large numbers of people (Black and White) coming into the area from outside, principally involved in looting, and a broader confrontation with the local Black community. The distinction between the two was, per-

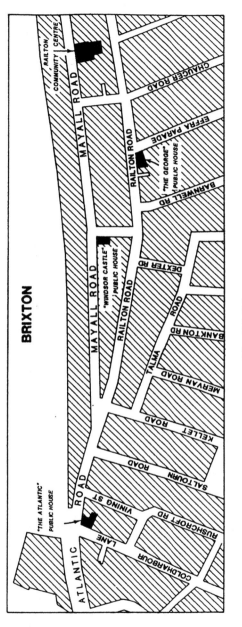

Map 7.3 Brixton.

POWER RELATIONS AND POLICING

haps unsurprisingly, less marked than previously, given the national symbolic importance of Brixton by this date. (Keith 1986).

This was even more clearly demonstrated on Wednesday 15 July when police raided 11 properties in Railton Road. The reason that was given for the raids was that senior officers had been told that caches of ammunition for further attacks on police were stored in these houses, although the element of revenge involved in this confrontation has already been described. Clashes followed that were both intense and, in contrast to the preceding weekend, highly localized.

The realization of social conflict in space

The differences between the three parts of London are significant because they illustrate the manner in which specific histories of confrontation were instrumental in the development of disorder in particular locations. These locations were not neutral spaces in which riots occurred. Instead they were resonant with contested meanings; the social relations of conflict between the police and local Black communities were sedimented through time in particular places lending these locations distinctive senses of "spatiality". The events of 1981 in these three places were only comprehensible if we understand the manner in which this sense of spatiality mediated antagonism. Such spatiality draws on the symbolic readings of these locations, but these readings were never transparent or universal; they were the sites of political struggle, constitutive rather than incidental to the patterns of violent conflict. It is through readings of this symbolism that the alternative senses of spontaneity, which were discussed in Chapter 3, become visible and that, in rejecting the material discussed in Chapter 1, a historically sensitive notion of police/Black conflict can displace the technocratic nonsense of so many theories of police racism at the heart of our understanding of events.

The reproduction of power relations in everyday life:
Given the nature of police work it is important for officers to keep control in any encounter (Smith & Gray 1983: 66). The ultimate sanction available to any police officer in dealing with members of the public is the legitimate use of force. In the final analysis this is the fundamental basis of "police power", a resource that underwrites every single contact between police and public. Ideally, the "control" alluded to by Smith & Gray is sustained by the professional management of encounters, the sort of micro-sociology of face-to-face engagements

154

THE REALIZATION OF SOCIAL CONFLICT IN SPACE

analyzed in exemplary detail in the work of Erving Goffman (1959, 1971 1972). In my own observations several PCs were highly skilled at weighing up situations and defusing potential problems through such pragmatism. (For the study of such behaviour in police generally see Cain 1973, Skolnick 1966, Manning 1977, Holdaway 1983). As Smith & Gray go on to suggest: "The strategies used by the best police officers are the ones that would emerge from a social psychology text book" (1983: 67), namely responses to a situation that are impassive, thoughtful, receptive, watchful, sceptical, not voluble and using eye-to-eye contact the whole time in order not to lose a grip on an encounter.

Manifest content: Functional policing (see the "purpose" of interaction: stop, arrest, caution, advise, etc.).

Latent content: Social reproduction (defining and redefining the rôle of police in society).

Reproduction of power relations (the "internal" relation between police and the policed).

The manifest content will normally only produce conflict with individuals transgressing particular "laws". The latent content of police action may involve conflict with social *groups*. This phenomenon may involve *potential* as well as actual conflict (raising questions of the perception of the police by the policed, legitimation, hegemony), and *covert* as well as *overt* conflict (concerning the "interests" of those groups involved, depending on the relation of the police institution to the state and changes in this relation). (For elaboration of concepts see Lukes 1974, Giddens 1984).

Diagram 7.1 Police and public : The "content" of routine interaction

---

Giddens (1984, 1979) has regularly stressed the point that it is such mundane performances that subsume the whole process of social reproduction. Institutional forms, social rules and norms, power relations and interpretative schema are all implicated in the durée (routine) of everyday life. In this way any single interaction involving a police officer can be seen to operate on at least two levels (see Diagram 7.1). On the level of manifest content a meeting may be purely functional, but through the repetition of such practice the police–policed relation is reproduced, reinforced or even, in the process of *structuration*, redefined. In the policing of a democratic society this power relation-

POWER RELATIONS AND POLICING

ship is in principle more complex than merely an exercise in coercion, resting ultimately on the institutionally embedded historical rôle of the police as both social *service* and an agent of social *control*. Hence in a non-Utopian society the police will always at best be the upholders of a transparently flawed *status quo*. It is this that creates a distinction between law and order, the police as both crime-fighters and enforcers of one particular social and moral order. This dichotomy echoes in the tension between the community of interest in combating certain offences and a common ambivalence towards a great many of the laws that define such crimes, the mismatch between what is criminal in law and criminal in popular sentiment.

The reconciliation of such uncertainties by the police constable forms part of the process by which "the job" is redefined and internally regulated within the police service (Fielding 1988). As in other "occupational cultures" the lower ranks, through a system of rules and norms, have a far greater license than the strict managerial structure would suggest (James 1979, McConville & Shepherd 1992). In this sense an issue such as stop and search by police officers cannot be understood in terms of its putative success or failure in catching criminals alone (cf. Willis 1983). Partly as a result of this, the behaviour of a police officer towards individual members of the public will be conditioned by a set of expectations based on the classification of that individual and the setting in which the interaction takes place.

The informal hierarchies of prestige and contempt that invariably operate alongside a formal rank structure is significant here. At a junior level, the "moral career" or peer group reputation of the individual PC (see Harre 1979) will, over a period of time, depend as much on the protection and enhancement of status in the expressive realm of respect and contempt in such encounters as in the practical realm of functional policing. Being "had over" or "wound up" by a prisoner will constitute a loss of face, but over-reaction will be ridiculed: on one occasion a PC driving in a Dalston car chase appeared to be more concerned with personal reputation than with the escaped "villain", particularly when, in an erro of judgement, we ended up driving down the road in the wrong direction! Kudos can take precedence over catching criminals. Within Dalston station one of the most respected PCs was a well built Scotsman, renowned for his displays of physical courage on Sandringham Road, his drinking and his generally gregarious manner. An industrious, conscientious but more reticent sergeant was scornfully referred to as "the wandering genie" (suggesting he had lost his bottle), while a WPS on the graduate escalated-promotion scheme was respected even less. The social hierarchy neither reflects the managerial structure nor conforms to the goals of that structure.

THE REALIZATION OF SOCIAL CONFLICT IN SPACE

The reproduction of power relations is thus not necessarily a conscious part of the PC's rôle but is built into the subcultural definition of doing the job well and being seen to sustain "the respect" of the police service, which incidentally reproduces the police rôle within society at large.

Spatial and social categorization

In order to sustain control and respect in encounters the police officer has to adjust his/her behaviour to the individual with whom he/she is dealing. Inevitably in reacting quickly to the whole cross-section of society a cast of "typical characters" that must be handled develops, a cast that is stereotypical by definition. Hence, as Holdaway (1983) points out, doctors, lawyers, teachers and social workers are often classified as "challengers" and, as the PSI (1985) confirmed, the poorer and powerless sections of society are often referred to as "slag". The struggle of the individual to elude his/her label is not confined to police work. It is a struggle in which racial stereotyping can falsely justify itself and it is a cultural process for which White society generally is as responsible as any alleged subcultural pathology within the police force.

Space too is categorized in this process. In James's (1979) comparison of senior and junior management definitions of "professionalism" (see Diagram 7.2), the attitude towards the area covered by the division is telling. Under the model of "practional professionalism" (junior ranks), "the police have a prior and absolute claim to control the geographical territory within which they work".

Ironically, the definition by PCs of spatial control and territoriality so stressed, often confirmed by serving police officers carrying out research (James 1979, Holdaway 1983, Young 1991), implies a self-image of the social control aspect of police work which closely resembles a radical or Marxian definition of the function of the British police force. More significantly here, this conceptual division of space, producing an imagined geography of the policed area, influences contact with ethnic minorities in two significant and divisive respects.

First, the normative division of the population is reinforced by a spatial division of expected routines. Expectations of the spatial "daily path" (Pred 1981) of distinct groups inform police conceptions of suspicious behaviour. A revealing comment is highlighted by Smith & Gray (1983: 129):

> If I saw a Black man walking through Wimbledon High Street I would definitely stop him. Course down here it's a common sight, so there's no point.

Quite literally, there is a place for everyone and everyone is expected to be in their place. Anyone who deviates from the expected social orbit

	Managerial professionalism	*Practical professionalism*
Theory of policing	Specialist squads of PCs. Local knowledge of patterns of offence vital.	Practical activity of policing (arresting offenders) takes priority over local knowledge.
Technology	Information storage based on technical aids assist in build up of information prior and subsequent to arrests.	Action orientation (scuffle, chase, fast drive) form basis of police work. Technology useful but of secondary importance.
Informed discretion	Slow build up of knowledge before arrests made. Discretionary decision to arrest based on judgement in relation to judicial evidence.	DISCRETION Speedy arrest of suspect, later questioned in confines of police station takes precedence over method of slow build up of evidence by observation.
Rule of law	Extra-legal techniques of control unnecessary; evidence gained before arrests and so questioning after arrest reduced. Policing can and should be performed within the rule of law.	Extra-legal techniques of gaining evidence accepted as necessary. Violence and pressuring of suspects are two routine examples of such techniques.
Criteria of success	Crime arrests one of several measures of success. Clear up rates takes second place to policing within the law	Arrests provide primary measure of successful policing and achieve esteem for the officers concerned
Criteria of control	*"The police share their function of control with other agencies; they have no absolute claim to control over a geographical territory."*	*"The police have a prior and and absolute claim to control the geographical territory within which they work."*
Race relations	Some policemen discriminate against blacks. The definitions of managerial professional help eradicate such discrimination	The police do not discriminate against blacks.

Diagram 7.2 The contrasting definitions and perceptions of "The Job" by senior and junior police officers. (Taken from D. James (1979), "Police–Black relations: the professional solution."; my emphasis.)

THE REALIZATION OF SOCIAL CONFLICT IN SPACE

is by definition suspicious. As part of this process the geography of suspicious persons can reinforce a perceived norm of social and racial segregation via the process of criminalization (see Gilroy 1982 on the relationship between SUS and ghettoization; Christian 1983).

Secondly, distinct "places" within an area will be classified in order to contextualize the appropriate police behaviour at particular sites. Holdaway suggests that,

The area policed from Hilton station, the ground as they call it, belongs to the police. They possess it; it is their territory and members of the force from adjoining stations have no right of entry into or patrol of the ground save by invitation . . . the view of Hilton as police controlled territory forms one central organizing principle of a mental map which officers use to order their work in the subdivision. (1983: 36)

He outlines a typology of sites of danger, sites of trouble, sites of work, mump holes (places to escape work), sites of interest and home territories. Again it is important to note that in intent and in its functional roots such practice is not deliberately racist. But yet again, through the form of the job, the essential perceptual mapping of space, along with all its divisive ramifications, is stereotypical incidentally rather than deliberately, racist in effect even if not racist in cause. On the grounds of these dangerous stereotypes, Black social centres and social events become labelled variously as foci for political agitators (1960s London); scenes of mugging; drug dealing and street crime (1970s London); and/ or potential sites of public disorder (1980s London), as the conflict between police and Black people becomes part of police routine.

Front Lines and the "sanctuary effect": power relations inverted
The suggestion is that this *necessary* characteristic of police work, when paired with the institutionally racist systems of collective consumption that reproduce ghettoization (Smith 1989), is crucial in the creation of centres of resistance focused on Front Lines of conflict. The social centres (locales) on Front Line were "places" where the rôle of Black people in Britain was acted, re-enacted, defined and re-defined, every day. An integral part of that rôle is the relationship with the police, which has deteriorated steadily for more than 30 years through the combined influences of racism, marginalization, labelling and criminalization already outlined. The fundamental point to grasp about the locales on Front Line is not that police/Black relations were *worse* on All Saints Road, Railton Road or Sandringham Road than anywhere else in the surrounding area. It is rather that these were the locales at which resentment of power relations was transformed into resistance of power relations. It is not just, as Giddens puts, it that, "back regions are zones

159

POWER RELATIONS AND POLICING

in which agents recover forms of autonomy which are compromised or treated in frontal contexts" (1985: 278), but that the power relation which is taken for granted across other parts of London is challenged as a matter of routine within a particular context. Crucially, such challenges became a part of everyday life long before any incidence of collective disorder in Notting Hill, Brixton or Hackney.

The form which such challenges assumed was fairly limited throughout the 1960s and 1970s on All Saints Road and throughout the 1970s on Railton Road and Sandringham Road. Somebody would be arrested, a group of people would gather and try, often successfully, to snatch back the prisoner. Alternatively, in attempting to effect an arrest, a PC would chase an individual, commonly young, male and Black, into a café or club and would be physically beaten off by the people using that facility.

The rhetoric and dramatic realization of struggles for the control of Front Line highlight the remarkable similarity between the perceptions of junior police officers and the voices of many Black people in such areas. The notions of Holdaway, James, Smith & Gray concerning police claims to territorial exclusivity are mirrored by the Brixton Rastafarian Collective's description to Scarman, described in Chapter 2, of the police as a force of occupation within Britain's internal colonies.

For the police, resistance of arrest and other attacks were normally rationalized in the stereotyping of Front Lines as *criminal* areas. Yet for people on Front Line the whole relevance of functional policing was overshadowed by the context of the encounter. The manifest content of a police action (taking action against criminal activity) was lost in the significance of the latent content of the same behaviour (enforcing social order). Typically, it is quite simply not possible to see Black reaction to any police action on All Saints Road divorced from a thirty-year history of injustice and repression. History weighs down on the present day. To take just one example, the Mangrove was a sign, a symbol of that history.

One result of such locationally specific challenges to authority was the creation of what might be called a "sanctuary effect" in certain areas on the Front Lines. When the prerogative of the police is challenged on such a regular basis the reality of the power relation is inverted. Junior officers will become afraid to make arrests in certain areas at certain times out of concern for personal safety. When senior officers, fearing public-order problems, build the precedence of public order over law enforcement into formal policy they effectively sanction this inversion. This change was at times openly exploited on the Front Lines.

"Challenges" become part of the routine because of what the police/Black interaction symbolizes. Often, all the challenging crowd see

160

THE REALIZATION OF SOCIAL CONFLICT IN SPACE

is a policeman chasing a Black man [sic] and the situation is immediately interpreted in a particular way for the reasons already cited. Petty criminals readily exploited this situation. The cases in Brixton of bag snatchers who were seen to use Railton Road as a safe haven and the open selling of cannabis are clear examples of this. The use of one pub for the sale of arms on one of the Front Lines, and the organized crime trade in heroin and cocaine, are more sinister, if also more evolved, forms of the same phenomenon. The fact that police moves against such operations are sometimes resisted by local people is greeted with bewilderment and cynicism by senior officers, who then subscribe to stereotypes of the whole area, often genuinely unaware of the context of their action, the existence of the "different realities" informing the life of Black Britain and defining the sense of history, or *the historicity*, of these places. This is not to suggest that confrontation is a simple function of "misunderstanding", only to suggest that a commonly held liberal ideology of policing cannot be squared with the empirical reality of Black Britain.

Once Front Line had developed into a sanctuary the conflict between the police and the Black community was driven further into the institutional practice of the police. Because authority was successfully challenged so regularly it became a priority for many police, of all ranks, to re-establish control in this *locale*. Symbolic "fishing raids" were often seen as one example of appropriate response. In Front Line areas both PCs and local Black people commonly regarded such operations as ostentatious demonstrations of police authority and some senior officers have suggested that it is important to "fly the flag" in this way (Keith 1988). It also has to be said that other senior officers in these three locations strongly disagreed with this tactic.

Even when the purpose of raids in Front Line locales may be wholly functional (e.g. Railton Road raids in July 1981, Sandringham Road raid July 1981) it is quite possible for PCs to subvert the manifest purpose of such actions by emphasizing their own latent purpose, settling old scores and "not paying too much attention to the furniture" (PC in Hackney). As explained earlier the concept of "front line deviancy" was developed by senior police officers themselves to describe such behaviour. Again it is noteworthy that there were signs of the development of such confrontations in all three case study locations long before 1981, although *rioting* was to intensify this tit for tat process.

At any one time there is a high degree of uncertainty about the "real" state of power relations in such areas and so both police officers and the many different individuals using the Front Line, are never sure "how far they can go". The relation is continually being redefined, the boundaries of "normal behaviour" continually renegotiated.

POWER RELATIONS AND POLICING

An illustration of this point occurred in Dalston in a police car in which I was an observer; on being asked about Notting Hill, I explained to the driver, the one time regulation about no cars being allowed to patrol on All Saints Road (see Ch. 6). The driver, who had not heard of this, was surprised, saying that he thought such policies disgraceful and that if ordered to do likewise on Sandringham Road he would refuse to conform with such instructions. We immediately drove to Sandringham Road (at about 1.30 am on a Saturday night/Sunday morning) and stopped a car in what was clearly a performance for my benefit. The Black driver of the stopped car could not prove that he owned the vehicle (he was not the registered owner, although the car was not listed as stolen), he had no driving licence, the car was untaxed and clearly not roadworthy. However, some ten to fifteen spectators had immediately gathered and their number was growing steadily. Although not physically threatening the police operator (the second member of the car crew with responsibility for such questioning), they were openly hostile to our presence. The operator, none too impressed by his own driver's demonstration, let the Sandringham Road driver off with a warning, clearly an abnormal decision in the light of his many violations, but as clearly understandable in the light of the attitude of "the crowd", which had by then doubled in size.

Although the events of July 1981 in Brixton, Hackney and possibly Notting Hill could be described as "riots", and although the sites of conflict were clearly similar in many respects, the respective clashes demonstrated the very different status of police authority in the three locations. The control of All Saints Road was never really contested by the police and this was much resented by many local PCs. In Railton Road in April 1981 a very common interpretation of events was that the authority of the police was clearly seen to be usurped. In Hackney, successful challenges to police practice had become common, but in the final analysis police were seen to be in the ascendancy that summer on Sandringham Road. Internal disagreements within the police in Stoke Newington can be seen, in part, as a re-evaluation of the status of Sandringham Road in the light of these disorders. In this sense, the very obvious animosity that characterized the minimal disorders of Battersea, Wandsworth and several other parts of London in 1981, could be understood partly in terms of the relative immaturity of the police/Black conflict in those areas, which had deprived both parties of a suitable scene for the transformation of manifest conflict into much more serious open confrontation. The status of the Front Line areas is not immutable, neither is the development over time of other sites of confrontation unexceptional.

162

THE REALIZATION OF SOCIAL CONFLICT IN SPACE

The collapse of "policing by consent"
Diagram 7.3 illustrates the pattern that has characterized the growing gulf between police and Black communities across London and throughout Britain. The central contradiction behind all police work (law vs order) will need an ideological support to sustain the police rôle as a widely accepted and legitimate social service. Faced with the reality of racism, and structurally positioned within British society to come out poorly from this central contradiction, a growing number of Black individuals, not just young, Black males, had withdrawn their consent to the police by the mid-1960s and early 1970s. The police/Black conflict dates back a long way.

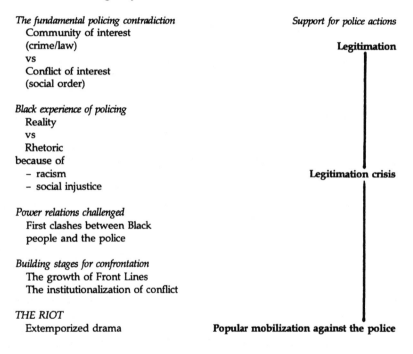

Diagram 7.3 The collapse of policing by consent.

However, the simple withdrawal of consent is never enough to provoke open confrontation. Conflict is bound up as much in the space in which it is realized as in the time in which it is generated. The element of time is crucial because it takes so long to progress along the path of the diagram. Because conflict is realized in space it becomes

POWER RELATIONS AND POLICING

"local" by definition, even when the experience of conflict is national, or at least metropolitan.

In evidence to the Scarman inquiry the CRE (1981) remarked that it was not that riots had occurred that was remarkable, it was that they had taken so long to occur. The reason for this is rooted in the fact that most people are reluctant to take to the streets. There is a wide gap that separates open animosity towards the police from a predisposition towards collective violent disorder. This evolution of conflict, spatially realized, preceded the incidence of collective disorder across London. Quite literally this evolution set the scene for rioting.

The stage: rioting as extemporized drama?

In arguing that the work of Erving Goffman should be considered as a major contribution to "grand" social theory, Giddens (1984, 1987) has suggested that the reproduction of social form is tied to the day-to-day routines that are themselves linked to the "stages" on which such processes take place. Yet one of the dangers of stressing the dramaturgical metaphor of Goffman is that space and particular places will be seen as explicitly communicative settings for social action. I would suggest that this is very far from the case; places act as signs but the symbolism is read in very different ways by those deciphering the "spatiality" of social life (Soja 1985, 1989). This is not simply a question of ambiguity but a matter of the proliferation of meaning, which can be reconciled with dramaturgical analysis by borrowing some of the concepts developed in the field of post-structuralism and semiology (Barthes 1967, 1973, Eco 1979).

"Places" as "signs"

"Places" form part of our cultural shorthand. Expectations of particular patterns of behaviour are contextualized by location, each location may have certain historical associations, trigger a Proustian process of recall. The memories bound up in a particular place may be the property of one, two or a handful of people. The significations of the Somme battlefield may be vicariously accessible to Western European culture generally, tied by the experiences of real and imagined relatives, while the symbolic power of Hiroshima is self-evidently universal. Places may act as signs but the messages they communicate will not be the same for everyone who reads them.

In terms of the linguistic paradigm derived from Saussure, the three "symbolic locations" can be seen as metaphorically linked. They are not

THE STAGE: RIOTING AS EXTEMPORIZED DRAMA?

precise replications of each other, but in terms of the sign systems involved they are almost mutually interchangeable (see Diagram 7.4). But it is the property of metonymy that most clearly renders comprehensible the set of actions that recur when police authority is challenged. For many Black people who lived in Notting Hill, Brixton and Hackney any police action at all triggered off a set of mental associations about the relationship between Black people and the police.

Clothing:	*Metaphoric*	*Metonymic/Syntagmatic*
	Blazer	
	Suit jacket	
	Dinner jacket	(a) A piece in the garment code, a part that is symbolically tied to the whole, i.e. bow tie, dress shirt, etc.
		(b) Symbolically tied to social protocol, i.e. the appropriate behaviour of someone in a dinner jacket
Spatial semiology:		
Front Lines in the 1980s, united by similarities, distinguished by differences, but broadly interchangeable		
	All Saints Road	
	Railton Road	
	Sandringham Road	(a) JJ's symbolizing an appropriate repertoire for a set stage (after Goffman); the appropriate behaviour at a particular "place" (syntagm).
		(b) JJ's as "part" symbolizing a whole history of police/Black relations in particular place (metonym).

Diagram 7.4 Two dimensions of linguistic and symbolic representation.

When any police action at all was set in the context of Front Line, the signification was that much more powerful, the sense of injustice at the "different reality" of Black Britain (see Bhavnani et al. 1986) overwhelming. For Black people in particular parts of London that reality was bound up in particular locations; history was deeply imbedded in the

POWER RELATIONS AND POLICING

places in which that history was enacted.

For the police, a completely different set of codes and messages were based on exactly the same set of locations. All Saints Road and Railton Road had a renown that stretched throughout the Metropolitan Police, the "canteen mythology" of Notting Hill that a senior officer there once described (Keith 1986). For junior officers these places were the sites of regular "attacks" on the police by Black people. Such associations may or may not be rationalized in terms of racist "folk psychology" depending on the individual; significantly these rationalizations (both the racist and non-racist ones) may well not alter police behaviour on such "stages". Moreover, even for those individuals keen to learn, the rapid three year turnover rate of senior officers frequently constricted any understanding of local history among senior management. For all ranks the inscription of history in particular places remains of little interest.

In terms of social theory a distinction could be made between the metonymic (historical) and the syntagmatic (operating principally in the present) modes of linguistic symbolism. Black perceptions are constructed as a form of "local knowledge" (cf. Geertz 1973, 1982) and are fundamentally metonymic in the reading of the social world; the police action is seen as part of a historical whole, invoking a 20 to 30 year history of Black experience in a particular "place". For the police, operational goals have priority and "place" as a sign is read syntagmatically; the action is part of an expected sequence, an anticipated repertoire of behaviour that occurs wholly in the present and characterizes a particular location. It is this very structure of police practice in such areas which guarantees that the policing institution acts as a "machine for the suppression of time", – history is lost.

Social relations are reproduced through the signification of places; conflict recurs as the power relations of a racialized social order are enacted, challenged and negotiated. In this process there is no straightforward one-to-one correspondence between places and the "true" meanings with which they resonate. It is of paramount importance to acknowledge that such symbolism, such evocative properties of places, are not "summoned up" by the individual. As Goffman and many others (e.g. Marsh et al. 1978, Harre 1979), have demonstrated, the reading of such spatial signs is not reflexively monitored but is either part of subconscious or "practical conscious" apprehension of the world in which we live. Such powerful affective connections between places and our understandings of those places are inseparable, precisely because we internally define these places by this set of mental cross-references.

166

THE STAGE: RIOTING AS EXTEMPORIZED DRAMA?

The fallacies of crowd psychology, the reality of rebellion?:
trigger events and the escalation of violence

> "sen fe de riot squad
> quick!
> cause wi runnin wild
> bitta like bile;
> blood will guide
> their way;
> an I say,
> all we doin
> is defendin;
> soh set yu ready
> fe war . . . war . . .
> freedom is a very firm thing."
>
> Linton Kwesi Johnson (from "All wi doin is defendin")

The most serious disturbances of 1980 and 1981 shared many similarities, particularly in the escalation of violence. Most descriptions of the major riots consider the events that immediately preceded trouble, the triggers to violence, as either irrelevant or inconsequential. They are normally characterized in terms of metaphoric combustibility, merely the spark that causes the inevitable fire (e.g. Hytner 1981: 33.6: "the spark that led to the conflagration"; Scarman 1981: 8.9, "the spark" that led to the rioting). Although it would be facile to overestimate the importance of the single instance, any explanation of "rioting" is incomplete unless it can account for the manner in which seemingly trivial incidents develop into major forms of collective destruction. Central to such a thesis is a rejection of the behaviourist conception of violence as some form of pressure release and an assumption that in crowd situations violence is both rational and meaningful. An understanding of the relationship between action and location can render "disorder" rational and meaningful, while simultaneously not losing sight of the wider material social context in which such behaviour is set.

I have argued elsewhere (Keith 1986, 1987) that in looking at the "triggers" to the uprisings of the 1980s we can make moves towards an *explanation* rather than just a *description* of events. The "flashpoints" model of disorder can be read in a similar fashion (Waddington et al. 1989, Waddington 1992). Arguably, the trigger is interpreted metonymically by those who either see it or hear about it. It is an act which is representative simultaneously of both a general situation and particular grievances; it is an act to which violence is a response sanctioned by a large enough crowd of people to constitute collective disorder. This

POWER RELATIONS AND POLICING

does not mean that violence is sanctioned by all present. As has already been suggested the propriety of violence does not vary arbitrarily between different age groups, genders or even times of day. Nor does it mean that this action of violence is considered the same act by all involved, the preferred descriptions of the same actions may be traced to differing intentional states. However, the reading of the signification of the trigger event must be sufficiently clear to induce collective action. Within the "social language" of a particular area at a particular time the trigger is read similarly by a large number of people.

It is because the trigger incident is taken as a single item, which in part symbolizes a much larger whole, that the question, "Do people riot because of police or unemployment or greed?", or any other neat reason, is quite literally meaningless. Such precise categorizations and partitions find no equivalents in the structure of action. So, although it is vital to understand the perception of those involved in the "uprisings", it is very difficult merely to cite a collective that is called "the rioters" and try and discern some straightforward average or communal "perception" for this group.

Similarly, as an eyewitness to serious disorder in Brixton in 1982, 1983 and 1985, and Tottenham in 1985 (Keith 1987), a common theme that ran through the chilling events on each occasion was the repetition of the claims that in avenging grievances, attacking the police in those particular circumstances was fully justified; the forceful and fearful realization that the gruesome events of those nights were not a consciously premeditated mass mobilization, nor the result of some criminal *force majeure* (not discounting the presence of large numbers of looters and others joining in "for fun"). The violence was being accounted for by fully rational individuals as the "proper" way to behave. It is not necessary to make a value judgement about such accounts, other than to establish their sincerity. Nor is there a suggestion that all rioters felt in this particular way; rather it is a contention that such feelings were common and crucially relevant to the transformation of such situations of tension and occasional resistance to arrest into scenes in which many hundreds of people became involved in full scale confrontations with the police. In this way such confrontations were, in the first instance, very often parochial and defensive in nature.

There is also clear evidence that when this confrontation occurs the collapse of public order will very often be seized upon to facilitate looting and other anti-social activities that can be more readily classified as criminal. In this way most riots tend to move toward some approximate equifinal product. Allowed to escalate, one looks very much like another, regardless of its roots. This is why the trends in the arrest data examined in Chapter 5, which highlighted differences between such

CONCLUSION

groups, remain useful in spite of all the inevitable problems that surround the data source. Therefore, the chronology of confrontation is important. Trigger events are not epiphenomenal or incidental to the development of violence. They provide a key element in the signification of action, the meaning of *the riot* set against its spatial and social context.

Conclusion

There are significant *theoretical* insights revealed in the realization of social conflict in space. The context in which police/Black antagonism briefly flowered in violent disorder in 1981 was unremarkable if the *spatialities* of the specific locations are understood. This conflict itself was a historical product, accessible to most of the Black community as a form of "local knowledge", violence only one of many manifestations of it. Most people did not seek out the violent clashes of 1981, they were just *appropriate* at a particular time and at certain specific places.

In this sense, conflict is not synonymous with confrontation. The historical product (conflict) has been reproduced and reconstructed in the *durée* of social practice, changing its nature but remaining as an embossed social division. The roots of violence remain.

Yet, perhaps more important than any theoretical advance, the justification of "realistic" analysis of "rioting" lies in the provision of a clearer perspective on this social schism throughout the whole decade and into the 1990s. Events before and after that summer fit into a particular local context in the evolution of this conflict. Power relations between police and local Black communities were acted and re-enacted daily across London and throughout the rest of the country. The nature of the historical conflict generated through the racial subordination and criminalization of those communities, resulted in these power relations being challenged at some places but not at others. These challenges, this particular type of racial mobilization, were political in the broadest sense of the term but, in part, were constrained by the very parameters of the law-and-order debates that had created the putative "social problem" of Black criminality in the first place.

This is why the spontaneity of the events of 1981 remains so important, even over ten years later. This is why the manner in which violent resistance was tied to particular places is crucial. This is why the 1960s racist portrayal of Black communities as centres of disorder became transformed into the momentary, but certainly not pathological, scenes of meaningful rebellion in 1981 and evolved into a much more

POWER RELATIONS AND POLICING

thoroughly articulated racial mobilization in 1985.

CHAPTER 8

Misunderstandings?
The resolution of conflict
by consultation:
assumptions and contradictions

"Consultation is the wavy line that squares circles."

Stuart Hall (1982)

In Chapters 6 and 7, I have attempted to argue that, in order to understand why it is that British Black communities confronted the police force in the horrific scenes of major uprisings and the daily cases of violent clashes throughout the 1980s, it is essential to develop a spatially and historically sensitive notion of police/Black conflict. As argued in Chapter 1, to focus on the communities alone, or on the police force out of context, can pathologize either in the production of invidious portrayals of Black culture or naïve notions of police racism (Keith 1991, 1992). In this chapter I attempt to refine an understanding of this notion of conflict, principally by suggesting that common liberal representations of police/Black antagonism as a form of "misunderstanding" seriously underestimate the material context in which such schism is founded.

The source material for this chapter is a study of the development of police–community consultative procedures across London throughout the 1980s. This material has been drawn on selectively here, the full results of the work being available in other forms (Keith 1986, 1988b, 1989).

Under Section 106 of the Police and Criminal Evidence Act 1984 (PACE), the Commissioner of the Metropolitan Police was obliged to establish statutory consultative groups in each London borough, which were to conform with both PACE and Home Office guidelines. These were initially issued in 1982, when their establishment was first mooted, and later in restyled form in 1985, subsequent to the passage

MISUNDERSTANDINGS?

of PACE through Parliament. It is not intended here to outline in any detail the history or debates concerning this passage (for full account see Jefferson & Grimshaw 1984, Morgan & Maggs 1984, 1985).

I have argued elsewhere that, in part, it is possible to analyze the consultative arrangements in the context of other exercises in institutional buffering by the state (Keith 1989), whereby symbolic reforms create new institutions with a high profile and few powers. A common argument has been that the central state can make token gestures of change without radically altering the structures through which racial inequalities are reproduced, creating an institutional fabric which promises much and delivers little. Popular movements that demand political change (e.g. police accountability) are thus co-opted into reinforcing the "city trenches" which defend the *status quo*. In this sense an organization such as the Commission for Racial Equality may become the focus of unrealistic expectations and the scapegoat for failing to deliver racial justice (Edelman 1971, 1985, Katznelson 1981, Solomos 1988). In other work I have suggested that such models of state intervention may be useful descriptively in an analysis of police–community consultation, but that they are unable to grasp the contingent and complex relations between consultative structures and the local police bureaucracy (Keith 1989).

As with so many legislative changes, consultation was not so much introduced as a planned satisfaction of an articulated demand, as conceived as part of a legislative package that was deemed appropriate at a particular time. Notwithstanding this, the primary political force behind its inception lay in the report of Lord Scarman (1981), who had recommended that,

a statutory framework be developed to require local consultation between the Metropolitan Police and the community at borough or police district level. (1981: 96, 5.69)

Crucially, Scarman placed consultation on the political agenda in a context which explicitly linked it to the prevention of public disorder and the resolution of the clashes between police and Black people in London.

This position was reinforced by government ministers in their public defences of PACE. As Douglas Hurd, then Minister of State at the Home Office, commented when attempting in Parliament to discredit some of the myths involved in the politicization of policing issues

We recognize, however, that behind the myth lies a real concern about the relationship between the police and the public – especially certain sections of the public such as the young and Black people. Every police force in the country is now working to meet that concern. The consultative arrangements which under clause 96

172

THE RESOLUTION OF CONFLICT BY CONSULTATION

will for the first time become part of the law are one way of working towards this purpose. (*Hansard* 7 November 1983: 106)

But if the broad political function of the reforms was clear, the central terms of these changes invoked two extremely problematic, politically contested notions. Both the parameters of "community" and the meaning of "consultation" endow the consultative process with crucial ambiguities at their very heart, which may create false expectations of the power and importance of consultative groups (Keith 1988). In reality, the institutional forms that emerge structure the ability of different groups to be heard, and the overall political context determines which agendas it is possible to address in such an arena (Morgan & Maggs 1984, 1985, Jefferson & McClaughlin 1989).

The reasoning behind Scarman's recommendation of statutory consultation was that at the heart of the disorders in Brixton were real grievances felt by an oppressed Black community, grievances which had no outlet other than violent street protest – essentially an echo of Martin Luther King's comment that riots are the language of the unheard. In providing an arena for such expression, the implication was that in the consultative group the Black community *could* be heard, and could explain their plight in person to senior officers. In this sense it was hoped to institutionalize conflict, taking it off the streets and into the committee room. It is upon this contrast between the ethnographic reality and the political construction of the process of consultation that this chapter focuses, by setting one incident, which perhaps came closest to achieving Scarman's goals, in its political context: a contrast of integrity with cynicism.

On three occasions in London in the period after 1981, it could be said that this goal was achieved, if not always in formal consultation, then in informal organizations that were close approximations to the official consultative structure. In 1984 in Notting Hill and in 1983 in Brixton, rising tensions, which had escalated to the point of nascent public disorder, were partially defused after public meetings on All Saints Road and Railton Road, respectively, when senior police officers (Whitfield in Notting Hill, Marnoch in Brixton) held public meetings where they explained the police position amidst general hostility and abuse.

A third occasion occurred in Brixton on Tuesday 1 October 1985 when, in the wake of the widespread rioting that had followed the police shooting of Mrs Cherry Groce (a middle-aged Black woman), a public meeting of the Community Police Consultative Group for Lambeth (CPCGL) was seen by members of the group itself, by senior police officers and by press present at the time, to be acting as a peaceful outlet for the anger of local people. Yet it is possible, without

MISUNDERSTANDINGS?

contesting this general description, to suggest that this meeting, rather than being the exemplary success of the CPCGL, highlighted the flaws that handicap its very existence.

Astel Parkinson was at the time chairman of the group. He had lived in Brixton since 1959, been a youth worker since the mid-1960s (full-time since the mid-1970s) and his son Horace was one of the Brockwell Park 3. This was one of the many *causes célèbres* in the Brixton history of clashes between the police and the Black community referred to in Chapter 2. Parkinson had been active in the campaign protesting about police behaviour. Friendly and generous, by the early 1980s he could talk with authority on the history of the area, because this sort of local knowledge was for him no more than autobiography. He was certainly no "mouthpiece" or "puppet" of the police and was one of the few members of the group who was well known and respected on Railton Road, where he was chairman of the Afro-Caribbean Community Association (ACCA). He was also a friend of the Groce family and, at the start of that night's meeting, introduced one of the members of the family to those present, while making a moving speech for serious but controlled discussion of the emotive issues that had occurred in the preceding few days.

The public gallery in the committee room of Lambeth town hall, which was being used for the meeting, had rapidly filled up and, before business opened, there had already been heckling of the police present. Within seconds of the start, three Black people (two men, one woman, all in their late twenties, early thirties and in paramilitary gear), shoved into the room, snatched the microphones from the committee table and began to harangue both Parkinson and the police. Every time either he or Commander Marnoch, the senior police officer present, tried to speak, they were shouted down by the slogan chanting of the intruders. Whenever Astel Parkinson tried to retaliate he was drowned in a chorus of "Uncle Tom, Uncle Tom, Uncle Tom" from the three paramilitaries, who had now placed themselves strategically around the room and controlled all the microphones. Their amplified vilification was often echoed from the floor and they frequently demanded that the meeting should be stopped because of the futility of even talking to "filth" like the police. About 50 people filled the room; a great many more had been locked out of the town hall and were noisily demanding to be let in.

The assembly continued fitfully in this vein for about half-an-hour until a group of about 15 to 20 from outside the town hall overpowered the security guards and demanded that all those outside be allowed into the meeting. The leader of this group made a scathing attack on Astel Parkinson, labelling him a parasite on other people's misfortune

THE RESOLUTION OF CONFLICT BY CONSULTATION

and a toady to the police. Visibly upset, Parkinson lost his cool and a further row followed. The back door to the committee room was now open. With the numbers of this second vociferous protest faction growing rapidly, the collapse of the gathering was avoided only when a council official allowed the meeting to move from the committee room into the main Lambeth function room, where between two and three hundred people filled the hall, many covering their faces to prevent identification.

There then followed a meeting more reminiscent of the tribunals of revolutionary France than the protocols of the twentieth-century committee, a gathering so intense that by the end of the evening, as an observer, I felt emotionally drained, after the most sustained display of mass anger I have seen inside a single room. It was not the self-righteous anger of politics. There was rhetoric, but not much. Only a small minority indulged themselves. It was the anger of the indignant, the wounded, the shocked. There was a feeling of incredulity, "How could they have done this?", and over everything a fury at the police shooting that regularly surfaced in overt and palpably sincere hatred.

In the larger hall the paramilitary group stepped back and Parkinson's authority as chairman was again usurped, this time by Tony Morgan, a local young member of the Black community better known for self-publicity than for "street credibility", who openly abused the members of the committee on which he had once served. Assuming command with a shout of "We're taking this meeting over Astel", it was under his aegis that the rest of the evening took the approximate form of a public interrogation of Marnoch, with individuals taking turns to come to the microphone to say their piece. Sometimes Marnoch was given a chance to reply.

Throughout this time a series of minor scenes were enacted just off the main stage. A television cameraman was bundled out of the room, not without force, after an impromptu vote ruled against his presence, while John Clare, the BBC correspondent, hid his tape recorder under his jacket and looked nervous. A group stood on one side of the room chanting, "Fire! Fire! Fire!". Occasionally the flow of the meeting would be interrupted. Once somebody ran into the room, advanced on Marnoch and accused him of having the building surrounded by police. Hostility and tension intensified dramatically and the numbers of those present who had kept on their anorak hoods and wore scarves over their faces, notably increased. At another time somebody interrupted the meeting with the cry, "Toxteth's on fire" to the prolonged cheers of the gathering.

But at the heart of events, one person after another came up to the front of the hall and explained their experiences and feelings of the past

MISUNDERSTANDINGS?

three days or the past 30 years. Their hurt and their bitterness turned the night into an abridged, but moving, account of a racist society. Occasionally this would become personalized. Two individuals threatened to kill Marnoch and another announced to the audience that the Lambeth Police Commander was responsible for jailing him eight times and that, "I will get you before I die, Marnoch."

In replying, Marnoch made some outspoken comments that included declarations of support for any public inquiry into the shooting of Mrs Groce and a democratically elected police authority in London, as well as the statement that,

I have stated several times in the past, and I still believe, that it will not be possible to have peace on these streets with the current high levels of deprivation.

But eventually it was all too much. Briefly, Marnoch broke down and was visibly in tears. Tough, gregarious, very large and very tall, the senior policeman in Brixton stood in front of a couple of hundred people in Lambeth Town Hall and cried. "Crocodile tears", somebody standing a foot away from him shouted in his face.

Neither Marnoch, nor Parkinson, nor the rest of the committee, who for the most part had remained silent throughout, could assuage the anger of those present at the horrific shooting of Mrs Groce; in fact most of their statements seemed instead to rouse most people further.

At about 9.45 pm a woman from the "Black Parents" support group strode to the microphone and demanded that everyone walk out of "this fiasco", at which point the meeting broke up in disarray.

In private interviews several months later both Marnoch and Parkinson suggested that this meeting was successful. The number of registered informants on Railton Road doubled within two days, which Marnoch took as a sign of some public support. The police had been called to account, in Parkinson's mind. Yet in reality both men had been trapped by the contradictions that undermine the whole value of consultation as a mechanism for the resolution of conflict between the police and Black communities in London. The roots and nature of this conflict were simply not susceptible to being talked away. Their remarkable actions might have served to buy time, but not to resolve conflict. Astel Parkinson's exemplary and principled position may well have persuaded many to be more reluctant to take to the streets. Marnoch's courage may have won friends and informers on Railton Road. But the level of sustained abuse, and the public humiliation of both men, revealed that such successes were merely tokens buying time at enormous personal cost.

Parkinson did not stand again as chairman of the CPCGL and in interviews in 1986 suggested that he saw his prominence in police–commu-

176

THE RESOLUTION OF CONFLICT BY CONSULTATION

nity affairs in Lambeth diminishing in the near future. Marnoch had a breakdown. When interviewed six months later, after prolonged medical leave, he still looked physically and mentally exhausted. Fine words cannot gloss over the fact that these two individuals had achieved so little yet paid so much. Certainly, antagonism between police and community had not "diminished"; almost certainly their equals in calibre could not be found in Brixton. As individuals they could not have invested more in the consultative process but they worked within an institutional structure that could offer only occasional palliatives to a social schism.

There is also a more insidious, connected problem that stems from the relationship between "committee officials" and the police. This was most clearly seen when, on 24 July 1986, the police staged a massive raid on the Railton Road ACCA, in what was known as "Operation Condor". With senior police management changing, Commander Lloyd stated several times in television and radio interviews that he had consulted with "community leaders" before the raid. Astel Parkinson was shattered. As Chairman of ACCA, and a vigorous anti-drugs campaigner, he had himself arranged for the club to be shut down over the bank holiday weekend a few weeks earlier, recognizing the rising tension on Railton Road. In spite of this, Lambeth Council, heavily involved in financing the centre, insisted that it was reopened and Parkinson was actively involved in trying to clean up the very real problems of criminal activity that were developing there. However, he knew nothing of the police raid in advance and confirmed in personal interviews that after Lloyd's public statements not a single person on the Front Line would believe this. He felt that his credibility had possibly been destroyed by the police. For him, his own alleged co-optation, once risible, had become a more plausible accusation.

The construction of co-optation is haphazard. It is difficult to locate the elusive "they", the personification of the power-bloc, the anonymous managerial "controllers" of dystopia. At the level of the consultative process itself, such Machiavellian types rarely, if ever, exist. If some of the police I observed and interviewed recognized pragmatically that "community relations" was "in vogue" and a promising promotion channel, the majority were working within a vision of society that incorporates the common-sense notion that if only everyone "understood each other" then the bitterness of police/Black conflict would dissolve. As it happens, this is a vision which is profoundly alien to both the personal views of the participant observer at the time, and all the arguments of this book

The institutionalization of the police/Black conflict, the inscription of antagonism in time and place, and the social context of racial injustice

MISUNDERSTANDINGS?

all undermine such ingenuous notions; the rhetorical assassinations of Alec Marnoch and Astel Parkinson were the product of this contradiction of common sense. This in no way negates the sincerity of many police involved in consultation. If co-optation was designed into the consultative process, it was designed in such a way as to deceive police as well as public. More plausibly, the flaws of functionalist sociology are once more exposed; cause and effect confused. In these circumstances co-optation may be an incidental facet of the consultative process, an equally alarming phenomenon. The case of Parkinson and the raid on ACCA is a clear cut example of this contingent property, yet this was produced by the insensitivity of the local Police Commander rather than by the institutional imperatives of the consultative process, although the result is no less unfortunate. In pairing the living tragedy of conflict with the protocols of the committee room, only the body bureaucratic can triumph.

Social theory and political reality

It was the manner in which police–community consultation appeared on the political agenda that made it symbolically so much more important than it really was. Because of the high profile of the Scarman recommendations, because of the whole debate surrounding the two Police Bills that preceded the PACE Act, and because of a misleading linkage between consultation and accountability, the political reality of consultation could never be an innocent reflection of institutional practices.

This was not simply the product of "radical left" fears of co-optation. The Police Bills of 1983 and 1984, widely seen as extending police powers, determined the context in which the statutory consultative measures for London were set. Consultation entered the stage as a rhetorical counterweight to such legislative extension. It was miscast. Precisely because the consultative machinery was given a symbolic political rôle, which was not consonant with the minor reform it actually represented, it became not only a political expedient in the short term but also a political imperative in theoretical terms for some groups to discredit and preferably to destroy the new developments.

Again the history must be traced back to Scarman. Scarman had set the agenda and his visions of the institutionalization of reconciliation and conciliation, frequently, in part, already present in many places in less than powerful "liaison committees", was given official endorsement. For the state, the riot commission may appeal because of its

SOCIAL THEORY AND POLITICAL REALITY

ability to buy political time, distance government from crisis and restore apparent neutrality to the penal system. Yet it also leaves a heritage in political discussion that may be difficult to discredit.

The principal official determinant of the two Police Bills was the Philips Royal Commission on Criminal Procedure, but the imprint of Scarman was also unmistakable. The combination of a fear of violent disorder, evinced in internal cabinet debate (Layton-Henry 1986), and the rhetorical power tied to Scarman, forced the government to act. In the insidious idiom of the time, the former problem demanded the incorporation of "alienated blacks" into the political system, while the latter required either high-profile action which could be represented as endorsing Scarman, or else a risky exercise in discrediting the report altogether. So Leon Brittan, then Home Secretary, had little choice when introducing the statutory consultative provisions in the second Police Bill but to claim that

> The fourth part of the Bill includes a provision underpinning arrangements for consultation between the police and the local community, following Lord Scarman's recommendations. (*Hansard*, 7 November 1983: 25)

The issue of consultation "solved" both problems and it is only against this background of "gesture politics" that the inception of the consultative groups can be understood. The edifice of the consultative machinery usefully symbolized a government "commitment" to reform. Once the edifice was constructed, the government were not afraid to deploy this symbolic power in fine rhetoric.

The politicization of policing issues from the late 1960s onwards (Reiner 1984, Jefferson & Grimshaw 1984), the events of 1981 and the new social movements that underwrote municipal socialism in the early 1980s (Boddy & Fudge 1983, Gilroy 1987), exemplified by the Livingstone regime at the GLC, all structured the political reactions to PACE. Grant aid from the GLC had by the early 1980s prompted the growth of police committees and police monitoring units across much of London (Fyfe 1987) and the two Police Bills served as an ideal vehicle for the mobilization of these forces. The GLC funded "Campaign against the Police Bill" produced almost 500,000 special leaflets and 35,000 copies of a special edition of the free paper *Policing London*. When the Bill was reintroduced after the 1983 general election the campaign was, to a large extent, repeated. Within the political culture of the city, in those areas where policing was a major political issue, the Bill was consequently seen in its entirety as a single package and to be opposed as such.

More specifically, within the policing debates in Parliament, any potential value of consultation was consistently undermined by the

MISUNDERSTANDINGS?

entanglement and misrepresentation of the reform in wide-ranging arguments. In one of the earliest of the PACE debates William Whitelaw, then Home Secretary commented

First, however, I should like to say a word about the need to counterweight the powers that we give to our police with safeguards against unwarrantable interference with the liberty of the citizen. It is in a free society that the police have to work, and it is a free society that they protect. It is possible to achieve order at too high a price in terms of freedom.

These counterweights were then cited

We have been able to provide additionally in the Bill for three important matters. These are the police complaints procedure, for which the provisions were foreshadowed in our White Paper; *a duty upon police authorities to make arrangements for public consultation on policing matters, with a view to securing help for the police*; and certain important aspects of the law of evidence in criminal proceedings, including the admissibility of confession statements. (*Hansard* 30 November 1982: 150–51; my emphasis)

Consultation has nothing to do with safeguarding the "liberty of the citizen" but this, apparently, was one of the criteria by which it was to be judged and one of the political justifications for its introduction.

It would probably be wrong to overemphasize the conspiratorial planning that lay behind statutory consultation. Perhaps it would be more accurate to suggest that in a prevailing atmosphere of "crisis management" and "damage limitation" which followed the 1981 events in Brixton, Moss Side and Liverpool 8, the consultative reform was, for the government, a political token exemplifying acceptance of the spirit of Scarman. The fact that special statutory arrangements were to be made only in London was an explicit recognition of contemporary debates on police accountability that were focused on the unique situation of the city and the nature of GLC politics. This tie is perhaps the single most important factor in structuring the subsequent history of consultation in London. Police consultation and police accountability became political Siamese twins. In almost every debating hall in London the two issues were to be inseparable and frequently confused. Consultation was placed in a wider context concerning the nature of the Police Bill as a whole, and it was a context and a confusion of issues that was accepted across the political spectrum (Keith 1988b).

Unsurprisingly, consultation as a political issue was not a straightforward reflection of consultation as a potential reform in the policing process. Unfortunately, potential advances in police–community understanding were always likely to be crippled by the potential rôle of consultative groups in legitimating police practice and by the history of the

Police Bills. It would be wrong to suggest that this was just an unfortunate incidental misunderstanding of the immanent properties of the consultative machinery. The political provenance of the consultative reforms was manifest and manifestly scarred by cynicism and bad faith, not on the part of those for whom the process was constructed (police and community), but on the part of those who were responsible for its design.

The vanishing state trick

The assumption that underwrites both PACE and Home Office guidelines on consultation was that there is, *out there in the real world*, a natural series of geographic, ethnic and religious groupings, hierarchically structured and answerable to the individuals who assume a position at the apex of each social pyramid. The expectation is quite clearly that, given ready access to consultation, the people who occupy these strategic positions will magically come forward.

Yet necessarily, where "representatives" willingly come forward to serve in consultation they will not collectively have any prerogative to act as the delegated representatives of the particular London Borough in which they operate. Many groups (younger people, the unwaged, the unmembers) will not belong to any organization that might possibly be involved; many of the members of the committee (e.g. clergy) cannot be said to "represent" any constituency, even if they have a valuable contribution to make to consultation. In such circumstances the consultative group can never claim any local mandate of democratic representation in a particular community, for to do so would be to parody democracy. This does not denigrate the groups' status: it only demands a more subtle analysis of consultation than the Home Office hierarchical model implies. Each individual may occupy a distinct rôle within the consultative structure – the religious minister as an advisor, the TA representative a delegate, the Black youth-club leader a possible middle-man or honest broker between the police and the people using his/her club – three of many different contributions. None controls a constituency, all may have something useful to say. In short, this sort of complexity validates the need for consultation but curtails the legitimate ambit of consultative group interests. In practice, this need for caution is readily flouted.

A more contingent factor often occurs where police are least popular and there is relatively little popular mobilization in community groups. In these circumstances there is a very real danger that the police (as

MISUNDERSTANDINGS?

government agents) are forced virtually to "create" a community by defining "community leaders". In this sense, the enactment of Section 106 represents, in part, a statutory recognition and enforcement of the pernicious "take me to your community leader" ideology which so bedevilled the early history of the race relations industry in Britain.

So, in a sense, communities are not only imagined (Anderson 1983), they are also invented. *The committee* is frequently the architect of this invention. This is not to denigrate the vitality of local cultures, nor to refute the validity of expressions of communal solidarity, only to suggest that such living realities cannot be condensed and reproduced faithfully, in microcosm, in the committee room. Although seemingly a truism, the implications of this were not, and are not, always taken on board by those who would legitimate either their own actions or their own status by reference to the dubious mandate of "the community".

There is a sense in which many of the disputes surrounding consultation across 1980s London may be seen as struggles to control the machinery behind this invention. As Fyfe (1987) has pointed out, the elitism of Conservatives in the Tory-held borough of Sutton, who felt that they alone should represent the community, was mirrored by the Labour group in Islington, who negotiated a constitution with the Home Office that gave the local authority greater power than in most other parts of London. Similarly, in Hackney, the protracted negotiations throughout the decade between the Metropolitan Police and Hackney Council tended to stumble repeatedly on the respective levels of council and "community" power.

Such negotiations are also significant for the way in which they reveal the hidden strings that are pulled at the highest levels of government. Again, competing notions of both "the community" and "consultation" struggled to form the structures in which social tensions, "misunderstandings" between the police and the Black community foremost among them, were to be "resolved". This is easily illustrated by comparison of the public and private faces of the Home Office.

In public the Home Office readily distanced itself from responsibility for the consultative process. Typically, in a letter to Hackney Council:

I entirely agree with Councillor Millwood about the urgent need for such consultative arrangements in Hackney. I understand that informal discussions have been continuing since Councillor Millwood wrote to you. *You will appreciate that we have no direct standing in these discussions. Under Section 106 of the Police and Criminal Evidence Act 1984 responsibility for establishing consultative arrangements throughout the Metropolitan Police District rests with the Commissioner,* and although in exercising this responsibility the Commissioner is

THE VANISHING STATE TRICK

obliged to take account of the Home Secretary's guidance (issued earlier this year) *the Home Secretary's direct powers are limited to calling for a report or a review of already established arrangements* if they do not appear to be functioning effectively. (Home Office letter to Brian Sedgemore MP from Giles Shaw MP, then Minister of State at the Home Office, 1985; my emphasis).

"The law" is used to establish a spurious distance between government and the executive. There is almost a tone of sympathetic regret from a minister seemingly handicapped by the tiresome but manifestly neutral bastion of the legal system.

This is in marked contrast to the more pragmatic vision implied by the 1987 internal Home Office assessment of the consultative process which cited the difficulties for the new groups, who needed to "establish their credibility" when often they did not have a "marketable product". In order to respond to this credibility problem, the same report commented that in the search for this marketable product

Police, local authorities and the Home Office can contribute to this by recognizing the value and status of the groups. (Home Office 1987: internal)

Several times throughout the decade, by changing official guidelines the Home Office moved the membership goalposts in order to minimize the influence of local councils (Keith 1988, Morgan & Maggs 1984, 1985). At one point in the protracted negotiations in Hackney, frequently stumbling on the question of who should chair the consultative group, the neutrality of Parliamentary legislation was used as an official justification for no agreement between police and council, even when a QC, Lord Gifford, called in to give legal opinion, suggested that there was nothing in many of the proposed compromises between the council and local police contravening PACE or the Home Office guidelines. At times politics hide behind the law, and it is not always the politics of particular police officers alone. The Home Office also controlled the power to recognize officially consultative groups – recognition which could be used as a carrot in negotiation – and formally acknowledged the need, and their responsibility, to sustain the credibility of the consultative process in the face of residual opposition in some parts of London and suspicion in a great many others. All this was set in the landscape of 1980s London, where a Conservative government was determined to curb the local powers and putatively "anti-police" stance of left-wing local authorities. Home Office actions were effectively exercises in buying political capital, structuring the consultative process in a context where the state can remain hidden; the invisible hand that camouflages the central contradiction at the heart of even the best cases of police–community consultation.

183

MISUNDERSTANDINGS?

This contradiction arises from the fact that, with the best will in the world, dialogue does not alter power structures. It is a contradiction that can only be resolved by those who would either make false claims on behalf of the consultative process or false statements on the necessary nature of even the best policing in twentieth-century Britain.

Superficially, the power to make a committee in their own image, and a community to their own taste, was conferred upon the police by PACE and resented by London local authorities. But this was only part of the story. The framework within which this process was set ensured that an inevitable conflict between central and local government over "democratic" control of one public service (Smith 1986a) was displaced, with the police set up, not always reluctantly, to take pride of place in a conflict of interests with local democracy.

Conclusion

In general, the case for consultation must rest on the grounds of modesty. As a showpiece counterweight to the increases in police powers embodied in PACE 1984, the consultative group was a paper tiger. As an arena for communication, complaint and explanation, it is a potentially valuable supplement to any sophisticated notion of local democracy. It has not had and cannot have a major impact on any of the crucial issues of policing in post-industrial Britain.

Yet in the 1980s the groups became political issues in their own right. Functional significance was overwhelmed by political symbolism. Both participating members and non-participating opponents tended to play up the importance of the consultative groups to the detriment of all. The groups were cited as major reforms (by the police) or as the locus of co-optation (Hackney and Lambeth councils), when in fact they are not *necessarily* either. Perhaps the best evidence of this was given when, in August 1991, Marnoch, in a later appointment as head of the Plus Programme, spoke publicly in an attempt to improve the service given by, and public image of, the Metropolitan Police. True to his word of a few years earlier he again spoke out, this time on behalf of the whole of the Metropolitan Police Force, in favour of an elected police authority for London. It is no sleight on his integrity to suggest that this corporate (as opposed to personal) *volte face* gave the merest hint that one of the core issues of policing politics in 1980s London, the accountability debate, was always tangential to the nature of police/Black antagonism in the capital.

Unfortunately, and paradoxically, the conflict that underscored the

CONCLUSION

events of 1981, which provided the impetus for "reform", remains a principal legitimation of the consultative process. Yet the historical depth and social basis of the conflict between police and Black communities ensures consultation cannot provide any solutions to this conflict, whatever such solutions might look like, but it does not mean that consultative groups invariably fail to provide useful arenas through which interests can come together. Generalization is elusive because personalities matter. A pragmatic, gregarious Commander of police dealing with one consultative group in one sensitive part of London may be replaced by an officious, pedantic successor. The chair of the same group may be at one time a sincere community activist with first-hand knowledge of some of the unpleasant realities of inner-city policing, at another time a moral entrepreneur playing at social science and politics.

More depressingly, study of one aspect of consultation confirms that the nature of police/Black conflict is beyond polite discussion, contradicting images of liberal-democratic Britain, institutionalized in the social divisions of the racist nation.

PART FOUR

DISCIPLINE AND PUNISH ?

CHAPTER 9

Strategies of control:
the local reality of racial subordination

"A new space cannot be born (produced) unless it accentuates differences." Henri Lefebvre in *The production of space* (1976/1991)

Introduction

An article in *Policing London*, published shortly after the riots in Handsworth, Brixton and Broadwater Farm, was headlined "1981–85: LITTLE CHANGE" (February/March 1986). The implication, supported by two very similar pictures of policing Brixton in 1981 and 1985, would appear to be that here we had the repetition of history, with this second appearance of uprisings possibly inverting the cruel axiom of first time tragedy, second time farce. The failure to combat those influences that had generated clashes in 1981 apparently led to a repetition of the same phenomenon four years later. Yet such a diagnosis would perhaps be very misleading. A central tenet of this work is that the deployment of common-sense notions of causality alongside simplistic portrayals of the police force have frequently led to a mystification of the reality of racism. In order to understand the multiplicity of *racisms* cited by Hall (1979), it is vital to deconstruct the processes at work which have reproduced and amplified the conflict between police and Black people, processes that have been structured in time and space. Consequently, it is possible to argue although while there may have been "very little change in black Londoners *experience* of the Metropolitan Police" (*Policing London*, op cit, my emphasis), this was certainly not produced by an equivalent stability in either the forces that underwrote these experiences or the forms of collective action that ensued.

Two problems, one descriptive one causal, appear to characterize much of the literature that quite rightly has attempted to highlight the grim, frequently horrific experiences of policing among Black communities. To link research with anti-racist campaigning and to confound

INTRODUCTION

accusations of political bias and exaggeration, there has been a tendency to document specific instances of confrontation and injustice. Yet the resultant case lists of causes both *célèbres* and forgotten (e.g. IRR 1987, 1988, HCRE 1983), although important, are necessarily constrained in their attempt to move beyond description of particular forms of institutional racism. The tendency, frequently evinced in the conclusions to casework lists, is to round off depressing catalogues by linking a common-sense notion of the causes of police/Black antagonism to a portrayal of a supposedly pathologically malevolent police force via a causal connection neatly bracketed as "police racism".

These lists of cases of injustice are necessarily problematic. They can only ever represent a small proportion of total cases of injustice, yet at the same time they will inevitably contain some cases that are in their detail dubious, one-sided historical reconstructions. Because of such reporting failures, it is also difficult to gauge the extent and nature of changes in confrontation over time. More significantly, they share with much of the liberal literature on policing an ambiguous, at times idealistic, notion of how day-to-day police work should actually occur.

A problem with many *radical* critiques of policing is that the perceived ideal does not square with the accompanying conceptualizations of the reality of inner-city life in contemporary Britain, conceptualizations that are usually tied to images of social injustice and poverty rooted in a divisive social order. Yet to concur with such images, as this text broadly does, necessarily discredits what might be described as the fallacy of polite policing. For although it would be invidious to stereotype melodramatically the inner city in the vocabulary of anomie and alienation, the reality of policing in those places, mutilated by various manifestations of "urban crisis", is *at best* rancorous, controversial and frequently violent.

There is thus a twofold failure. On the one hand it is crucial to move beyond the politically significant but descriptively dead-end character of casework lists. On the other it is essential to sustain analysis of the specific processes of policing without losing sight of the wider social context, with specific reference to the policing rôle within the penal system as a whole.

Consequently, this chapter attempts to demonstrate that through analysis of racially institutionalized power relations in time and space, it is possible to put forward an argument that ties notions of conflict between police and Black people firmly to concepts of criminalization and racialization, rather than to common-sense constructions of crime and race. Perhaps it is only in this way that it is possible to avoid the dual trap of either "being dragged – with varying degrees of reluctance – to the right by the attempt to even speak about policing and crime"

189

THE LOCAL REALITY OF RACIAL SUBORDINATION

(Gilroy & Sim 1985) or the alternative of relying on disingenuous and implausible caricatures of the police institution.

The notion that the struggle over power relations in particular places formed a central theme in "rioting" is reinforced by the policing strategies adopted in such areas since 1981. It is not the suggestion here that all such policies have been the successful product of centralized control. Indeed a principal element of the Metropolitan Police reorganization of the early and mid-1980s was to focus managerial power on the division, decentralize policy-making, and, theoretically, make it responsive to local needs. Rather it is the contention that such changes have been the almost inevitable product of the localized collapse of policing by consent that has already been described. Senior officers who co-operated with this work have openly disagreed with certain specific policies employed in other "symbolic locations", yet, while often differing in form from one place to another, these strategies share the common goal (content) of re-imposing the power prerogative implied in the internal relation between police and the policed described in Chapter 7.

Such strategies are of major significance for two reasons. First, because they recognized the *de facto* inversion of power relations within the context of the need to consider maintaining order as a higher priority to law-enforcement on those occasions when the two are mutually irreconcilable. Secondly, they exemplify the imposition of social order on a particular place. The exigencies of policing without consent make such an imposition part of all police action in such areas.

The nature of policing without consent

Certain policy initiatives were common to one or more of the locations analyzed in Chapter 6. They were generally initiated in the early 1980s and they embody a significant part of the institutional Metropolitan Police response to the official geographies which sought to identify the places at which there was the greatest potential for incidents of *disorder*.

Immediate Response Units / District Support Units

Immediate Response Units, normally 11 PCs and a sergeant in a van, were introduced in the immediate aftermath of the 1981 riots in order to provide quick support on occasions of spontaneous outbreaks of public disorder. Their name was later changed to District Support Unit and subsequently, following merger with the SPG, they were separated between units within the Tacticai Support Group and Police Support Units (Waddington 1991: 307–308). Two of the earliest occasions on

THE NATURE OF POLICING WITHOUT CONSENT

which they were deployed, in Brixton and in Notting Hill, have already been described.

One of the problems arising out of the creation of such groups was that the sort of police work in which they are involved is quite obviously closer to a military model than to the traditional independent function of the police constable. Superintendent Murray at Brixton talked at length about what he saw as the growth of a "DSU mentality", the habits and norms that grow out of the close teamwork, amplifying the subcultural evaluations of "good policing" that may centre on action, speed and ostentatious operations involving the gathering of large numbers of "prisoners". As has repeatedly been pointed out, seeking such expressive rewards in the practical realm of any job is a normal not a pathological trait, but with the DSUs the rewards of "action" may be particularly welcomed because,

The problem with these units is that most of the time there is no public disorder for them to deal with and there is therefore a difficulty in finding them something to do. (Smith & Gray 1983: 37)

Potentially such difficulties had a particular impact on the symbolic locations such as Railton Road and Sandringham Road. For the moveable squad represent the custom-made response to challenges to police authority, a presence that is often seen by junior officers as enforcing the sort of symbolic control already discussed, which may or may not operate outside the management goals of senior officers. Brian Hilliard, the editor of *Police Review*, has remarked,

There are areas in London which are recognized as potential trouble spots where serious disorders might break out at any time, the areas are almost fully manned, all the stations are up to strength, not only that but the District Support Units, which are supposed to patrol a wider area, tend to congregate there so you have a more visible presence of policemen, . . . also, because there's more police about, they feel they have to do more and so more people get stopped in the street, more motorists get checked, more roadblocks are held. (London Weekend Television: 11 July 1986)

This clustering has important ramifications. Not only are the sort of "cowboy policing" incidents that were described in Chapter 6 on the Moorlands and Holly Street estates an almost inevitable part of policing without consent, but also they are most likely to occur where they can do most damage, entrenching mutual antagonism, making the transformation from conflict to confrontation that much more common.

Dog patrols

Watching dog patrols on Sandringham Road in both 1982 and 1983 there is no doubt in the author's mind that it is almost impossible for

THE LOCAL REALITY OF RACIAL SUBORDINATION

any social contact to occur between local residents and police using dogs. Most people, Black and White, steer well clear of the dog patrols; several complaints arose from those people who had been mistakenly bitten (see *Policing, London, passim* 1983). One such complaint arrived in Stoke Newington police station when I was present in July 1986. I spoke at length to two PCs, one a dog handler, who had been involved in these patrols on Sandringham Road. Again it was remarkable how close were the views of both the junior police officers and the resentful people who used Roots Pool and other social centres along Sandringham Road. The dogs were seen as explicitly establishing police control of the Front Line.

In his inquiry into the Brixton disorders, Lord Scarman said,

On two occasions . . . dogs were deployed in an undesirable way in the handling of a crowd. All officers who gave evidence to the Inquiry recognized that dogs are not appropriate instruments for dispersing crowds in sensitive situations. Chief Superintendent Marsh clearly recognized as much . . . Arrangements must be introduced to prevent the deployment of dogs in handling major crowd disorders in the future. (1981: 4.84)

Although dogs have rarely been used on Railton Road under normal circumstances, in spite of this stipulation such deployment occurred in disorders in Brixton in 1982 and 1985 (personal eyewitness). In the micro-sociology of police patrols, the implicit or latent resource of the legitimate use of force is normally hidden; with the dog patrol it is manifest. That it should be manifest on Front Line was quite clearly a "pre-emptive response" to possible challenges to police authority.

Again, ostentatious police control resorts to practices that inevitably reproduce antagonism, practices that are endorsed from the highest levels in spite of Scarman's censure. In a letter to Ernie Roberts, local MP, on 22 December 1983 Douglas Hurd, then Minister of State at the Home Office comments

Concern was expressed about the use of police dogs in Hackney. Patrolling by dog units is a feature of policing in North East London and is regarded by the police as an effective part of their response. The police believe that in general the public welcome these patrols. I understand that earlier this year there was an incident when one dog bit three people during a meleé caused by a crowd which had gathered to watch an arrest. I am satisfied that the incident was dealt with sensibly at local level by the police and does not indicate that the use of dogs is either provocative or should be curtailed.

Ignorant of the past, insensitive to the present, Hurd's letter highlights the impossibility of reconciling the nature of the conflict between police

THE NATURE OF POLICING WITHOUT CONSENT

and Black people with the vocabulary of even the more liberal forms of law-and-order politics. Most importantly, the notion of a public that will "welcome these patrols" necessarily begs all the important questions about the nature and purpose of using dogs and the apparently extraordinary attitudes of those that might object to them.

Special patrols, special orders

The existence of special patrols in Notting Hill, Brixton and Dalston has already been outlined in some detail. Although the common resistance to police actions in such places provides a severe handicap to police work, the level of crime alone, which may often be higher than in other parts of the division, seldom, if ever, justified the level of policing that such patrols involve. Quite clearly, the secondary function of police work, the latent content of interaction, was of singular importance in the deployment of such groups. They again establish the police right to police all of London – an ostentatious refutation of no-go areas.

However, the contrasting opinions of Commander Marnoch, Chief Superintendent Whitfield and Chief Superintendent Barr are revealing. All three were in fact friends, similar intelligent, personable characters with a more pragmatic approach to policing than many of the notorious "Bramshill club" (not this author's term), commonly identified in formulating public-order contingency plans from above. For Marnoch and Whitfield, one of the principal functions of such patrols was that they demonstrate police control of symbolic locations while obviating the need for the "mob-handed" tactics, which become necessary when failed arrests and lost prisoners lead to sudden fights, and when making demonstrative raids in particular premises. The latter task was to be handled not by police action but by co-operation with local government in the removal or closure of premises which provide a locale for criminal activity and regulation of those premises involved with "anti-social" activity. Certainly, in all three Front Line areas the failure to distinguish, or even to try and distinguish, between the "anti-social" – late night (often illegal drinkers), street gatherings – and the genuinely criminal – hard drugs, arms dealing – in such Front Line areas has cost dear in terms of police–community relations. Significantly, Richard Allen, one time acting head of Lambeth Police Committee Support Unit, suggested that in the past Lambeth Council should have taken an initiative to provide an arena for the social functions of Front Line in order that the Council could be involved in preventing the attraction of criminal activity to such places (personal interview). The feasibility of such a strategy was, of course, debatable.

In contrast, Barr's scepticism about the Sandringham Road patrol and his keen pursuit of a policy of selective raids suggested a very different

THE LOCAL REALITY OF RACIAL SUBORDINATION

sort of policing in Hackney. Yet, several points can be made in his defence. First, and perhaps most importantly for Barr, Stoke Newington had for obvious reasons never achieved the same privileged status as Brixton and Notting Hill in the allocation of manpower. The heavy personnel commitment required by such special patrols clearly hit an understaffed police station such as Stoke Newington (and its subdivision of Dalston) much harder than it would do in Brixton or Notting Hill. Secondly, unlike the compliant Conservative council of Kensington and Chelsea, and the "special relationship" that Marnoch built up with Ted Knight in Lambeth, the Hackney Council in the mid-1980s were not prepared to involve themselves with multi-agency approaches of any sort until changes in the accountability of the Metropolitan Police had been made, particularly after relations had been soured even more by the Colin Roach affair. Thirdly, and perhaps most significantly, was Barr's concern that his officers might become obsessed with Sandringham Road as Front Line. This was a revealing attitude, not only because it reflects the hostility of many PCs towards such patrols but also because, given the many constrictions applied to PCs on special patrols (e.g. no stops for minor offences, limits on car patrols, no inflammatory arrests), it is hard to avoid the impression that, even in the ostensibly enlightened policies of Marnoch and Whitfield, the police on the streets are never more explicitly acting as agents of *social control* rather than as a service of *law enforcement*. The conflict between the Black community on the Front Line and the police becomes accidentally built into police practice.

In such circumstances the positions of committed senior officers such as Marnoch, Whitfield and Barr were not enviable. Prisoners of history, they ran the risk that whatever action they took would emerge on the streets as an intensification of conflict. Personality is important, but it is always trapped within the institutional structure in which the individual operates.

In the late 1980s the separate treatment of all three symbolic locations became officially recognized in all the case study locations, with the special patrols elevated to the status of being removed from the ordinary scheduling of daily reliefs. A spatial categorization of all three divisions was institutionalized in police practice.

Symbolic raids

Although officially discouraged by many at the highest level of management, the raid on Front Line is often seen by some senior officers as establishing the police right to operate there. If all such raids were in accordance with the rule book, such a policy might be defensible.

At their worst, such exercises in ostentatious control turn into "fish-

THE NATURE OF POLICING WITHOUT CONSENT

ing raids" – cases of police raiding premises in the expectation of picking up prisoners. Although all senior officers I spoke to quite clearly disapproved of "fishing raids", not one denied that such raids had occurred on sensitive premises in the past, nor that such "outings" could be used to settle old scores; one senior officer suggested that such raids epitomized the sort of behaviour covered by the concept of Front Line deviancy. In spite of such, doubtless sincere, protestations, the distinction between a "fishing raid" and the raid designed to "remind the frequenters of a particular café of police presence" (senior officer, personal interview) is a fine one; notably, both operate on the level of explicit symbolic communication rather than at the level of what is normally considered functional policing.

Again, it is important to identify the variety of opinions that may co-exist within police management. Over this policy in particular, none of the named informants would justify the notion of "the fishing raid", while other senior (anonymous) officers in the divisional management structures at times expressed a resentment that this sort of high-profile action had been curtailed in the post-Scarman policing climate.

Targeting and surveillance

The connection between targeting and surveillance operations and the criminalization of Black communities in Britain (Christian 1983) is discussed in more detail below. It must be acknowledged that the principal reason for the introduction of such techniques was initially to replace the sort of disastrous operations such as SWAMP 81 with its arbitrary stop and search, tactics that brought such massive numbers into hostile contact with the police and reaped such little long-term reward in fighting crime. However, for the communities who live in such areas, who often spot the observation vehicles used by the police, who know the houses (and sometimes the owners of the houses) which are used for observation and who occasionally see the cameras and binoculars that are used (Gifford 1986), there is often a bitter resentment that their lives are monitored, scrutinized and spied on in this way. It is hard to gauge how strong these feelings are, but several representatives of Black organizations in both Brixton and Notting Hill have regularly expressed great bitterness about such "Big Brother" tactics.

It is also important to stress that the introduction of special policing strategies in symbolic locations occurred, to a large extent, in a singularly inchoate fashion. Many of the police officers, in the three locations studied, expressed open and honest disagreement about the effectiveness and value of policies advocated by senior staff at Scotland Yard or divisional staff in the other symbolic locations. Targeting and surveil-

THE LOCAL REALITY OF RACIAL SUBORDINATION

lance is expensive in terms of staffing, as well as frequently being boring and unpopular. Not all places are easily overlooked.

Yet one central thrust of these policies is consistent. The routine and the organization of police action become structured by the conflict between the police and Black people. Ordinary police actions are structured by a policing conception of the potential for disorder. Policy relating to symbolic locations can take no account of the history which produced that symbolism: organization becomes organization to control specific areas and "win" in any confrontation. In short, conflict becomes institutionalized.

The institutionalization of conflict

The policing experiences of the three symbolic locations highlights the nature of changes in police practice in the 1980s. At each stage in the escalation of conflict, dating back to the 1960s, police policy can be seen reacting to events rather than analyzing them. In large part this is no more than the precedence of "reactive" over "pro-active" policing that has been debated within the police service itself (e.g. Alderson 1979, 1984, Newman 1983, 1986).

However this does not accord well with some vision of the police as not only the willing accomplices of, but also a significant conspirator in, a drift towards authoritarianism. There is a less premeditated process at work here, which is instrumental in the progressive adoption of policies by police forces across the country which in their implementation, if not in their design, reproduce the racial subordination of one section of society.

At the level of implementation, one significant feature of this phenomenon is that the historical context of changes in the form of policing is not considered (cf. Reiner 1980, 1985). Quite possibly this derives from the singular concentration of management on present-day objectives, taking the worst incidents of yesterday as the worst possible case that might be handled today.

Routine and the escalation of violence
After the experiences of Notting Hill and Lewisham in the mid-1970s, police trouble with "Black youth" became considered as normal and the police were equipped with shields to deal with future incidents. With increased clashes at the scenes of arrest and the disorders of 1981, "rioting" by "Black youth" was considered permanently on the agenda and the Immediate Response Units, protective clothing and militaristic

THE INSTITUTIONALIZATION OF CONFLICT

training were introduced to cope with this phenomenon. By 1986, following the armed insurrection on Broadwater Farm Estate and serious rioting in Brixton and Handsworth in 1985, the response was the use of "riot cities" for more training, new truncheons for public-order situations and the mooted use of baton rounds (plastic bullets), stun guns and water canon, most of which were dismissed as unfeasible (see Waddington 1991 for an extensive technical account). In London alone the incremental accumulation of riot equipment in the form of shields, special truncheons and armour protected Land Rovers was not enough to satisfy Peter Imbert, who, when he first assumed the office of Commissioner of the Metropolitan Police told the 1987 annual conference of the Howard League that there was still a need for more equipment to prepare for civil disorder.

The police are seen to go hand in hand with the escalation of violence. At each level, police take the new public-order phenomenon as given, one of many natural phenomena of contemporary society, unaware, or unwilling to be aware, of their own causal rôle in this process. The anticipation of public-order problems is obviously one essential part of police management. Yet it appears that the primary managerial goal is to ensure that in situations of public-order conflict the police "do not lose". Incidental to this anticipation, in preparing this capacity to control disorder, police management build into the very structure of police practice the conflict between police and Black people. The distinction between cause and effect is again vital. It is this managerial task itself that, like the modern myth, "transforms history into nature" (Barthes 1963: 129), treating riots as "natural" phenomena, divorced from history, not cultural products of particular times and places.

In exactly the same sense, it is important to understand the locational interplay of power relations ("stage building"), which preceded the rioting of 1981, as part of this process of institutionalizing conflict. As with every other institution that has been subjected to research scrutiny, there is plenty of evidence of overtly racist behaviour and overtly racialist beliefs in the Metropolitan Police (see PSI 1983), although it is not possible to quantify how common either actually is. In participant observation for this work, this author saw plentiful evidence of the latter but very much less of the former (if it is possible to separate the two), yet, as Chapter 1 suggested, any attempt either to quantify attitudes and actions that are racist, or even to distinguish between them, perhaps diverts attention from more important related social processes that are at work.

Such behaviour, however common, was of only secondary importance in the immediate genesis of violent conflict, precisely because,

197

THE LOCAL REALITY OF RACIAL SUBORDINATION

long before 1981, in places that witnessed serious confrontations, the conflict between Black people and the police had become part of the daily routine of police practice and Black "resistance", even before a majority of PCs had arrived at the respective police stations. The relative significance of personal racism in the inception of this conflict in the late 1950s and early 1960s is a different issue. The effect of the rioting was to hammer this conflict yet further into this institutional structure. The uprisings of 1981 were about the whole history and social context of policing Black Britain, not about the cultural deviancy of racialist police officers (however many such officers there are), nor about a violent clash of "personalities".

Routine and stigma: the labelling process

The process of stigmatizing outsider groups (Becker 1963, Goffman 1972, 1981, Young 1974) both precedes and is reinforced by the incidence of rioting. On a very simple interactive level, the mutual suspicion between police and young Black people can reproduce and even amplify such hostility. In the time I was involved in participant observation at both Brixton and Stoke Newington stations, I saw little deliberately racialist behaviour by police officers. This was quite possibly related to the obtrusive nature of the "fly on the wall". What was extremely common, and was admitted quite openly by many of the PCs, was that in dealing with young Black men "on the street" a degree of caution and expectation of trouble characterized the approach of officers in the "focused interaction" of encounters (Goffman 1963). Almost invariably correct and polite in every technical respect, this level of suspicion remained obvious to both the observer and the Black individuals concerned. Virtually all such encounters passed off peacefully, yet the tension and hostility remained built into the "micro-sociology" of the meeting, the antagonism between Black individuals and the police hardened. It is only one very small step from this level of suspicion to the "knock-on offences" already described. Such behaviour, not deliberately racist by intention, is manifestly racist in effect, criminalization being not "the fault" of police officers concerned but still the direct consequence of their behaviour.

Similarly, the rôle of the police has become clearly defined in the minds of very many Black people in London, especially in Brixton, where most police actions I witnessed met with open hostility and vociferous abuse, whatever their nature. It is consequently important to identify the processes by which social relations are reproduced, while at the same time not losing sight of the material context which always underlies the conflict in the first place.

Exactly the same processes operate at a spatial level. Areas of conflict

THE INSTITUTIONALIZATION OF CONFLICT

between the police and the local community become stigmatized by both the police and many other groups as "criminal" or "undesirable" areas; the violent realization of this conflict (not necessarily full-scale riots) rapidly drives those residents who can to escape. Rioting in Sandringham Road in 1981 prompted an exodus of about half the people who lived there, according to the local residents' association; the resultant substantial increase in the number of vacant properties prompted a concomitant increase in the level of squatting, and the social and petty crime problems which accompany an itinerant population, and reinforced the creation of a "problem road". Labelling and criminalization by area assume the nature of a self-fulfilling prophecy, a cumulative spiral of decline that callously victimizes the poorer and powerless groups in society.

Personality traits vs institutional practice: the nature of institutional racism
All police must operate within the context of this labelling process. The degree to which both police and public are able to distinguish between the cultural classification of "places and peoples" and their actual experience of those same people and places will obviously vary greatly between individuals. The perception of the Railton Road home beat officer of Front Line compared to other police in the same division is a classic example of this. Most significantly, the behaviour that was conditioned by classification of time and space confirms the fact that this classification had, by 1981, been shaped by the long history of police/Black conflict in London, a conflict built into the institutional practice of police work, operating at a different level to the personality traits of individual police officers.

In the awareness of these tensions between structural forces and the integrity of individuals, Anne Dummett has commented that:

A racist society has institutions which effectively maintain inequality between members of different groups, in such a way that the open expression of racist doctrine is unnecessary or, where it occurs, superfluous. Racist institutions, even if operated partly by individuals who are not themselves racist in their beliefs, still have the effect of making and perpetuating inequalities.

Taking these lines as the specifications of institutional racism, it could be argued that the Metropolitan Police Force and all other police forces, local and central government, and the higher educational system, clearly display all the salient characteristics of this definition.

This at once highlights both the frightening dimensions of racist practice in British society and the limited utility of the concept of institutional racism. At present a description – an indictment of British society generally – the notion of institutional racism, when placed on the politi-

THE LOCAL REALITY OF RACIAL SUBORDINATION

cal stage, too often becomes no more than an all-embracing term of abuse; a rhetorical accusation of guilt.

It is a contention of this work that anti-racist analysis can justify itself only when the concept of institutional racism is supplemented by an explication of the specific institutional context and practices which leads to racial subordination.

Spatial control

Much discussion in the wake of the events of 1981 centred on why there was apparently no immediate repetition of "that summer" in 1982 and the first few years that followed. Explanations ranged from the perverse to the naïve, from the suggestion that 1981 was somehow cathartic (Kettle 1982), to the occasional displays of idealistic naïvete seen in the suggestions that this social problem, intractable and difficult though it was, might in some way be moving down the road to resolution. It is suggested here that a contextualization of police/Black relations throughout the 1980s exposes such explanations as fanciful in the extreme.

The management of space took two, rather distinct forms. On the one hand certain policies were initiated with the central aim of facilitating state control of particular places and areas. Simultaneously, the day-to-day negotiations of the policing prerogative continued, as they had done throughout the past 30 years, but this time set against the symbolic precedent of "riot". Collective insurrection was no longer merely a hypothetical scenario. Consequently, the Front Lines of London in the wake of the summer of 1981 witnessed a continually renegotiated stand-off rather than a reluctant reconciliation of two parties. The stand-off itself perpetuates stances of conflict, there is no simple equivalence between *bad* police/Black relations and violent uprising. On the Front Lines of London the Metropolitan Police bought time with space.

Again it is important to emphasize precisely what is meant here. Two traps in particular must be avoided. As Lefebvre (1991) is so keen to stress, space is *produced* rather than a mere *tabula rasa* on which social relations are played. The production and reproduction of power relations and social conflict are tied up in the space in which such relations are exercised. But this in no way implies that such spatial production is permanent or immutable.

Yet simultaneously, over time the symbolic associations of particular sites of conflict, rhetorically so powerful, may rapidly become historical-

SPATIAL CONTROL

ly anachronistic. In all three symbolic locations examined here the powerful forces of gentrification, in the mid- and late 1980s, have exerted a major influence on the social fabric of the streets surrounding all three Front Lines, if not always on the specific roads themselves. Simultaneously, other sites of confrontation have come to the fore both in connected and different parts of London. However, there is also a shadow process necessarily lagging in time behind such changes. For the institutionalization of policing policies for particular Front Lines, by its responsive nature, has institutionalized particular demarcations of space. Strategies of control, often pioneered in the three front lines examined here, may be transferred from one part of London to another, but do not necessarily take on board this contingent nature of social relations.

A second, related misconception, is the suggestion that, because throughout the 1980s there was such a locationally specific theme to challenges to the right to police, this represents some sort of ethological expression of territoriality. The casting of uprisings as some sort of proprietorial animal behaviour has had a powerful influence on police discourse, examined in the following chapter.

There is more than just an academic misunderstanding here. The locational specificity of resistance was particularly important in the early 1980s and is of crucial importance in refining the understanding of the spontaneity so central to most violent conflicts of the time. Yet, the police/Black conflict has continued to evolve, and there is no suggestion in this text that spontaneity remained so important in understanding the events of the second half of the decade, or will be reproduced throughout the 1990s. The salient characteristics of mobilization changed as conflict evolved in time and space. The Front Line as such, myth and reality, may become less significant with this mobilization.

Instead, the importance of the production of particular geographical patterns of police response can be tied to the nature of the police force as a major bureaucratic institution. The policing bureaucracy digested a particular conception of the phenomenon of collective disorder. The policy responses to this conception were perforce represented as the logical response to the events of 1980 and 1981. In the years following these disorders, it was particular trouble spots that were identified as potential scenes of disorder, and therefore subject to particular forms of high-priority public-order policing. To corrupt a well known phrase of Stuart Hall's, space was the modality through which racial subordination was naturalized.

THE LOCAL REALITY OF RACIAL SUBORDINATION

The riot as a natural policing problem, paramilitarism as the inevitable solution?

The existence of particular local realizations of the conflict between police and Black communities should not be taken as implying that either policy responses to this conflict or the antagonism itself is in some way parochial in nature.

In fact it would be more accurate to suggest that, in the process of escalating conflict already outlined, these initiatives had ramifications of major significance for any understanding of the drift into policing paramilitarism, which has been cited by, among others, both Kenneth Newman and his immediate successor as Commissioner of the Metropolitan Police (Imbert 1987). Although the affirmation of power relations of control in space evinced in the policing of Front Lines turned a conflict of "race" into a problem of space, specific individual confrontations of yesterday have often been taken as the natural national policing problems of tomorrow. Consequently, a whole array of policy responses to civil disorder in both 1981 and 1985 transform "the riot" into a universal contingency, to be considered by all police divisions.

The extent of this national planning has been examined by Northam (1988). Northam outlines the developments that have followed from the production of the "Public Order Manual" by the Association for Chief Police Officers (ACPO) after their conference in 1981, and the more widely disseminated "Public Order Manual of Tactical Options and Related Matters", which drew on colonial methods of crowd control and lessons taught in Ulster as a prime, if not sole, reaction to the events of 1981.

It has to be said that at no point does Northam concede the logic of such preplanning. While it is not the intention here to defend ACPO, no understanding of policing can be complete unless it is acknowledged that, in the 1980s, the reality of specific forms of violent conflict between police and British Black communities rendered the development of some sort of contingency planning not only inevitable but also completely rational, within the bureaucratic context within which police were operating. The implications of the adoption of such strategies for the policing of all other forms of social conflict, from industrial disputes to the most basic rights of assembly, were altogether different. The deployment of the ideological imagery of sundry *enemies within* in the political common sense of the 1980s (Hall 1988, Solomos 1988, Northam 1988) was thus reflected in the material reality of paramilitary policing potential.

THE RIOT AS A PROBLEM, PARAMILITARISM AS THE SOLUTION?

Symmetrically opposed to Northam's work, Waddington (1991) has taken the naturalization of the problem of rioting to its logical extreme. Working within a managerial notion of public-order problems, Waddington stresses that the apparent paramilitarism that results in police practice may accrue advantages both in efficiency and the disciplinary control of the police themselves. His highly technocratic discussion of public-order situations is extremely informative about the logistical detail of policing, but divorces such practices from their history, logically (in its own terms) recommending the early use of baton rounds and CS gas in all public-order situations (1991: 209). Waddington's work is useful precisely because it reveals such a logic so clearly and disingenuous because it conflates all sorts of distinct civil-order problems – *naturalizing* the riot, ignoring the history which generated confrontation and *mystifying* the manner in which different groups, including the police, competitively rationalize such confrontation in public (Waddington 1991: Ch. 7).

Ironically, public-order contingency plans may incorporate an anachronistic vision of the context of violent resistance to policing action. During the early 1980s, one of the standard police riot-prevention tactical games used in senior officer training was based on scenarios of events that might occur in Sandringham Road in Hackney. Disorder was tied to spontaneous resistance to police actions. In 1985 the reality of disorder was very different. In both Brixton and Broadwater Farm, violent disorder was linked to the mobilization of people protesting at police actions which resulted in, respectively, the shooting and the death of Black women. The exact nature of this changing form of mobilization is addressed in Chapter 11, but the ramifications for police strategy were also significant. Subsequently the hypothetical riots of the planning games were based, in the post 1986 era, on disorders that had occurred in Brixton and Broadwater Farm. Strategy again is reactionary, in the literal sense of the term, and it aims to win the battles of yesterday rather than address the confrontations of tomorrow.

Police/Black conflict is institutionalized in police contingency planning, but as an unquestioning fact of history. At one level this may be defensible, in terms of both the specific policing function of maintaining civil order and the real human costs of violent uprisings. Yet at another level a notion of territorially demarcated, racially explicit crucibles of disorder becomes officially embedded in policing policy. Typically, by 1987 the Chief Inspector of Constabulary could remark with little controversy that "tensions which can so easily lead to disorder" are so common that "a relatively low level of disorder is a constant feature of life in these areas together with high levels of crime, muggings, burglary and the subculture of crime associated with drug taking and

THE LOCAL REALITY OF RACIAL SUBORDINATION

dealing" (as quoted in IRR Police Media Research Bulletin number 1987, number 36, 7). The pathological space of the inner city serves as the imagined territory on which a conjunction of social problems are grounded and an officially sanctioned conflation of these issues defines the correspondence of problems of race, rioting and criminality.

Another way in which localized conflict is translated into a national preparation for civil disorder is through the whole range of equipment designed to combat riot situations. In Britain the range is too extensive to document here in any more than a cursory and partial fashion, but covers both the logistical support required for public-order operations and the major advances in surveillance and control technology. In the former category might be placed the deployment of helicopters, the rapid response carriers already described and also the high-tech forward command vehicles introduced across London in 1987 (see Waddington 1991). The forms of high-power surveillance among the latter array of equipment crosses the range of advances from the more well known, such as the hoolivans, close circuit monitoring of streets, and helitele (air-to-ground cameras in helicopters), to the more esoteric, such as PROD (photographic retrieval from an optical disc) and WISARD, which is used to identify individual faces from a crowd (*Policing London*, January/February 1987).

Ironically, the acceptance of paramilitarism, along with its corollary, public disorder, as coherent concepts, and therefore logical objects of scrutiny, can also readily permeate Left discussion of the same phenomena. Hence, in an important book, Tony Jefferson, taking Cohen's (1979) work as seminal, draws up an analysis of paramilitarism which powerfully connects changes in policing to its social context, suggesting that

the "moment" of paramilitarism broadly coincides with the "moment" of a crisis in police accountability and a more general hegemonic crisis and breakdown. (1990: 40)

The stress on hegemonic contingency and the empirical contextualization make the book a welcome advance on some of the useful but sometimes crude state logic analyses (e.g. Bunyan 1976, Scraton 1985). The clashes in Southall, which led to the death of Blair Peach, the riots of 1981 and the uprisings of 1985 are cited as the three watersheds that prompted reorganization of public-order policing. Yet, almost in spite of itself, the book turns paramilitarism itself into an object that becomes in Jefferson's book as analytically unproblematic as it is morally objectionable. The inevitable result of this is that, in part, all challenges to civil order become equivalent. The events of 1985 consequently emerge as a repetition of the events of 1981 (1990: 12), obscuring the evolution of police/Black conflict over this period of time. Such an analysis cannot

THE RIOT AS A PROBLEM, PARAMILITARISM AS THE SOLUTION?

answer the fair question of how, were he in the police, Jefferson himself would deal with a riot. Paramilitarism, as a form of centralized rather than individualized police organization, is, on one level, no more than the logical response to the scale of civil disorder witnessed in Britain. Received opinion, buttressed by the sorts of police ideology analyzed in the next chapter, make such a response unavoidable. What is objectionable is not paramilitarism itself but its rôle in reproducing and amplifying conflict.

Likewise, one of the problems with conflating Black uprisings with other incidents of public disorder, whether technocratically (as in the invidious slippage into football hooliganism endorsed by Scarman), or politically (as in the sympathetic comparisons with the miner's strike), is that the particular historical rôle of the police as a constitutive feature of conflict is obscured. In this technocratic world, crowd psychology represents the antagonism between police and crowd as standardized: the two actors, crowd and police force, are uniformly antagonistic. In linking uprisings to police / Trades Union clashes, the structural position of the police as the embodiment of an unjust social order is shared. But, while labour history is clearly saturated with incidents of confrontation between organized labour and police, these confrontations have only very rarely, notwithstanding the important parallels in the 1980s coal mining disputes, been *primarily* about policing, arising from specific police actions as in the cases of Swamp 81, the shooting of Cherry Groce or the death of Cynthia Jarrett. For Black communities the police have always been a constitutive part of *the problem* as well as an implausible arbitrator.

This is clearly demonstrated by some of the attempts to analyze public order as a phenomenon in its own right. The volume by Waddington et al. (1989) is valuable in its attempt to provide a critique of both sociological and psychological studies of crowd behaviour and the concerns of contemporary legislation, and in its determination to contextualize public-order situations. As with several other studies (Brewer et al. 1988, Card 1987, McCabe et al. 1988), it demonstrates successfully the manner in which an unproblematic notion of disorder has been taken on board in the 1986 Public Order Act, thereby restricting civil liberties. Yet, in conflating issues of public order, it cannot come to terms with the scale of Black uprisings in the 1980s: the useful typologies of policing strategies are juxtaposed in this volume with erroneous histories (as for instance of the Handsworth uprising), and pathological generalizations with the lame and dangerous comment that the police "are not directly responsible for the structural location and *cultural disposition* of Afro-Caribbean youth in British society" (1990: 152; my emphasis). Public order as a "social problem" interests, the objects

THE LOCAL REALITY OF RACIAL SUBORDINATION

of disorder become blurred or stereotypical. This is compounded later in the work when, in a discussion of police masculinity, the authors comment that certain masculine ideals "are not unique to the police force and can be found in other subcultures". It is precisely when the police are confronted by groups who share this masculine ethos, such as miners and Afro-Caribbean youth, that disorder is most likely. (1990: 186)

In contrast, local manifestations of specific conflict are significant precisely because they embody the manner in which particular policy initiatives are first tried and tested. In addition, because they are the arena in which it is possible to reconcile a portrayal of common police integrity with the nasty reality of policing in late-twentieth-century Britain. Local experiences are consequently taken on board by the policing bureaucracy and translated into force-wide policy.

Bureaucratic rationality

Throughout the implementation of all these policies, a leitmotif that recurs again and again is the manner in which a particular policing conception of civil disorder is fed into the bureaucratic machinery. In this context, if the metaphor of the bureaucracy is taken as a central explanatory framework for understanding policing in Britain, then the putative benevolence or malevolence of the institution is largely irrelevant. In an understanding of the evolution of police practices, the conspiracy takes precedence over the "cock-up" only exceptionally; yet the architecture of the policing institution itself is structured by social context, the material preconditions and historical reproduction of "policing" a multi-racial and multi-racist nation.

The sort of bureaucratic rationality displayed by most police forces in the 1980s was not so much the cold efficiency envisioned by Weber in the first half of the twentieth-century as the confused, often contradictory, organization of a corporation designed by Kafka. As several authors have observed (Gilroy & Sim 1987, Jefferson & Grimshaw 1987), the contradictions, the complexity and the symbolic nature of much policing prevents neat measures of bureaucratic rationality. In a sense, the structural organization of the police mediates changes in the nature of police work (see also Grimshaw & Jefferson 1987). The bureaucracy transmits "downwards" changes in relations between the state and the police force and also rationalizes "upwards" the trajectory of relations between the police and British Black communities.

CONCLUSIONS

Conclusions

In this way it is impossible to explain the manner in which police practice institutionalizes racial subordination unless clear-cut distinctions are made between acknowledged and unacknowledged conditions of action under which individual police operate and between intended and unintended effects of policing policy as a whole.

The crucial metaphor is not one of a myriad police officers wandering around in varied states of false consciousness. Such a simplistic and fundamentally arrogant diagnosis is manifestly implausible. What is instead the case, is that the organization of routine policing stems from the interaction between the structural circumstances within which police operate, and the manner in which such circumstances are rationalized and translated into day-to-day behaviour by police officers themselves. This crucial, if obvious, duality highlights two sets of processes that, by definition, the individual cannot transcend: on the one hand the situation of policing within the penal system as a whole, on the other the existence of what might be referred to as "police discourse", which describes the limits of what can and cannot be said and done, and which sets the boundaries within which police history can be written and police practices may be rationalized.

It is a central contention here that the acknowledgement of individual police integrity alongside a critical diagnosis of institutionalized racial subordination, can be sustained by tracing practices back to these two sources, avoiding any resort to notions of "rotten apple" policing problems. The empirical demonstration of practices in this chapter might be considered descriptively adequate to support exemplary charges of institutional racism, but such charges, although politically significant, can remain only descriptive. In short, if academic discourse is to serve any useful anti-racist purpose, it is less important to list genuine cases of malicious individuals in blue than it is to analyze the processes by which the efforts of the well intentioned may become implicated in the grim reproduction of real conflict. By 1993, Chief Constables such as Kenneth Oxford in Liverpool and James Anderton in Manchester, look very much like characters from a different age, and did little for their own service and even less to prompt sophisticated analysis of the politics of the police bureaucracy. Both men represented ready-made caricatures for sloppy critiques from the Left. They are too easy targets.

CHAPTER 10

Policing reconstructions of reality

"Truth is only that which is taken to be true. It's the currency of living. There may be nothing behind it but it doesn't make any difference so long as it's honoured. One acts on assumptions."

Tom Stoppard

Introduction

In a television programme broadcast on 1 December 1985, a few months after the violence in Birmingham and London, a well known liberal sociology professor was talking to the renowned guru of the New Right, Alfred Sherman

Professor Halsey

. . . it's a problem of social education . . . solidarity must depend upon a sense of shared citizenship. I think this is so terribly important because if you think about the inner city and the riots and that kind of thing: surely one must see that as a breakdown of the idea of membership one of another, and a group of people who are seeing themselves as not belonging to their society.

Sir Alfred Sherman

People look at the terrible situation in the inner city. Why don't we ask how that came about. It is a result of the welfare state: first of all the new towns which deliberately decanted large numbers of native-born Englishmen, the more energetic and competent, to new towns, breaking the social structure; then the invention of a labour shortage which never existed (merely the labour market had been made inefficient) to bring in large numbers of people, many of them from primitive countries. And as Machiavelli said, any country's institutions reflect the nature of the people.

The comments are revealing, not so much for Sherman's objectionable and fallacious notion of a contaminated race of Englishmen, as for the similarity between the visions of inner-city Britain, which were to be conjured up in much police discourse, and the explanation of violence

RACE & MIGRANT MINORITIES: RECONSTRUCTING CONFLICT

offered by Halsey, a reputable member of the liberal establishment. It is extremely important to clarify exactly what is being said here. Issues of citizenship and alienation are legitimate concerns. There is also no intention of understating the reality of inner-city poverty. Yet Halsey's comments are dangerous not because they are patronizing, nor because they come close to endorsing a conception of urban life that borders on an inner-city pathology. It is the manner in which Halsey chooses to validate this vision that is crucial. By placing what interests him most – poverty – into a causal relationship with that which interests him least – violent conflict – "the riots" are safely (ir)rationalized.

The link is crucial. In large part it is based on the simplistic and misleading notions of causality that have already been examined. But its importance derives from the historical diagnosis, policy ramifications and theoretical prognosis that stem from such conceptions of violent disorder. For again it was to this sort of liberal social science, not to the explicitly racist ideologies of the New Right, or the authoritarian invocations of the Old Right, that the police most often looked for explanations of the violence of the 1980s. In this chapter, I argue that such liberal social science is important precisely because it is one of the most powerful influences on society's understanding of itself. Specifically, neutral social science rationalizes policing reconstructions of reality.

Race and migrant minorities: reconstructing conflict

There is a social basis to the conflict between Black communities and the police. It is rooted in the material causes of institutionalized racial injustice, realized in particular historical and geographical contexts. However, it is the manner in which received wisdom mirrors this situation that structures popular and official reactions to this conflict.

What is of concern here is the relationship between writing about policing, and the social context in which that writing is set. It is essential to analyze the way in which particular accounts of processes and events are proffered, heard, authenticated and, most importantly, remembered or forgotten.

The prevalence of "pathology sociology" in the explanation of police/ Black confrontations has already been alluded to; there is no intention here to repeat the criticisms of an earlier chapter or other work (e.g. Lawrence 1982). I have also discussed elsewhere in detail (Keith 1991, 1992) one specific instance, in which an eminent sociology professor, Michael Banton (1972), produced descriptions of West Indian culture which, it was argued, provided rationalizations for police/Black conflict.

POLICING RECONSTRUCTIONS OF REALITY

Banton's work *Police–community relations* (1972), which takes as a central objective the task of "informing the police what they should know about community relations", became a constitutive element of the common sense through which British police understood British Black communities. The pernicious notion of a cultural disposition to crime is made explicit through the *objective* realm of academic description. So it is hardly surprising if notable police officers reproduce such notions publicly (Marshall 1975), or the Commissioner of the Metropolitan Police echoes such received wisdom in public when analyzing the difficulties of "Policing and social policy in multi-ethnic areas in Europe" (Newman 1983).

The reason for drawing attention to this sort of work is not to malign Banton or Marshall, only to draw out the connections between theory and practice. Through the respectability and status of "objective" academic accounts an *authoritative* explanation is derived. Logically, clashes between police and Black communities focus attention (and policy reaction) on *the problem* of migrant communities, in situations that are exacerbated by the occasional incidence of "rotten apple" racism (Brown 1977). Such clashes are *to be expected* in situations where mutual cultural misunderstanding is paired with economic deprivation. In this vein, as early as 1978 Robert Mark suggested that

The police have no influence on employment, housing and education. The problem of alienated black youth is dumped on their lap without any means to resolve it. (Mark 1978: 286)

It is not that such generalizations are *true* or *false* in any straightforward sense of these terms. An academic gloss is painted over the major problems of (good or bad) policing in a racist society and the deviant nature of the social problem category "Black youth" is legitimated. It is the context in which cultural generalizations are used that is as problematic as their (in)accuracy.

"Riots"

Memory is important. It is important because the way in which events are remembered becomes the stuff of folklore, informing common-sense understandings of riots, how they occur and how they should be prevented. Here again, like Keynes's famed businessman labouring under the influence of the economist of yesteryear, the police themselves often echo the axioms and generalizations of past sociologists. When coupled with the notion of causality as blame allocation, "social theory", in the loosest sense of the term, becomes one of many arenas

"RIOTS"

in which institutions are not only vindicated or condemned but are also defined in terms of legitimacy, neutrality, and vague but significant measures of social utility.

In such circumstances there was, after 1981, a clearly felt need in some police quarters to reassess the rôle of the police, most readily evinced in the many statements and essays, including a high-profile submission to Lord Scarman, of John Alderson, an individual at various times Commandant of Bramshill Police College, Chief Constable of Devon and Cornwall, and criminologist academic. It is not possible here to do justice to the scope and significance of Alderson's many interventions on the political stage in the early 1980s. Nevertheless, it is significant that, while often decried at the time, the Alderson line epitomized a conception of technological, sociologically informed policing that was to become, in large part, 1980s orthodox thinking in London under the aegis of one of his successors at Bramshill, Kenneth Newman. It was Alderson, in his submission to Scarman, who focused on the need to create a new "social contract" between police and public, and it was Alderson who was repeatedly to situate the riots of 1981 as a social problem, not divorced from policing practice but beyond police control:

> Not only were the traditional social controls of family, school, reli-
> gion and culture weakened in the affected areas but the idea that
> the problem of social disorder could be cured by the police was a
> gross error. (1984: 41)

The contingent nature of social description here is crucial. The attempt to draw in a wider social context is laudable, as is the refusal throughout Alderson's work to duck the issues of policing, but it is worth noting that in such analysis lay the potential for the shift of attention away from the police force, a powerful political tool.

The events of 1981 raised questions about police legitimacy, and liberal social science provided the resources through which these questions could be answered. By 1985 Kenneth Newman, in his reaction to the uprisings in Brixton and Tottenham, was quick to draw on both the Kerner Report and liberal models of social conditions causing riots. In the 1980s, similar diagnoses were increasingly to be found in the journals, which attempted, at various levels of sophistication, to address the nature of the policing function. In periodicals such as *Police Journal*, *Police Review*, *Police* and, latterly, *Policing*, this shift of focus could be completed by the mobilization of academic models of crowd psychology (Brindley 1982, Trivizias 1983), or the credentialist expertise of sociology (Waddington 1982, 1984b).

Although not always the case, this too was a task not irreconcilable with sympathetic visions of city life (Wells 1987). At one level such an

211

POLICING RECONSTRUCTIONS OF REALITY

approach may appear unexceptionable:

Senior police officers have a difficult path to tread in being sensitive to a variety of differing and conflictual pressures upon them. They have to exercise their professional judgement and make decisions which have to finely balance these conflicting pressures. It would appear that as our society is becoming more socially divided and ideologically divided the policing job will become more difficult not merely in terms of physical violence which the police will have to face but also in making decisions that strike a balance that can help to continue the tradition of policing by consent. (Vick 1982: 277)

Yet even here the contrast between police professionalism and political ideology renders the two mutually exclusive. The politics of policing become an exercise in common-sense diplomacy rather than the problematic routine enforcement of a contentious social order, a process hidden by appeal to a tradition of policing by consent (cf. Brogden 1982, Reiner 1985).

Moreover, compiling an historical record of the events of 1981 was at times recognized as more than an exercise in cataloguing and comprehension. This can be seen in Thackrah's study of "Reactions to terrorism and riots" (1985). Here the tension between theory and practice is particularly marked, and the relationship between academic discourse and public policy is of particular concern, as the author writes as a lecturer at Bramshill Police College. Thackrah does not advance an explanation of the rioting as such; yet the assumptions he makes about the disorders throw light on a conception of the phenomenon that may structure policy-orientated reactions to it.

The rioters are classified as an irrational and cohesive "crowd" that must be subdued: policing *per se* is to be removed from the political agenda, as the attacks on police are classified as unprovoked, and the focus is returned to British society as a whole.

Police intelligence has to work against the Left trying to link the question of policing to what is seen as the underlying causes of recent rioting. (1985: 155)

The transformation from violence as politics to violence as crime assumes the status and incontrovertibility of received wisdom.

Notwithstanding the significance of such examples, any generalizations about the dominant modes of explanation of civil unrest necessarily take on the veneer of simplicity when constrained by the amount of space available here. Struggles between memories and countermemories permeate civil society at all levels from the grand institutions right down to the individual. Here it is intended to note only three points.

(i) The importance of memory. It is how uprisings or riots are re-

"RIOTS"

membered, rather than how they actually occurred, that dictates policy reaction and future popular mobilization. It is not reality alone which structures the political agenda of today and tomorrow (cf. Edelman 1971, 1988).

(ii) It is possible to define the existence of policing conceptions of rioting which are, sufficiently broad to cover the range of opinion from Anderton to Alderson, yet simultaneously remain firmly within a police perspective on the nature of social disorder. These conceptions were not necessarily conscious exercises in self-justification. The single uniting theme was an implicit equivalence between "cause" and "blame", no more than an acceptance of the common-sense notions of causality examined in detail in Chapter 4, often incorporating mainstream social science in the production of accounts which in varying degrees exculpated police in allocation of "responsibility" for civil disorder.

(iii) It has been demonstrated elsewhere that a major theme, which differentiated 1985 from 1981 in the foremost spheres of public discussion, was the removal of the problem of policing from the public agenda (Solomos 1986, 1988). Such a change has to be related to a changing perception of policing in an unjust society. These perceptions are themselves tied to a cultural construction of the policing function in the writings of police discourse. This does not mean that the study of policing should relate exclusively to the nature of civil (dis)order. There is no call here to resort to a reversal of the process of blame allocation or, necessarily, a demand for the privileged recognition of alternative counter-memories of uprisings. It is only important to realize that, in the arena in which explanations of "riots" competed against each other for recognition, like a collection of "avant-garde artistes", some achieved greater recognition than others.

The leaking into the vocabularies of the political agenda and common sense of some forms of academic explanation of disorder and not others is at least in part due to this competition. This in turn has structured the social realities of the years that followed 1981 and 1985.

It would be impossible to map out with any great precision the formation of public knowledge in this way. However, to support the contention that the institutionalized nature of racial subordination is tied to the discursive field through which police practices are generated, it is useful to illustrate one of the key concepts through which the conflict between police and British Black communities is manipulated, rationalized and reproduced.

POLICING RECONSTRUCTIONS OF REALITY

Police/Black clashes, "no-go areas" and the inversion of history

The terms "no-go area" gained increasing currency in the 1970s, for example:

"No-go area": attribute of an area impossible to enter (because of barricades etc.); to which entry is forbidden for specified persons, groups, etc.
The UDA organized the Protestant "no-go" areas in Belfast last weekend. *The Times* 24 May 1972
Oxford English Dictionary Supplement 1976

The use of the term "no-go area" was significant in political debates of the 1980s because of the subtle changes in inflection that developed, and the outright inversion of the term's connotations that were produced, through discursive competition. Following both the disorders at Notting Hill Carnival in the mid-1970s and the St Paul's uprising in Bristol in 1980, the no-go area was a term of rebuke, used against the police. Both Robert Mark, then Commissioner of the Metropolitan Police, and the Chief Constable of Avon and Somerset defended their forces on these occasions by ridiculing the possibility that a term which had leaked into Britain from Ulster could have anything other than rhetorical relevance to the policing of British cities. The term itself in these early years connoted only police failure.

Yet, less than a decade after St Paul's, a new deployment of the term was seen in the early 1988 stories surrounding the emergence of alleged organized crime by "The Yardies", already described in relation to Stoke Newington. Early reports explicitly related the rationale for establishing Operation Lucy to a fear of nascent no-go areas. Hence a *Times* story that was headlined "YARDIES 'MAY SET UP NO-GO AREAS'" claimed that

Yardies, the criminal gangs which originated in Jamaica, could establish no-go areas in British cities as a cover for their increasing cocaine trafficking, a police assessment says. (*The Times* 8 February 1988)

The possible existence of a no-go area, once evidence of policing failure, is now proof positive of the monstrous task facing the police force.

Elsewhere I have described in greater detail these gradual changes in parliamentary, press and popular coinage of the term (Keith 1991). Significantly, the protean symbolism of the no-go area does not arise out of nowhere. To understand the context in which the Metropolitan Police could themselves use a term they had once feared is to see how police/Black conflict has come to be rationalized as a manageable social problem, digested by discourse.

CLASHES, "NO-GO AREAS" AND THE INVERSION OF HISTORY

It is here that the powerful nature of historical revisionism is revealed. For, of course, the "reality" of so called no-go areas has already been described. There are places where the conflict between police and Black communities has become so historically mature that the regular challenges to the police–policed power relation and the consequent nature of policing in these particular places is qualitatively different from that in other parts of the same city. In the early 1980s, All Saints Road, Railton Road and Sandringham Road would have topped the lists of many senior Met officers asked to identify such places. It is also worth remembering Kenneth Newman's public reference to these same streets, quoted in Chapters 2 and 6, which acknowledges this perceived priority while simultaneously explaining it within a police frame of reference.

To repeat the substance of Chapter 7, the defining characteristic of such locations is that national conflicts are locally realized. It is not that these are the places where police/Black relations are worse than anywhere else, only that it is here that the policing prerogative was most frequently challenged.

Whether or not such localized social relations in space warrant categorization as "no-go areas" is ultimately a meaningless and naïve question. The phrase is akin to any linguistic term which has an arbitrary referential property. What the phrase actually means is flexible within the constraints imposed by the anarchic reference at its heart. The term can symbolize either police failure or the enormity of the task facing the police force, and it is the struggle to decide which of these meanings will prevail that is more important than any isomorphic relationship between the term itself and "the real world". This struggle is conducted through the process of historical recording.

To get from the pejorative use of the no-go area epitomizing policing inadequacies, to the Metropolitan Police prophecies of tomorrow's Britain, requires three stages of reconstruction. Through these three stages, policing problems are defined and rationalized within an orthodox vision of social consensus. It is necessary to forget history and then reinvent it, but only once, in an intervening second stage, the background chronology of more recent events has been suppressed.

First, forgetting history: popular resistance to both the introduction of the British police force and the practice of "policing by consent" dates back a long way, as many of the revisionist police histories of the past decade or so have shown (Box 1983, Brogden 1982). The spatial realization of such resistance produced a series of historical precedents to the negotiated stand-offs that often characterized the Front Lines of the early 1980s. In those areas where opposition to the police presence was at its greatest,

POLICING RECONSTRUCTIONS OF REALITY

[police] negotiated a complex, shifting, largely unspoken "contract". They defined the activities they would turn a blind eye to, and those which they would suppress, harass or control. This "tacit contract" between normal neighbourhood activities and police objectives was sometimes oiled by corruption, but more often secured by favours and friendship. This was the microscopic basis of police legitimacy and it was a fragile basis at best. (Ignatieff 1978)

That such conflicts have tended to be written out of history by most of the more conventional accounts of the British police (see Reiner 1984: Ch. 1) has inevitably contributed to the process of historical amnesia. To mask the central contradictions of policing always requires a major ideological exercise in the fiction of consensus, and the need for "tacit contracts" is at variance with the notion of a straightforward social contract based on the universal acceptance of a police service.

As we have already seen, police discourse can transform major disturbances into social scientific "problems" of societal deprivation and crowd psychology. The medical metaphors most often used in such analysis are usefully ahistorical. It is by turning civil disorder into a social problem, a societal blight regularly witnessed in nascent form in the symbolic locations of conflict, that the historical context of unrest is suppressed. Once this has occurred, the locational resistance of police operations, the seeds of "no-go area" descriptions, become a medium through which the problem of civil unrest can be rationalized. Hence, in a piece for *Police Journal*, a Bramshill lecturer suggests that

In such areas as Bristol, a chief constable is placed in a most invidious position. If he seeks to enforce the laws as they stand, and rioting and disorder results because of a reaction by that community, he may be accused of provoking the riot. If he does nothing and turns a blind eye to what are often open and flagrant breaches of the law, then he is accused by others of operating double standards, and failing in his duty to uphold the laws of the land. (Vick 1982: 275)

Here there is frank description of the real problems of policing without consent but, significantly, no reference to the history of how consent was lost. Confrontation is a problem of policing, but it apparently stems from the refusal of unnamed groups to accept the rule of law.

The final stage of this process is to reinvent the "no-go area", and restore the history that was lost. In this process of reconstruction, Sir Kenneth Newman has provided an explicit "police rationalization" (an official account) of the existence of symbolic locations in sensitive parts of London where police actions are most frequently challenged – the streets he did not shy from naming. For Newman it was in these places that the challenge to police authority was most pronounced.

CLASHES, 'NO-GO AREAS' AND THE INVERSION OF HISTORY

This brand of destruction and hostility is at its height in certain parts of ethnic areas which have become a focal point for congregation and association by Black youths. In these locations confrontations with the police are deliberately engineered either to make a political point or to create a diversion in order to facilitate organized crime in relation to drugs or stolen property. If allowed to continue, locations with these characteristics assume a symbolic importance, a negative symbolism of the inability of police to maintain order.

The youths take a proprietorial posture in this location; they regard it as their territory. In general they will regard the police as intruders . . . (1983: 9 and 13).

Two connected themes provide the backbone for this conception of clashes on the Front Lines of London. The first is the notion of disorder as purely criminal activity. Rather than merely suppress time, Newman's statement goes further and turns time on its head. Notwithstanding the long record of officially "illegal" social activity in such places, history shows that some serious crime tends to exploit disorder, moving in on the collapse of policing by consent into the Front Line areas. As Chapters 2 and 6 have stressed, Black challenges to police action pre-date the very real major crime problems that grow up in these symbolic locations; such challenges are not caused by that crime. The chronological inversion is an example of criminalization by area which simultaneously discredits the "validity" of violent protest in symbolic locations by categorizing it as a form of criminal behaviour in the same class as street crime and drug dealing.

The notion that "all rioters are criminals" is a powerful ideological classification that has obvious policing implications. It is only fair to Newman to acknowledge that as an individual he might not concur with such a simplistic equivalence; certainly DAC Wells, one of his closest advisors, publicly contradicted this sort of classification (London Weekend Television, 11 October 1985). However, the refusal to acknowledge any element of protest in the rioters' actions was common within the Metropolitan Police Force throughout the 1980s.

Typically, a notion of disorder is revealed in the assumptions underlying the Stoke Newington Divisional Report for 1985:

Perhaps a useful barometer of social tensions within an area can be the level of violence. If this is the case then perhaps we can be a little optimistic. Crimes of violence have dropped over the past year and there is evidence that we are solving more of them.

The policy implications are obviously significant. If it is believed that the author of this report was writing in good faith – and that is something that the author of this book does believe – then the violent resistance of the policing prerogative can be accounted for only in the clumsy vocabulary of common-sense criminality.

It is important to differentiate between the individual and the nature of police discourse as a whole. The latter is characterized by a whole set of linguistic rules that render the questioning of police legitimacy contradictory, almost literally unspeakable.[1] Classification of violent disorder has to be squared with the vision of policing demanded by police discourse. In such a situation there is no attempt here to impugn the integrity or insult the intelligence of specific police officers involved in such official conceptualizations, particularly given the less than admirable record of much "academic social science" in exactly the same area. The individual police officer is placed in a relation to police discourse akin to that between agent and structure, the two are recursively tied to each other. In these circumstances there are necessary rules behind official rationalizations. The limits to police accounts of civil unrest are just one manifestation of these rules.

The second theme in the quotation from Newman's paper is one of territoriality. There is a very real difference between the ethological conception of the human "territorial imperative" (Ardrey 1961) and the dramaturgical concept that the behaviour of individuals will be conditioned by scene, a scene-setting process that will include the social sanctioning of violence in particular contexts (Marsh 1983). Both might be described as conceptions of "territoriality", yet the former connotes a vision of human behaviour which is essentially pathological, or at best bestial, a powerful political transformation (Miller 1982). The failure to make this distinction is not rare (e.g. Sack 1983). It is the contention here that the employment of the ethological concept of territoriality is often mistakenly used in the "theoretical" analysis of police behaviour (e.g. Holdaway (1983) explicitly uses Ardrey's model), suggesting a misleadingly pathological view of police culture. It is also the contention that the connoted view of Black culture implied by Newman employs an identical approach, an approach which incidentally devalues the form of location-specific Black resistance by transforming the social into the natural (Barthes 1971), the rational act into a manifestation of animal nature.

Again, it is interesting and important to note that the lineage of Newman's remarks is much closer to a liberal social science perspective than to a caricature of Right reactionary law-and-order politics. This proximity was exemplified in an article written by *Guardian* journalist Stephen Cook in 1984, who, in a piece that reproduces much of the sympathetic, but orthodox and predictable, liberal vision of urban life in Britain, suggested that

What has developed, in my view, is essentially a conflict between police and blacks over occupation and control of the inner-city

CLASHES, "NO-GO AREAS" AND THE INVERSION OF HISTORY

streets. It is like a tribal, territorial conflict, with strong overtones of sexual curiosity and jealousy, and fear and contempt of the other side's totems and ju-jus. (*Police Review* 3 August 1984)

Terms such as "riot", "crime" and "territoriality" may connote whole value-systems and social orders; they do not exist simply as fixed objects, open to study. In this sense the phenomenon of academic appropriation of "rioting" outlined in Chapter 4 is repeated by Newman: the explicandum "riot" is determined by the preferred explanation of the phenomenon rather than vice versa. So, while holding back from any concession of the existence of "no-go areas", Newman's account provides the explanatory framework through which such phenomena should be understood. If, of course, they *were* to develop in the future.

There can be no dialogue with "criminals". The claims of "uprisings" to political substance are compromised by classification. Beyond this classification, such criminal activity can either be put down to the deviant propensities of individuals, as the New Right might prefer (see Lewis 1988 on "Race and riot"), or to look to liberal social science for rationalization.

Reinforcing a central contention of this chapter, that policing discourse is structured more by the tenets of liberal academic social science than by reactionary law-and-order politics, a central organizing metaphor of police discourse in the late 1980s has been "the metaphor of the dustbin". The notion that society delegates to the police force the task of "keeping the lid on" the cauldron of ills that is the modern inner city is both emotively persuasive and ideologically useful. It is a metaphor that has been used both inside and outside the police force to describe the genuinely difficult nature of the policing task, normally set against a list of social problems that need to be tackled. (e.g. Wells 1987, Imbert 1987; Mark 1978: Ch. 24).

As already suggested, this notion of discrete social problems is itself disingenuous; in refusing to tie various facets of urban deprivation to their societal context there is a danger that root causes are obscured by academic reification. The policing outcome of this sort of vision is also contradictory. Couched in the vocabulary of "keeping the lid on", the dustbin metaphor for British city life implicitly recognizes the injustice that is being legally enforced, yet there is also a refusal to address publicly the ramifications that follow from the regulation of a disputed and institutionally racist social order. A real and recurrent difficulty all police face is how to enforce this unjust social order, but this task can barely be expressed in police discourse because it cannot be reconciled with notions of *policing by consent*. This is another example of "the fallacy of polite policing". Those who resist police actions must still take

219

on the classification of "criminals" by their necessary position within a particular discursive field. Ultimately, it is not possible for individual police officers publicly to transcend this discursive field, whatever their private opinions, for to do so would be to question the relationship between state and police that lies at the very heart of police legitimacy. The selective amnesia that discredits violent conflict in symbolic locations and Front Lines exemplifies Foucault's notion of history as "a mode of mobilizing power"; the power of naming so crucial to the mapping of popular geographies or the common-sense territorialization of the British city. There is no attempt here to romanticize or even to justify violence, only to prohibit classification of disorder as straightforwardly criminal or causally irrational. Memory of the history of particular places may differ between people who live in them and those that write official geographies of the city. It is not the purpose of this text to provide the counter-memories to substantiate such alternative history, only to point to their existence.

When social relations in space are classified in terms of "no-go areas" the phrase assumes connotations that are highly normative. The rôle of the medium of space is itself interpreted and deployed to rhetorical effect. The "no-go area" is a term full of fearful images but devoid of causal meaning. It is rhetorically so useful because it is possible simultaneously to evoke the one and imply the other. Powerful symbols are combined with a reassuring vision of society that is connoted by the wider context in which the term is used rather than by events and processes in the real world.

Public debate tends to be constructed around a tapestry of assumptions and myths concerning the history of the British police. The reality of the so-called "no-go area" is just one place where on close inspection the seam that holds this tapestry together begins to show.

Hegemonic discourse?

If it is accepted that police discourse provides a field in which the relations between the police, the state and the public are contested, defined and legitimated, then a great many of the developments in the politics of policing in 1980s Britain become more readily comprehensible. Presentation and perception of policing is socially constructed but also plays an integral rôle in the generation of police practices. In short, popular images of police work may bear little relation to reality but have very real effects. The public react to a notion of policing rather than to the reality of police work.

HEGEMONIC DISCOURSE?

The fiction of consensus . . . selling consensus

One of the commonly recited features of British police tactics has been the apparent ability to win by seeming to lose (e.g. Mark 1978). The suggestion, commonly made by police spokespeople, has been that a popular reservoir of support for the institution is sustained by the public appearance of police tolerance in the face of frequently violent "provocation". The explicit recognition by the police themselves of the significance of images of policing in the eye of the beholder immediately highlights one of the less analyzed areas of police activity – the need continually to reproduce sympathetic interpretations of their own institution through plausible public rationalizations of their own behaviour.

Given the place of the police in the late capitalist state, there will always be, simultaneously present, large pools of support for and opposition to the policing function. These contradictory tendencies cannot simply be tied to particular groups; those most hostile to imposition of an unjust social order will perforce still look to the police for enforcement of the large parts of the criminal justice system that command popular support.

In crude, slightly simplistic, terms, support for the police will depend upon the highlighting of those tasks that command popular support and the muting of those tasks that do not. Such perception is never within the control of the police alone, divorced from the material changes in the configuration of the political economy. However, in the definition of the police–policed internal relation (see Ch. 7), the field of public relations is for the police force much more than an arena for polishing up an image. The ethical ramifications of such a position are considerable.

In the early 1980s Kenneth Newman was fond of suggesting that a society that felt well policed *was* well policed. In the academic counterpart to this school of thought, "fear of crime" has been taken as both a legitimate *object* of study and a reasonable *subject* to campaign on (e.g. Smith 1986b). The images of a society may be as important as reality in determining people's reactions to institutions (e.g. the police) and situations (e.g. crime rates).

For the police–policed relation is always internal, but the level of antagonism constituted by it depends on the successful legitimation and rationalization of policing practices. Given the contradictory, conflict-riven nature of society, *policing by consent* can only ever be a half-truth, and has never been more than a partial historical reality; it is in large part a powerful myth. But the proportion of society that accepts this notion of police work will, by definition, qualitatively affect the nature of policing in a society. On one level, police have a necessarily vested interest in "selling consensus".

POLICING RECONSTRUCTIONS OF REALITY

There is a very real sense in which, through significant periods of the post-war era, the British police have been considerably more successful in enhancing this myth than the police forces of comparable capitalist societies (Reiner 1984, Roach & Tomacek 1986). In part this must be tied to the nature of consensus in British politics generally; more significantly it should be tied to a particular history of policing.

Moreover, it would also be unwise to rush immediately to support either the sustaining or the destruction of the connoted vision of British policing such qualified success implies. For in defining their own rôle the police must necessarily engage in a form of explicit or implicit political campaigning if the rhetorical possibility of policing by consent is to remain a plausible strategic option.

In this sense the morality of consensus is always moot. A perennial question of moral philosophy and political strategy is tied to the pay-off between social reform and societal stability. The flaws of society can necessarily be reformed only by suffering the social conflict through which such change occurs. There is no attempt to resolve such intractable problems here, only to draw attention to the fact that all police have a legitimate and understandable interest in the one (social stability), knowing that they will always bear the sometimes unpleasant, frequently violent costs of the latter (social reform). Other people, equally legitimately, do not share this interest.

Robert Mark, Kenneth Newman, John Alderson and many other equally sophisticated individual police operated in the world of public relations (PR). They won awards for communication skills, as they sold their police force to the public. In the context in which they were operating this was both a legitimate and necessary task, if the notion of "policing by consent" was to be bought by the British public. The popular image of police, the social construction of policing, is not merely a question of PR. It is part of the process by which a police force is reproduced through time and police practices are generated.

It was Oscar Wilde who suggested that:

the worst slave owners were those who were kind to their slaves and so prevented the horror of the system being realized by those who suffer from it and understood by those who contemplated it.

The crisis of the British state of the mid-1970s threatened the popular acceptance of virtually all the major institutions of the state apparatus. This was recognized not only in the groves of academe, but also by many of the institutions themselves. As the outgoing Commissioner of the Metropolitan Police has suggested, the crisis was manifested so severely in the policing field that the viability of "winning by seeming to lose" came under scrutiny and a new range of measures to secure police legitimacy was demanded in response to the politicization of

CONTESTATION AND "POWERFUL" RECONSTRUCTIONS?

policing" (Imbert 1987).

The need for state institutions to seek legitimacy in the changing times of the past decade provided the arenas of contestation for all political campaigning from the Thatcherite project of the right to the upheavals on the left that resulted in the splitting of the Labour party. Many of the public debates over the nature of policing were tied into these processes of political contestation (Keith & Murji 1990).

Arenas of contestation
and the most "powerful" reconstructions?

Only in this light can many of the changes in police policy be assessed. The practices involved in policing and the writing about policing, which constitutes the loosely defined field of police discourse, have a manifest and a latent content. On the surface they may be objectively defined exercises in either theory or practice. But there is a latent, often incidental, rôle which they may fulfil. In the case of police practices, the early and mid-1980s saw rapid changes in policing which embraced not only the provisions for social control examined in the last chapter but also a full range of PR-orientated policies that, *inter alia*, comprise in large part the attempt to reconstruct Newman's social contract. There is no time or space to analyze each measure individually here, but community consultation, neighbourhood watch, the publication of divisional plans, crime-prevention initiatives, and the "prioritizing" of multi-agency policing together formed the principal components of this change (Wright 1986). As Gilroy & Sim (1986) have suggested, it is always important not to underestimate the symbolic function of police performances,

In the field of writing, the literature of the major journals of policing (*Police, Police Review, Policing Journal, The Job*, etc.), although occupying distinctive ideological positions, do, amongst their other functions, provide arenas in which the rationalization of these changes may be theorized. Accounts of police practices are generated which may be later used in the public domain.

Sometimes this function was recognized explicitly. *Police Officer Magazine*, established in 1981 by the Superintendents Association, had an opening editorial which included the statement that:

On Sunday 13 November 1981 *The Observer* published a National Opinion Poll which, the newspaper says, "Suggested that public confidence in the police is beginning to erode for the first time, especially among the young, and is not nearly as high as is

POLICING RECONSTRUCTIONS OF REALITY

popularly imagined." If the poll is a true reflection of public opinion then 1982 should be a year in which the Police Service will intensify the efforts it is already making to put its house in order and to improve its professionalism. I hope this magazine has a part to play in that process. (*Police Officer Magazine*, December 1981)

Again, such relationships between rationalization and reality are not unusual. They merely serve to highlight the significance of police discourse, and are cited here purely because of their relevance to the discursive rationalization of "problems of race and racism".

One of the key concepts by which these rationalizations are constructed is through competing notions of police "professionalism", of much current interest to debates on policing and police training, which stem from attempts to define examples of good police practice. This in itself is not altogether a bad thing, but has remained a persistently problematic theme in much research on policing, most notably in the studies carried out on the Metropolitan Police Force by the Policy Studies Institute in the early 1980s and by Wolf–Ohlins PR consultants in the late 1980s.

Attempts to define police professionalism cannot be seen as a socially neutral process. For it has to be said that professionalism in the police, as in all branches of the civil service, is in part a notion through which practices are standardized and consequently drained of any political or moral content.[2] One of the definitive uniting features about police discourse is the manner in which widely differing perceptions of police work may co-exist in journals, in books and in social science, as long as the fundamental task of *policing* itself is not subjected to scrutiny. Significantly, if problems of the relations between police and Black communities are cast *solely* in terms of notions of professionalism (*Police Review*, 9 December 1988), then the core issues that underscore *all* policing in a multi-racist society are obscured rather than openly addressed. Yet it is in the arena of police discourse that precisely this sort of rationalization may be proffered.

Moreover, it is in these arenas of contestation that the reconstructions of reality may be generated which lend a sense to past and present. It has already been suggested that the process of proffering official memories and rationalizations performs a powerful rôle in the reproduction of social relations. Police discourse is one medium through which such power relations are exercised.

Ideal policing?

A core problem here, so rarely addressed, relates to notions of "ideal policing". It has to be said that there is something slightly disingenuous about some of the criticisms of police attempts to win public consent,

CONTESTATION AND "POWERFUL" RECONSTRUCTIONS?

to form a new "social contract". In an important article about such projects Wright has suggested that, "In essence, multi-agency policing seeks to mobilize non-police resources towards policy-defined goals" (Wright 1986: 76), and that:

The police PR campaign, irrespective of the value of any specific changes in operational policy which it reveals, is designed to counter the demand for accountability by representing the self-regulating mechanisms of the police as adequate for the task. Wright (1986: 77)

In one sense the police cannot win either way. They are criticized either because people do oppose their actions or for the hegemonic influence of their attempts to win community support.

Wright's argument may indeed be correct. But it is certainly logically hermetic. If policing by consent involves the enforcement of an unjust social order with the agreement of those policed, then it inevitably requires an element of dubious "hegemonic persuasion". The conflation of law and order, which ties popular suspicion of policing to popular support for a major part of the policing task, provides the arena in which this may occur. The accentuation of the common interest in law enforcement at the cost of the social significance of order enforcement is precisely the function of a long line of police supported public relations exercises, from Dixon of Dock Green down to the construction of Kenneth Newman's social contract. As Reiner has put it:

Whereas Mark manipulated the media to politicize law-and-order issues, Newman is using them to cultivate legitimacy – "a new social contract", in his words (Reiner 1985: 146-7).

The sort of policing practised in society depends, in part, on a manufactured cultural identity of the British police. Short of Utopia, the police are always ultimately the active enforcers of an unjust social order. In terms of police practice (as opposed to social reform more generally) the issue at hand is the *nature* of this enforcement. So, when Newman in the early 1980s wrote and spoke of designing a new social contract, he was almost explicitly referring to the construction of a new hegemony. The syntactical rules of police discourse do not allow for such frankness, but the degree to which it is possible to find Newman culpable on grounds of deceit depends not only on his personal belief in the idealistic myth of social consensus but also on a condemnation of Oscar Wilde's benevolent slave master.

Exactly the same processes of mystification and legitimation of policing occurs in the ostensibly more objective world of writing about policing. Significantly, there is an equally long line of academic studies of police work which, normally unquestioningly, use academic or quasiscientific credentialism to reinforce this mystification of the necessary nature of the policing task. Whether or not it is acknowledged publicly,

POLICING RECONSTRUCTIONS OF REALITY

there will always be a politics of policing as well as social scientific investigation of the police.

There is nothing exclusive to the police about the need to invent tradition in order to cultivate an historical legitimacy. Tracing the nineteenth century forging of nationalism, Hobsbawm has commented that:

> Quite new, or old but dramatically transformed, social groups, environments and social contexts called for new devices to ensure or express social cohesion and identity and to structure social relations (1983: 263)

Similarly, revisionist schools of criminology (Brogden 1982, Box 1983) have deconstructed many of the myths behind the history of policing in Britain. Yet the myths remain significant because, even if they do not represent a particularly accurate picture of the historical past, they are still part of the cultural present.

The fictional status of liberal visions of society creates a situation in which the nature of real policing depends upon common acceptance of normative images of the function of the police institution. Policing practices too have a dual status. They are both tied to the images of policing they connote and to the real effects they may produce. To take just one high-profile example: the "value" of neighbourhood watch schemes is, quite understandably, measured for the police not solely by their success in reducing arithmetically measured crime rates.

But this relationship between police theory and practice is not unidirectional. Theoretical abstraction reveals the logic underlying hegemonic police discourse; it says nothing of the good faith of those individuals working within its boundaries. The ideologies of police officers that are used to rationalize their own work, their own relationship to the central state, are no more examples of false consciousness than those which explain and excuse the rôle of the state-funded researcher within a national education system. In this sense again the recursive relationship between policing practice and policing discourse is revealed.

One anecdotal example might be cited from the highly dangerous evolution of a "Yardies" problem in London. At one public meeting in 1988 the newly installed Chief Superintendent of Stoke Newington division stated that the Metropolitan Police must not allow press hyperbole to create a dangerous stereotypical image of British Black communities, acknowledging that this had occurred in the mugging moral panics of the 1970s. The significance of the statement and the historical concession may not have been relevant to many present. Nevertheless, aside from a certain sense of irony in seeing the words of Stuart Hall et al. paraphrased by a senior police officer, here was a clear example of the manner in which writing about policing, in time, fashions the rational-

CONTESTATION AND "POWERFUL" RECONSTRUCTIONS?

izations of police work even of those involved in "the job" itself.

The complexity of police interest groups and the public agenda
One final point must be stressed: the attempt to suggest that there is an important relationship between policing and writing about policing, best analyzed in terms of a notion of police discourse. This concerns the diversity of opinions that can be sustained within the one discursive field. There is no attempt here to undervalue the power of the individual name to attract attention in the political arena, nor to understate the significance of individual personalities in history. Those with credentials, position or prestige obviously carry more weight in the nebulous process of agenda building than those who do not.

Michael Banton's work in the 1970s was underwritten by academic "expertise", Commissioners such as Robert Mark and Kenneth Newman have long recognized the value of media access, and a pronouncement by Lord Scarman invariably receives far greater publicity – in a real sense exercises far greater power – than a differing opinion voiced in the editorial columns of "The Job". As Foucault has suggested

Discourse that possesses an author's name is not to be immediately consumed and forgotten, neither is it accorded the momentary attention given to ordinary fleeting words. Rather, its status and its manner of reception are regulated by the culture in which it circulates. (Foucault 1977, *What is an author*: 123)

Moreover, a central theme of this work is that it is extremely misleading to analyze the police either locally or nationally as a single cohesive unit. The reason so many conspiratorial theories of police practice lack plausibility is that they fail to take on board the institutional complexity of the British police. Each group within the wider unit may speak with their own voice, even if they are not all received and heard with the same respect.

Even a very simplistic typology can be divided by hierarchy, function and geography. Each division in such a typology would have many subdivisions. In terms of hierarchy, the *de facto* "officer class", which is produced by Bramshill Police College, has been subject to relatively little research. Often speaking through the columns of periodicals such as *Policing* and *Police Journal*, many who have passed through the Bramshill police graduate entry or the senior command course are frequently seen to hold opinions very different from other middle and senior management, not to mention the very different perspectives and objectives from the police rank and file. Chief Constables, often using the institutional endorsement of ACPO and media notables, former policemen such as John Alderson and John Stalker, for example, also have a real power to command particular attention (Reiner 1990). The

POLICING RECONSTRUCTIONS OF REALITY

regularly aired debates about installing an officer class within the police is no more than an acknowledgement of this. Yet the rank and file also now have the means and the will to enter into this same realm through Police Federation activity (see *Police, The Job*) as Tony Judge (editor of *Police* and former Labour Party councillor) has acknowledged:

> Ironically, many of us who were around in the days when the police was indeed a silent service, recall being criticized by such bodies as the NCCL for not speaking out and giving the public the benefit of police experience! It is the Federation's success as a communicator which has made other pressure groups, and some politicians, reach for their gags. (Tony Judge, *Policing* 1985 1: 308)

Yet this should not obscure the commonalities that unite different interest groups within a definition of policing discourse.

In short, police forces are typical late-twentieth-century bureaucracies standing in a specific relation to the state. Factionalism and patronage inevitably become part of managerial politics, and the multiplication of departmental divisions and subdivisions promotes institutional communication more akin to something out of Kafka than to a Weberian notion of bureaucratic rationalization.[3]

A case in point might be taken from the various well documented efforts, which preoccupied certain senior officers and elements of the Metropolitan Police, to discredit the Scarman Inquiry at various times before, during and after the publication of the final report.[4] The selective release of racially coded, disingenuously constructed crime statistics on "mugging" in 1982, which occurred under the aegis of Assistant Commissioner Gilbert Kelland, was just one example. Yet to suggest that this move represented the united actions of the Metropolitan Police as a whole, and was not contentious inside as well as outside the force, would be misleading. A few years later, in what was widely seen at the time as a public snub of Kenneth Newman's attempt to discourage freemasonry in the Metropolitan Police,

> The Manor of St James's Lodge was founded by Brethren, all of whom had served as police officers in "C" or St James's District of the Metropolitan Police.

One of the original members is listed as W. Bro. Gilbert J. Kelland.

Any analysis of policing actions, particularly at the corporate or institutional level, that does not take on board these personal and departmental complexities, and conflicting interests will inevitably lack plausibility.

To recognize that individuals acting in all integrity may purvey notions and explanations of society that are inadvertently iniquitous and dangerously policy-prescriptive, is not to succumb to the reassuring vision of contemporary society as an essentially benevolent system, it

CONTESTATION AND "POWERFUL" RECONSTRUCTIONS?

is only to recognize the ideological power of particular rationalizations of violent conflict. In this hypothetical world, where Popper meets Pangloss, the legitimate tasks of the bureaucratic arms of the state are restricted to a neat array of "social problems", discretely listed one apart from another.

In this context police discourse can assume the definitive characteristics of technocratic language (mystification), professionalism (over politics) and amnesia. Cast not so much engineers of human souls as plumbers who must make do and mend, the police are one of many institutions holding together a confused and malfunctioning urban society. As Robert Mark's collection of essays was titled in 1977, the problem becomes one of "Policing a perplexed society".

Notes

1. This point has been well made by Jefferson & Grimshaw (1987), when suggesting that all police discourse is structured by the three organizing principles of law, work and democracy, with "the law" the ultimate determining feature. Given that the law in part codifies a particular social order, it is obviously morally, politically and academically desirable as well as feasible to question its legitimacy. However, the notion of a police force operating within a discursive field, structured around the translation of such questioning *regularly* into all operational practice (a moral police force?) is not without alarming aspects. Arbitrary challenges to the rule book are not the tasks usually ascribed to the civil service arm of the state by many from anywhere on the political spectrum.

2. "Police professionalism" is a concept that warrants much more attention than can be paid here. Like many notions that can evoke a powerful rhetorical power, "police professionalism" can be used by a variety of interest groups to further a wide range of interests. Any history of the use of the term in Britain would have to look at the very least at the following purposes this chameleon concept may serve: Robert Mark's "professionalization" of the Metropolitan Police as a means of combatting corruption; the use of "professionalism" as a credentialist strategy in the police wage campaigns of the 1970s; the use of the term as a measure of "expertise" mobilized by senior police and police associations (the Federation, ACPO, the Superintendents' Association) in lobbying and political mobilization; and the cost-cutting drives "to measure" police efficiency in the late 1980s by evaluating standards of good police practice.

3. Similarly, the different priorities of community involvement, CID, special squads, ordinary reliefs and other functional divisions will also be evinced in the process of agenda building. The different perceptions of particular clubs and social centres by drug squad, relief (street patrol) and community involvement/community liaison officers in Stoke Newington would be one example of this, the very different conceptions of Operation Swamp offered to Scarman by uniform and CID officers in 1981 would be another. At times it might be said that the whole game of "agenda building" is a Wittgensteinian nightmare, a "game" that everybody plays but few know the rules. It may be easy to identify people playing the game but it might be misleading to pretend that even within the narrow ideological spectrum of the British media any one group knows exactly what they are doing.

POLICING RECONSTRUCTIONS OF REALITY

4. There is no suggestion here that a highly efficient, co-ordinated campaign was or has been organized to discredit Scarman. Such an assertion would itself be an example of the sort of conspiratorial portrayal of state bureaucracies which it is suggested here is normally not a particularly accurate description of the workings of the bureaucracy itself. It is not that the typical post-industrial bureaucracy is particularly benign, it is just not particularly efficient. Rather, the suggestion is that there were and are assorted groups inside and closely associated with the police who see an interest in using whatever influence available to combat the operational and policy legacies of the Scarman report.

CHAPTER 11

Constructing characters: racialization and criminalization into the 1990s

British, that's me.
I was British in the 1960s
  Because arses needed wiping.
I was British when
  The factories needed maintaining.
I was British again when
  The wars needed fighting.
But I was West Indian Black
  Once the trouble began erupting.
I was British yet again
  When gold medals I was winning.
I was British again
  When the community needed policing.
But I was West Indian Black again
  When the media spoke of the mugging,
  The looting,
  The raping,
  The scapegoating.
        From "Going For The Jugula" by Kendell Smith

There is a shot from the scenes on Broadwater Farm in 1985 of a massive wheeled bin on fire, pushed towards police lines, blazing contents cheered on by masked rebels. It is a powerful image. It is a shot that seems to have been replayed endlessly on news footage and documentary, imitated repeatedly in popular and serious drama. From the opening scenes of *Sammie and Rosie Get Laid* to the climax of the film *For Queen and Country*, the television series *GBH* and the novel *The Satanic Verses*, the riot has become a metaphor for 1980s Britain. But, as with

RACIALIZATION AND CRIMINALIZATION INTO THE 1990s

all such symbols, it is replete with multiple and often contradictory meanings.

The riot is invested with significance and, so endowed, enters into political discourse in a highly symbolic form. The meaning of the symbols are, as always, contested. Official accounts struggle against counter-memories. Nobody triumphs absolutely but some voices are louder than others. Significantly, people and places become known for these events. At its most extreme this process defines a place, for instance *Brixton*, or a group of people exclusively in the language of a moment of rebellion.

It is a process of constructing characters.

Lore and disorder: Subject positions and mobilization

There is a consistent thematic element to the reproduction of racism in Britain seen in the combination and permutation of the variables of race, crime and public order. Waves of moral panic, phases of criminalization, the stark reality of violent conflict – all point to the same end: the entrenched and reinforced subordination of one section of society.

It is possible to see this pattern as the straightforward outcome of an alliance of police and government – the intention of state policy. But this book has tried to argue against the simplicity of conspiratorial models of the massive bureaucracies of late twentieth-century Britain. Political strategy and anti-racist campaigning demand more. The police force will not just disappear, even in the most optimistic of political scenarios. Instead it is suggested here not only that criminalization is the logical outcome of the racialization of British society but also that this process of racial criminalization is in part consonant with the restructuring of the British economy in the past decade, that it lends a legitimacy to the measures of social control this restructuring requires and also that the very reproduction of racial divisions in society is in part a function of this process. The outcome is no less invidious, the reality no less morally obscene, but the processes at work belie easy categorization.

In the 1980s the variables of race, crime and public order did not just interact, they came in part to define each other (Diagram 11.1). Not one of the key variables is an essential concept. They have no core reality. Each of the three constitutive elements of the discourse of *lore and disorder* is decentred, drawing its meaning from a position in relation to other key themes through which society is constituted.

232

LORE AND DISORDER: SUBJECT POSITIONS AND MOBILIZATION

The axis between crime and public order describes the terrain on which police legitimacy is constructed and contested. Public support of police actions depends on minimizing the perception of the police as enforcers of a particular *social order* by the social construction of a consensual interest in *crime fighting*.

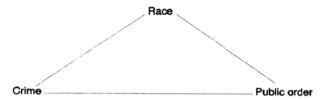

Diagram 11.1 The discursive field of lore and disorder.

The manner in which the police are respected or resented is a historical product of the manufacture of consent. This consent is a historically contingent goal which relies on convincing as many people as possible that they share a common interest in a set of consensually derived *laws*, and that the benefits of social tranquillity outweigh the costs of disruptive challenges to the *status quo*. Hence, in the British case, the particular success of this ideological exercise, coupled with the post-war settlement context of consensus politics, led to what Reiner (1985: 61) has described as the "high point in police legitimation" in the late 1950s.

All three axes describe grounds on which reality and rhetoric intertwine in a process of mutual definition. This is why the historical voice which provides *an authoritative account* is as important as empirical or reflexive evidence. The axis along which police legitimacy is contested provides the raw material for revisionist accounts of British policing (Box 1983, Brogden 1982, Reiner 1985), and is also the axis along which the gamut of police practices, from policing by consent (hegemonic policing?), through proactive, community, reactive, multi-agency, paramilitary and neighbourhood styles, shape the nature of contemporary policing. There is no single definition of *the police task*. Contradictory representations of the police are simultaneously present at different places and times among different communities, and it is both the popular perception of the police (the social construction of *police work*) and the material conditions within which the Force operate that dictates the character of all policing from the mundane and everyday to the violent and politically contentious.

Yet there is little new in suggesting that the contentious and ideologically contested presentation of police work conditions the reality of policing. The suggestion here is that similar relations characterize the relationship between this axis and "race" and are the root of racist criminalization of Black communities in Britain.

Because the constituent elements of this unholy trinity draw their meaning, in part, from each other, they can at times, in context, be substituted one for another. For example the couplet *Black youth* can be employed in racist discourse to signify *criminality*. Similarly, just as the polite conventions of contemporary racism may demand that racist discourse is connoted implicitly by discussion of an agenda of social problems, which sends coded racial messages without mentioning "race" (e.g. the underclass), "crime" and "riot" have become similarly racially loaded. This is not a universal connection; neither all discussion of criminality nor all discussion of civil unrest necessarily connotes racialized meanings, it is instead the case that such subjects have a propensity so to do.

The arenas in which these practices of signification evolve are part and parcel of the material conditions in which they occur. But there are two fields that have played a particular rôle in the reproduction of conflict between police and British Black communities; one is a national context which has threatened to destroy decades of assiduously constructed myths about the necessary nature of policing society; the other is the process of criminalization which has come to so define the very life-chances of a large section of the Black community. They involved, respectively, a naturalization of radically changed public expectations about public order in civil society and the reproduction of a subject position which flexibly defined "Blackness" as constitutively criminal.

Naturalization and the central state context: Thatcherism and authoritarian populism

This is not a book on Thatcherism, but it is a book in which the Thatcher years provided an important backdrop to many of the events and much of the research material. Face to face with the realities of today it is sometimes easy to forget quite how far the ground of common-sense debate and normal assumptions has shifted in the past decade. Whatever the judgement on fourteen years of Conservative rule, it is intended here to suggest only that two features of this changing national context have proved particularly relevant to the evolution of a single discursive field of *lore and disorder*.

The sustained economic depressions of the post-1973 years, coupled with a sense, and possibly a reality, of the growth in civil strife and

NATURALIZATION, THE STATE, AUTHORITARIAN POPULISM

popular dissent, threatened to discredit the consensus politics of the post-war era and to question the legitimacy of the state in the eyes of the British electorate. Yet if the 1970s were the years of CRISIS, the 1980s were to see the SOLUTIONS to this crisis.

Few would question the need for a massive restructuring of a British economy dominated by the anachronisms of a past world. But the methods by which such goals were to be achieved were inevitably more contentious. Whether or not Thatcher's strategy is described as radical modernization, or an attempt to integrate Britain within the new global circuits of capital, the logical implications for society are much the same once it was decided to achieve these changes without any pretence of a resort to consensual decision making. Hence, at the heart of the Conservative manifesto of 1979, and the party's political project of the following decade, was an attempt to redefine the rôle of the state in all its forms from economic intervention to arbitration of personal and collective rights. The aim was to produce what Gamble has described as "The Strong State and the Free Economy".

But if the British economy was to be dismantled and reconstructed in the image of postmodern capitalism somebody had to pay the price. Structurally, locationally and historically some groups were to suffer more than others.

> Within the working class the groups that stood to lose most were women and Blacks and particular regional communities. The costs of restructuring the economy, however, could be loaded much more easily onto such groups if the political credibility of their case for equal rights had first been destroyed. Conversely, if social democratic arguments retained their dominant place in public debate on welfare provision, it would be less easy to ignore the claims of Blacks and women and other disadvantaged groups to assistance and subsidy from the state. (Gamble 1988: 16)

It is at this point that the racialization of British society becomes so significant to the national changes of the past decade. The reorganization of society by Conservative Party fiat would inevitably provoke resistance, and the logical reaction to such resistance involved not only a programme which changed the social ground rules through which such resistance mobilized, but also a denigration of the rhetoric and rationales which motivated such mobilization.

The progressive criminalization of dissent in the Thatcher years, exemplified by a series of legislative measures from restrictions on Trade Union rights through to the Public Order Act of 1986, highlights the manner in which the legal apparatus for the new regime was to be furnished. But more significantly, the experiences of British Black communities provided the ideal testing ground on which such changes were to be justified. This took two forms.

The first was the ideological project, analyzed extensively elsewhere (Gilroy 1987, Hall 1983, 1988, Jessop et al. 1988, Gamble 1988), which questioned the nature of a whole series of social changes in post-war Britain, most obviously, the growth of feminism, a questioning of conventional family, age and gender rôles, and the development of some notions of a multi-racial society which had been achieved in the pre-1978 years through the struggles of respective minority groups, most notably the British Black community.

The threat to the patriarchal family and the White nation that these alternative values embodied coincided with the end of the post-war boom and the discrediting of many of the institutions and policies used to manage social democratic society. The very cohesion of society appeared to be endangered. This was the social corollary of economic crisis and the rhetorical onslaught on such changes – commonly couched either in attacks on permissiveness or nostalgic reference to a Victorian past of dubious provenance – were central elements of "Thatcherism". British Black communities could readily be used as symbols of this vilified recent past, held up pejoratively in racist discourse as the quintessential product of the permissive society, a society in need of moral reconstitution.

So a new identity, a new national pride was to be forged. There was nothing particularly novel in the manipulation of nationalism to bond society. As Hobsbawm has written about the nineteenth century,

nationalism became a substitute for social cohesion through a national church, a royal family or other cohesive traditions, or collective group self-presentations, a new secular religion, and that the class which required such a mode of cohesion most was the growing new middle class, or rather that large intermediate mass which so signally lacked other forms of cohesion. (Hobsbawm 1983: 303)

Again, there is not space here to detail in more than a brief, incomplete list the frequent resort to nationalist rhetoric and sentiment which have characterized the past decade and more, from the resuscitation of immigration as a political issue in the 1979 election campaign, through relations with the EEC, the Falklands War, the Nationality Act, and the Rushdie affair. The distinctive facet of British nationalism in the 1980s was that it conveniently excluded British Black communities from these newly invented traditions (Gilroy 1987), just as the reassertion of *family values* implicitly denigrated the equal citizenship rights of women, young people and gays.

However, more significantly for this work, was the almost fortuitous incidence of civil disorder with which the decade opened. The

NATURALIZATION, THE STATE, AUTHORITARIAN POPULISM

mystification of the relationship between race and crime (see Chs 1 and 10) rendered possible the transformation of civil disorder into a *natural* social problem, demanding solutions couched in the vocabulary of social control. This process of *naturalization* (turning history into nature) suggested that if scenes of violent unrest were a necessary characteristic of contemporary society it was, after all, only natural that preventive measures should be taken.

The "nature" of authoritarian populism

The clarity of hindsight sometimes suggests an inevitable logic to this process that is misleading. That there was a logic underscoring the drift towards popular authoritarianism does not detract from the extemporized nature of the Thatcherite political strategy. In this sense, Stuart Hall's (1988) diagnostic analysis of Thatcherism as an incomplete ideological project does not necessarily imply a coherent strategy thought through from its inception.

Social change is more random. Random developments occur which lend themselves to particular forms of manipulation. The crisis of legitimacy and economic restructuring lent themselves to a form of new authoritarianism in 1970s Britain, and it was New Commonwealth migrants and their children who provided an important medium through which this logic was extended into an invidious process of systematic criminalization. The historical groundwork of racist (criminal) stereotyping, dating back many decades, coincided with a shift away from liberal consensus nationally and a need to *explain,* or at least rationalize, the early 1970s crisis in police/Black relations. A specific conjunction of issues provided the raw material for a more general drift of history.

The conjunction here between state racism and state authoritarianism is important. There is no necessary suggestion that the increasing intolerance of dissent by the central state implies a nostalgic reference either to a period of racial equity before 1979, or to an era in society when police legitimacy was not contested (cf. Cambridge 1978, Gilroy & Sim 1985, Gordon 1983). It is rather that the post-1979 restructuring of British society demanded both the suppression of dissent from the victims of this change – a wide cross section of society – and *the enemies within* who could serve to legitimate necessary changes in patterns of social control. Although Black people were just one fraction of the former, they provided the exemplary *objects* to fulfil the rôles of the latter.

RACIALIZATION AND CRIMINALIZATION INTO THE 1990s

It is in this context that public reactions to major clashes in the coalfields and the Wapping Printworks in the 1980s, the much more common occurrence of rioting in the late 1980s and early 1990s up and down the country, and the incidence of civil unrest surrounding the introduction of the poll tax, have to be understood. The quite different struggles of Black communities, and the consequent uprisings, had already radically changed what was understood as "normal" social order, as well as the police force's ability to deal with such unrest.

The poll tax riots were exceptional, as much for *where* they took place – in the heart of the public spaces of civil society, outside Town Halls and even in Trafalgar Square (the historically symbolic centre of the capital) (Vogler 1991). Yet, unlike the events of 1981, later incidents of violent unrest are notable for prompting relatively minor state reaction. By 1992 rioting was seen as so unexceptional that it featured barely at all on the agenda of that year's General Election. The specificity of particular disputes could readily be lost in the dangerous conflation of very different issues within the rubric of "public-order problems", a blurring category that analytically was as much about football hooliganism as about mass protest.

Superficially, this process of naturalization of civil unrest might appear to run counter to the second concern of this chapter, the manner in which both criminality and rioting can invoke or even define notions of "Blackness". Certainly by the early 1990s "the riot" was not identified exclusively with Black communities alone. But the argument of the chapter is that it is not just demographic sections of society that are being described in the discourse of lore and disorder, it is instead an imagined subject position of "Blackness" which is invented within it; an invention that retains its political power and has to be understood within the history of the racialization of British society.

Racialization

Social divisions which appear self evident or neutral are frequently inseparable from normative judgements. Demographic divisions of sex and age are commonly value loaded with tacit assumptions about gender rôles and rites of passage. Similarly, with the notion of "race" little is quite as it appears on the surface. The concept of "race" assumes different meanings in different contexts. It is imperative to question how debates about civil order and crime produce and draw on particular coinages of this concept before accepting a straightforward correspondence between the term itself and some taken for granted

CRIMINALIZATION, RACIAL FORMATION AND MOBILIZATION

empirical reality.

"Race" is not an essential characteristic. The pervasive practices of racism, however, and the evolution of racial formations over time and space (Omi & Winant 1986), guarantee some correspondence in the harsh reality of the day-to-day world between the ideological fictions of racial divisions between people and the empirical circumscription of specific groups in society. The generation of racial divisions in society is most easily grasped by use of the notion of racialization, which stresses both the reality of the group formation process as well as the social construction of the differences between the racial collective identities so formed. The process of racialization is also of particular significance because it is one of the principal means through which subordination is produced and reproduced in an unjust society.

Action and reaction:
criminalization, racial formations and racial mobilization

The sheer scale of criminalization of Afro-Caribbean people in Britain is hard to exaggerate (Herbert & Omambala 1990). A Home Office report in 1989 highlighted the stark figure that, between 1984 and 1985, there were 521 prosecutions for indictable offences per 1,000 of the young (aged 17–20) Afro-Caribbean male population in the Metropolitan Police District - that is, over half of the age cohort.

If it were not for the proportion of those involved, this pattern, although an indictment of British *justice*, might not be surprising. After all, there is a long tradition in Britain of certain communities being scapegoated by the criminal justice system. But with British Black communities this scale is now without precedent, so much so that it is suggested here that whereas the Criminal Justice System was once an arena in which migrant communities came face to face with British injustice, it now provides one of the racializing institutions by which "racial difference" is reproduced.

The second half of this chapter attempts to put this case by advancing four connected propositions. The first is to suggest that the history of relations between British Black people and the police must be set against a theoretical analysis of criminalization. The second is to suggest that this process of criminalization must in turn be placed in the context of the racializing discourses that circumscribe British Black communities. The third is to suggest that the process of criminalization itself now constitutes a significant racializing discourse. Through racist constructions of criminality the Criminal Justice System has become a locus of racialization, manufacturing a criminalized classification of "race" which co-exists with alternative, often contradictory, invocations of "race" that derive from other racializing discourses. Finally, I want to propose that it is possible for so many contradictory constructions of "race" to co-exist because of the deployment of social relations as products in time and space.

The term "Black" has been used in a consciously ambiguous manner throughout this text. It does not, in any straightforward sense refer to a specific demographic fraction of society. Although it has been used here principally, but not exclusively, to refer to the experiences of people of Afro-Caribbean ethnicity, it is a term that draws its meaning instead from the context in which it is used. In short it is a category that is discursively constructed.

The discursive field with which this chapter is concerned links together the themes of criminality, policing and race. This discursive field thus connotes its own construction of race. It is a construction which is racist in the most invidious sense of the term and cannot be equated with any natural social divisions of society or rendered equivalent to any single (old or new) articulation of ethnicity. It can and does connote a racist and sexist *definition* of the meaning of Blackness. It is for this reason that it is important to differentiate between the notion of criminalization advanced here and standard labelling theory. In standard labelling theory a demographic fraction of society is picked out and victimized. Here it is not so straightforward. A construction of criminality which draws on the glossary of racial difference is applied to define the varying subject positions of Black communities at particular times and places.

(a) Racialization . . . multiple processes of racialization

Within a framework that broadly accepts his critique of "race relations sociology" (1982, 1984a), I want to take as a starting point Miles's axiom that the

> process of social (i.e. ideological) construction, of attributing meaning to particular patterns of phenotypical variation, must always be explained rather than assumed to be unproblematic.
> (Miles 1984b)

In short "race" cannot be taken for granted. Yet, at times, this fundamental can lead analysis to the point at which it is the ontological status of "race" which, explicitly or implicitly, becomes "a problem". Even within various currents of modern Marxian analysis of "race" (Hall 1980a, Miles 1982, 1984, 1988, Solomos 1988, Green & Carter 1987) the analytical problem has generally been that some empirical phenomenon exists, whether as natural social grouping, racialized class fraction

CRIMINALIZATION, RACIAL FORMATION AND MOBILIZATION

or outcome of racist constructions of social identity. Consequently, with the theoretical imperative to explain this phenomenon, there is a theoretical prerequisite to classify the ontological status of the phenomenon. In this sense, within a broadly critical perspective, it is now considered normal to trace patterns of racialization in history (e.g. Carter et al. 1987, Sherwood 1984, Miles 1984b)[1]

I want to suggest here that to periodize processes of racialization is not always enough. To understand how it is possible for several, often contradictory, constructions of "race" to permeate society simultaneously, it is necessary to tie the evolution of racial formations to particular places as well as particular times. The advantage of such an approach is that the ontological status of the concept of "race", which has so bedevilled critical analysis, is resolved by acknowledging that "race" exists, has causal powers, and epistemological validity, but is not necessarily reified.

Throughout this chapter it is stressed that constructions of race are the outcome of this array of different processes of racialization. At any one time a plurality of processes of racialization may co-exist. In part, the multiplicity of racisms cited by Hall (1980a) can be equated with an array of connected but distinct processes of racialization. The racism which mediated the insertion of migrant labour into the political economy of post-war Western Europe differs from the racism associated with the racial divisions of labour of post-Fordism, which is not quite the same as the racism of the authoritarian state, which is not quite the same as the racist politics of nationalism. Yet all are empirically realized as processes of racialization.

Several of these processes relate to the shared experiences of migrant minorities – expressions of ethnicity, collective struggles around community and processes of collective consumption, mobilizations of racial solidarity – common experiences of British racism. As has been suggested, race effectively gains ontological status by its positioning at the intersection of all these discursive fields. Abstracted, race assumes a reality that is the sum of these racializing discourses. The different but inseparable processes of racialization which relate to the common cause and common Black experience in Britain are consciously not addressed here. All social groups, or collective social identities, including the British Black community, have flexible parameters defined by various forces external and internal to the collective. In this sense the boundaries of a racial formation are stalked both by racism and solidarity. Hence, the emphasis on the production and reproduction of racism in this chapter is not intended in any way to diminish the significance of the forces of mobilization in racial formation (Gilroy 1987), or the salience of new ethnicities (Hall 1988) and identity politics

241

RACIALIZATION AND CRIMINALIZATION INTO THE 1990s

in the overall determination of race in economy and society, only to acknowledge that this chapter is centrally concerned with only one discursive field of racialization, that of the criminal justice system.

A plurality of identities is the logical result of the creation of subjects set in discursive formations. This is the power of Laclau & Mouffe's statement that

all identity is relational.... It is not the poverty of signifieds but, on the contrary, polysemy that disarticulates a discursive structure. That is what establishes the overdetermined, symbolic dimension of every social identity. (Laclau & Mouffe 1985: 113)

What is crucial to an understanding of a decentred conceptualization of race is that a multiplicity of end products of racialization may be simultaneously present. The term "race" takes a specific meaning when multiple, frequently contradictory, discursive attempts to define a racial identity are stopped in a moment of closure.

The process of racialization is of particular significance because it is one of the principal media through which subordination is produced and reproduced in an unjust society. Criminalization of Black people in Britain is only one of several processes of racialization

(b) Punishment . . .

There is little purpose here in once again specifying in detail the obscene treatment of migrant minorities by the British Criminal Justice System throughout history, or the overt and wholesale racist nature of this same experience for British Black communities over the past 30 years. In every single part of the system there is well documented evidence of the racism of British society incorporated into the arenas of some of its most powerful institutions.

The broad contours of the historical processes of criminalization of migrant minorities are now relatively uncontroversial, whether the group concerned is the Irish at the turn of the century, Maltese and Cypriots in the 1930s and 1940s, or the British Black community over the past 30 and more years. Racist stereotypes of racial difference feed into public knowledge and policing practice. A conflict with the reality of "unjust" policing echoes through the "due process of the law" into courts and penal institutions, and reinforces the portrayal of migrant groups as involved in particular forms of criminal activity and legitimates particular repressive policing strategies targeted on these communities. The potential for the perpetuation of this pattern is exacerbated by the institutionalization of stereotypes in the fabric of the agencies of social reproduction.

Therefore, criminalization is a process that is tied to production relations as well as to consumption relations; empirically tied to the

CRIMINALIZATION, RACIAL FORMATION AND MOBILIZATION

institutional racism of housing, education and social services as well as to the major institutions of the Criminal Justice System such as the police, the courts, the prison service and the probation service. Constructions of criminality are linked to racially circumscribed processes of criminalization.

Yet at the heart of most analyses of criminalization a group is picked out of society and victimized, an analytical tradition which consciously echoes and expands the theories of labelling and social deviancy (e.g. Becker 1971 & Goffman 1963). In the seminal work on the social construction of Black criminality in Britain, Stuart Hall and his associates (1978), when deconstructing the ghetto, regularly resort to the metaphor of the "Black colony" as both victim of these racist practices of criminalization and (apparently) social reality (*Policing the Crisis*, Ch. 10). Yet there is an imaginative uncertainty at the heart of their work. The ghetto is sometimes a stage, sometimes a metaphor for the Black experience, and sometimes a metonym for racist practice. The authors point out the way in which racist classification of mugging can be connoted by place, by highlighting Black areas of settlement. A case in which a White youth assaults a Black bus conductor can still reproduce the racialized imagery of mugging because, "The specification of certain venues reactivates earlier and subsequent associations: Brixton and Clapham" (Hall et al. 1978: 329). Crime, race and the ghetto could be conflated as social problems after incidents such as the Brockwell Park clashes because they "located and situated Black crime, geographically and ethnically, as peculiar to Black youth in the inner-city ghettos" (Hall et al. 1978: 329).

The slippage between race and crime is here seen to work both ways; each may connote the other. It was in taking up many of the themes of *Policing the Crisis* that Hall developed the notion of authoritarian populism in his landmark Cobden Lecture of 1979, which outlines a political project that uses the "forging of a disciplinary common sense" (1980b: 3) to undermine welfare rights, notions of citizenship, and the freedoms of organized labour. At its formative stages Hall's analysis takes as its driving force the realization of urban crisis (1980b: 13) with "the use of police powers to contain and constrain, and in effect to help to criminalize, parts of the Black population in our urban colonies" (1980b: 3) defining the Black community again as the victim of these changes.

There is obviously a danger that a perception of Margaret Thatcher as the personification of injustice will obscure the continuities of racial injustice in British society. Paul Gilroy (Gilroy & Sim 1985, Gilroy 1987) has questioned the notion of "a drift" into a law-and-order society, preferring to explain criminalization more in terms of continuities

RACIALIZATION AND CRIMINALIZATION INTO THE 1990s

within the construction of nationalism. In broad terms, if not in detail, this approach squares more with a general historical invention of tradition within the imagined community of the nation state (cf. Hobsbawm 1983, Anderson 1983) and which ties in with Benedict Anderson's concept of *imagined communities* (Anderson 1983) which, contrary to Anderson's own argument, manipulates racist ideology as an exclusionary mechanism.

The ability of law and the ideology of legality to express and represent the nation state and national unity precedes the identification of racially distinct crimes and criminals. (Gilroy 1987: 74)

Black law breaking supplies the historic proof that Blacks are incompatible with the standards of decency and civilization which the nation requires of its citizenry. (Gilroy 1982b: 215)

It is precisely this unified national culture articulated around the theme of legality and constitution which Black criminality is alleged to violate, thus jeopardizing both state and civilization. (Gilroy 1987: 76)

At this stage it is not necessary to arbitrate between the different emphases of Hall and Gilroy here. The point is more simple. Both analyses contain a tension which is not clearly resolved between the empirical reality of racial groupings who are victimized by racist processes of marginalization/criminalization and the invention of cultural significations of race as criminality. The tension is not so much a flaw of the analyses as the point at which the processes of criminalization and racialization become one.

Random developments occur which lend themselves to particular forms of manipulation. The crises of legitimacy and economic restructuring lent themselves to a form of new authoritarianism, whether rhetorical or real, in 1970s Britain. New Commonwealth migrants and their children provided an important medium through which this logic was extended into an invidious process of systematic criminalization. The historical groundwork of racist (criminal) stereotyping coincided with a shift away from liberal consensus nationally and a need to explain, or at least rationalize, the early 1970s crisis in police/Black relations. A specific conjunction of issues provided the raw material for a more general drift of history.

(c) Discipline . . .

It is not easy to specify a particular historical watershed in the encounters between Black people and the British Criminal Justice System but I want to suggest that a change in the nature of these encounters has become increasingly distinguishable over time. Heuristically, if not literally, it might be possible to conceptualize this

CRIMINALIZATION, RACIAL FORMATION AND MOBILIZATION

change in the following terms. Whereas once migrant communities were the object of racism in the criminal justice system, today's Black communities are in part a subject created by the racializing discourse of criminalization. There is, of course, no suggestion that this subject exhausts the empirical description of a British Black community,

A criminalized subject category, "Blackness", is one racist construction of the British Criminal Justice System. Yet this subject position, an imagined racial identity, does not refer exclusively and immutably to any empirically defined section of the population. It is an invidiously powerful categorization that connotes an imagery of "Black criminality", which achieves empirical realization in particular times and at specific places.

Certainly, the folk devils of the mugging panic in *Policing the Crisis* were the creations of racist discourses. Yet the initiation of the Urban Programme in 1968 can be traced further back, at least to folk images of civil disorder linked not only to Powell's "Rivers of Blood" speech but also to particular common-sense understandings of the American urban crisis in the 1960s.

The relationship, never one way, is rarely predetermined. At a micro-level such constructions are the outcome of day-to-day interactions and mobilization, exemplified both by the sorts of real social movements of resistance witnessed on Front Lines" in the 1980s and by the manner in which these movements are reconstructed and represented as conventional rhetoric in the sort of discourses of common sense discussed in Chapter 10.

Through time and over space the dominant themes in racializing discourses fluctuate and contradict each other. The precise nature of "Blackness" that is connoted evolves. In Britain, at a crude level, the succession of racist images of (gender specific) Afro-Caribbean criminality have followed on from the pimp of the 1950s, to the Black power activist of the 1960s, to the mugger of the 1970s, to the rioter of the 1980s and, quite possibly, to the ultimate folk devil, the underworld "Yardie" of the 1990s.

At another level, the existence of a degree of gang violence in all youth cultures across Britain is undisputable. But a phenomenon of more recent times has been deployment of the tropes of Black criminality in the simplistic portrayals of the violent subcultures of both Punjabi youth in Southall, West London and Bengalis in the East End. In spite of the more dominant racialized imagery of reputed "Asian" entrepreneurial skills, a medium of localized criminalization opens up the potential for particular localized forms of (racial) criminalization, drawing on the structures of sensibility established by the discursive field of lore and disorder.

245

RACIALIZATION AND CRIMINALIZATION INTO THE 1990s

The central point about this process of criminalization is that it may run concurrently with more sophisticated political projects which relate to the ostensibly contradictory nature of policies of "economic regeneration", accompanied by the ideological construction of "ethnic" entrepreneurial skills. In the eyes of the White majority it is now, and may continue to be, quite acceptable for crudely racist constructions of Black criminality to co-exist alongside a social reality of young upwardly mobile Black professionals, a Buppefied minority; indeed the existence of the latter lends a legitimation to the former.

"Race" is constructed as a facet of criminality through the institutionally racist channels of White society. Criminalization must be conceptualized with reference to *both* social practices and the accounts given publicly and privately to make sense of these practices, with reference to both the more obvious rôles of police and other elements of the criminal justice system, and to a whole series of normalizing institutions from educational provision to welfare service delivery. And of course the restructuring of British society in the 1980s has radically altered the social context in which such organizations operate. It is now unexceptionable to acknowledge the routine nature of regulation of populations that is embossed on all of these institutions from the discipline of the classroom to the surveillance of the welfare state. But significantly, in an era rhetorically committed to deregulation in all spheres, a contradictory outcome of social policy has been the ever increasing demands placed on explicit and implicit institutions of social control (Gamble 1988).

It is against this context that common-sense understandings of criminality, civil disorder and race are inextricably interconnected. *Analysis* of any single element of this trinity commonly conjures up overt or latent images of these connections. This was a central theme of Part Two of this work, the *public* and *private* lives of disorder. Consequently, with social constructions and representations of violent uprisings, there are at least two processes of racialization going on at the same time, which appear complementary but may be nothing of the sort. The signification of *riot* in terms of a racist construction of the social problem group "Black Youth" may come to permeate common sense through the combined influences of political, media and academic discourse. The configuration of White dominated institutions, particularly the Criminal Justice System, may appropriate this common sense as a central organizing theme in their imaginative representations of muti-racial Britain, setting up one process of racialization. Indeed it is suggested here that the rôle of the Criminal Justice System, in particular, over the past 30 years has been so profoundly significant that a class of subject positions has been created by its influence. A *de facto*

CRIMINALIZATION, RACIAL FORMATION AND MOBILIZATION

racist partitioning of legal rights in the courts, the prisons, the offices of lawyers and barristers and the probation service reflects this.

Yet simultaneously another process operates which derives from the forms of mobilization that emerge from the crucible of violent conflict, derived from the manner in which uprisings are signified positively as acts of popular resistance. It is these movements that set up the counter-memories which claim rebellion as part of an alternative history of resistance, which places scenes of uprising on municipal murals and personal recollections. Signified positively, the 1980s riots are claimed as part of British Black experience. So, when the early 1990s witnessed disorder in predominantly White estates, it was not insignificant that the cultural forms of expression adopted by the young on the estates of Meadowell in the North-East drew on Afro-Caribbean musical forms to celebrate insurrection. This chapter is not about such movements, but this does not imply that they are not at least as significant an outcome of the events of the 1980s as the various responses of the White establishment.

The potential racial formations emerging from disorder are complex. It is not just that, as the misleading notion of "the average rioter" discussed in Chapter 5 suggests, civil disorder was not the historical property of, even an empirically defined notion of, Black Youth, although this is important. In the 1970s the *articulating principle* through which dominant society understood the rich diversity of British Afro-Caribbean communities was through the tainted debates around this imaginary Black Youth (Solomos 1988), and in the 1980s this principle became increasingly focused around rioting. More significantly, the manner in which disorders are taken as expressions of Black solidarity in the face of oppression sets up multiple agendas of political and social strategy and mobilization. Violent conflict is again the medium through which racialization occurs, but the racial formations which emerge are more than likely to contradict notions of "race" established in other arenas, not least in the discursive construction of "Black Youth" itself.

At a simple symbolic level British Black communities are, for White society, associated with racist stereotypical notions of law and disorder, powerfully connoted by the images of burning buildings and angry crowds so frequently seen on the screens of British television sets in the 1980s.

Yet just as the invidious stereotypical force of such imagery is manifest, the painful reality of those clashes is undeniable.

Similarly, it is impossible to conceive of an objective empirical reality of "Black crime" which can be investigated by social research. This is because criminality, a chameleon concept defined by the histories of legal whim and political fashion, is at once both social reality and

RACIALIZATION AND CRIMINALIZATION INTO THE 1990s

emotive myth. Clearly, demographically concentrated both in social areas and economic classes structured by material deprivation, it is no surprise to find individuals from migrant minority backgrounds committing individual crimes. But this does not mean that "Black crime" can be reified, subjected to scrutiny as a subject category in its own right, without reference to the broader social, political and moral context in which such scrutiny occurs.

It is precisely this disingenuous divorce of the statistical from the empirical that periodically emerges under occasional calls for hard evidence of the extent of Black involvement in crime. So it was unsurprising to see the *Evening Standard* on 4 June 1990 touting a story on "How 60 Muggers Hold Us to ransom", reporting that some police research had suggested that violent theft was caused in the main by a very small minority. In spite of the police deliberately refraining from playing the race card, the *Standard* comments that "Commander Stevens was at pains to play down *the fact* that the majority of muggers in the area were Black" (my emphasis), following this up with a comment that barely hides its racialized agenda; "the typical mugger is not a poor youth. He wears £100 tracksuits, the latest trainers and is streetwise and style conscious". The identikit rioter, the alienated criminal, the designer mugger; there is no need to say *they* are Black because *we* already know it.

As the Home Office statistics on the relations between young Black people and the criminal justice system already alluded to demonstrate, there is something much more significant going on than putative disproportionate involvement in criminal activity. Lives are structured by a notion of Black criminality.

In short, the rôle of the criminal justice system in the reproduction of a racialized society has changed. Where once the criminal justice system was an arena in which migrant minorities came face to face with the racist injustices of White society, the system itself has now assumed a determining rôle in constructing particular racial groups. These processes must also be set against the dramatic material and social restructuring of British cities that has accompanied the Thatcher years.

(d) Space mediating racialization

As several authors have suggested (Hall et al. 1978, CCCS 1982, Gilroy 1987) there is nothing particularly new in linking the construction of racist notions of Black criminality with the massive restructuring of society that followed the economic crisis of the 1970s. In broad terms the creation of a criminalized racial formation accentuated the ideological scope of authoritarian populism (Hall 1980b), lent a spurious legitimacy to social control innovations (CCCS 1982, Bridges 1982), and

CRIMINALIZATION, RACIAL FORMATION AND MOBILIZATION

provided raw material for the racist projects of the New Right (Gilroy 1987).

But this restructuring demanded the spatialization of such changes, a new city radically transformed from the economic contours of the era of post-war settlement and labour shortage. And it was a city that also demanded more than the control of labour surplus in the era of 3–4 million unemployed (Keith 1993, Keith & Cross 1993).

The urban crisis of the 1960s and 1970s rapidly acquired the status of political reality, even if the concept often masked more about social change than it revealed. A great many issues were subsumed in and connoted by the evolution of the inner city as a social problem in the 1970s and not all of them can be addressed here. However, rooted among the images of the decaying metropolis was a series of debates that drew on a picture of late twentieth-century urbanism which recalled the Hobbesian nightmare of life as "solitary, poor, nasty, brutish and short." Obviously this provided the raw material for the political rhetoric of the law-and-order lobby. Implicitly, what was needed was the "safe city"; Oscar Newman was to provide everyone's salvation by designing "defensible space". In the UK by the end of the decade the then minister of state at the Home Office, John Patten, decided to play heir to Baron Haussman, who so dramatically reshaped the urban fabric of Paris, backed by the full resources of Home Office Crime Prevention and the newly created "Safer Cities" programme.

There were both obvious and less obvious ramifications for such political projects. Race could be used systematically to conjure up the urban crisis. Neighbourhood watch and active citizens, along with fear of crime based on the public knowledge generated by the ever reliable tabloid press, all quite clearly invoked arenas in which the reproduction and legitimation of racist images of Black criminality could flourish (Christian 1983).

Less apparent, but equally significant, were the overarching trends which are still influential in shaping the overall form of the city. The call for safe streets, which has surfaced on both sides of the Atlantic in the movement for Crime Protection through Environmental Design, involves a conception of social control which is complete in embracing both formal and informal structures of surveillance. The focus on "defensible space" and secure "urban fortresses" invokes the one just as the stress on the informal structures of socialization and the alleged breakdown of community responsibility and involvement invoke the other (Cohen 1985: 214). The community itself has become the site of models of social control, most crudely witnessed in the UK in the liberal prose of high-profile police officers such as John Alderson and Kenneth Newman.

RACIALIZATION AND CRIMINALIZATION INTO THE 1990s

Of course this ties in with many of Foucault's examinations of the nature of what he describes as carceral cities. As Cohen puts it

For Foucault, the city was not a place for other metaphors, but was to provide a powerful spatial metaphor itself. Here could be observed the new dispersed discourse of power actually spreading itself out, passing though finer and finer channels. He continually uses the spatial metaphors of "geopolitics" to describe the dispersal of discipline: city, archipelago, maps, streets, topology, vectors, landscapes. (Cohen 1985: 210)

This project of reshaping the city for the postmodern relations of social control also needed legitimation. The manipulation of "fear of crime" as a legitimate social problem throughout the 1980s has obviously provided one source for such projects. But there is also the demand for the ready made folk-devil and here there was already a dreadful metaphoric continuity. In a work that barely touches on issues of race and racism Cohen inadvertently goes on to sum up the appeal of demands for a safer city as emotively tied to

the dreadful realization that while the medieval fortress town has been a place of safe retreat against the external enemy, the enemy was now within the gates. (1985: 211)

Full circle. The enemy within. In multi-racial, multi-racist British cities the connotations of race too readily transferred the notion of Black youth as this self same "enemy within".

There is no space here to detail the sort of analysis that is required in understanding the racialized landscape of the contemporary city. It is now a commonplace to periodize the manner in which race becomes significant, to trace the way in which the articulating principle of racialization has changed from the naked colonialism of the "coloured migrant" of the post-war years to a much more subtle set of racisms with associated racial formations. Likewise, whereas the popular mobilizations once emphasized the strength of a Black unity that corresponded to the monolith of the colonial legacy, the distinctive experiences of different migrant minorities has more recently prompted a stress on the *new ethnicities* so developed, united by difference within a post-colonial context of such a plurality of racisms.

All these developments have their spatial referents. There is space here only to point to the sort of analysis that is required. I can only suggest that such mapping is a direct equivalent of the periodizing of processes of racialization which is now considered so essential (Harris 1987, Carter, Harris & Joshi 1987). The street, the tower block and the council estate are just three examples of how the socially constructed sites of social relations are loaded with barely hidden racial codes.

In part such spatialization represents the differential focus of the

CRIMINALIZATION, RACIAL FORMATION AND MOBILIZATION

process of racialization, what Gilroy (1987: 230) suggested was the displacing of "race" and "class" by the language of "community". But it is also about the manner in which space provides one of the principal means by which competing constructions of "racialized identities" can co-exist simultaneously. Although the two can never be completely separated, such racialized identities are created both by collective action and by the inventions of racist discourse. The discursive field of lore and disorder is just one example of the latter; racialization and criminalization are conflated in a set of rationalizations and practices that are articulated at specific times and particular places.

Criminalization may create subject positions but it does not create real people. The struggles of community provide only one very important set of sites of racialization. For there are other forces shaping the social form of the contemporary city. As Cooke has remarked, current labour process changes suggest high levels of labour market segmentation;

> the sociological profile of the postmodern era, the development of an hourglass shape to the social structure with a burgeoning service class, an attenuating working class and a burgeoning underclass of unemployed, subemployed and the "waged poor" of part time and/or casualized labour, classically found in fast food outlets and service stations. (Cooke 1988: 485)

The highly contingent fault lines along which urban society divides to provide this sort of division of labour in the postmodern city, are precisely the places at which a sophisticated theorization of racial formation is required in an urban political economy

The liberal common-sense image is one of the ghetto and the underclass, the privileged and the dispossessed, the free riders of postmodern capitalism controlling the total exclusion of the truly disadvantaged. Such notions frequently contain a straightforward understanding of ethnicity as a defensive cultural reaction to the forces of change (Keith 1993). Here I am trying to work towards something slightly more subtle; such naked exclusions are mobilized on some occasions but not on others.

The logic of racial exclusion in liberal texts is consonant with certain dystopian visions of the future which invoke a social control rhetoric of suppression. Cohen, in a work generally more subtle, evokes a vision in which

> we arrive at a vision not too far from Orwell's. Middle class thought crime is subject to inclusionary controls; when these fail and the party members present a political threat, then "down the chute". Working-class deviant behaviour is segregated away and contained; if the proles become threatening, they can be "sub-

251

RACIALIZATION AND CRIMINALIZATION INTO THE 1990s

jected" like animals by a few simple rules. (Cohen 1985: 234)

It is here that the realms of social control become so relevant to a conceptualization of racism. For the architecture of models of punitive cities expresses quite clearly the possibilities of forces of exclusion operating *simultaneously* with forces of inclusion, not in opposition to each other but both towards the end of social control in the widest sense of the term.

In the past the insertion of migrant labour at strategic points in the British political economy was facilitated by the creation of a racialized fraction of labour mediated by the force of racism. The apparent long term economic irrationality of such divisions prompted Sivanandan to predict in the mid-1970s that "racism dies that capital may survive" (1976: 367) and today underscores the optimism of some liberal analysis of racial formations (Banham 1988).

But workplace identities and the racial divisions of labour they promote tell only half the story and it is perhaps here that the notion of change implicit in conceptions of the postmodern city are analytically most powerful. This is the era of flexible accumulation and highly demarcated market segmentation. The identities of the workplace are not necessarily those of the community, which are not necessarily those of the family. The new racial divisions can be tied functionally to the related notions of disciplined communities and flexible workplaces. The racism expressed in the imagery of a criminalized underclass co-exists alongside a form of racism, different in form if not in kind, which constructs racial divisions of labour. This is at the root of why a leitmotif of notions of Asian entrepreneurial skills can co-exist alongside a contemporary criminalization of Bengali youth in the East End and young Punjabis in Southall which draws on notions of Blackness constructed by the discourse of *lore and disorder*.

The partial nature of the process of racialization as criminalization may simultaneously allow the evolution of a symbolically more successful racialized fraction which serves publicly to rebuke the immiserated majority, and divest White society of any responsibility for such immiseration.

Into the future?

Just as the inner-city policy of the past 30 years rested on an imagined city which naturalized a whole set of contingent social processes (Keith & Rogers 1990), policies of social control in British cities have stemmed from the naturalization of police Black confrontation and extending this

INTO THE FUTURE?

to an almost universal status. In this sense the processes of racialization have extended beyond the orbit of racialization alone. In the early 1980s "the street" provided both the articulating principle of social control and the naturalization of the "social problem" of rioting in British cities (Keith 1988). This fed into the new policing practices that were seen in the miners strike, the Wapping print workers dispute and other industrial conflict at the time (Fine & Millar 1985, Coulter et al. 1984). The rationalizations of these practices was in part achieved by the manner in which violent conflict came to be seen as a natural aspect of contemporary Britain.

Later in the decade disorder in Brixton and Broadwater Farm followed protests at the shooting and the death respectively of two Black women. Although particular places provided an important backdrop this was not the same sort of spontaneous violence tied to Front Line locales that had characterized 1981 in particular and so many clashes of the 1980s in general. The 1985 uprising in Handsworth, Birmingham was more similar to the events of 1981 in London, perhaps significant given the relative quiet that had prevailed earlier in the decade. In contrast, senior officers in Brixton considered the relative calm on Railton Road an encouraging oasis amidst disaster in 1985. Yet this could also be interpreted slightly differently. For the sort of disorder that was witnessed bore a much closer resemblance to other conscious collective political movements than had any of the events of 1981. The conflict between police and community was yet further inscribed in the definition of the relationship between the two parties, this sort of Black mobilization both at the time and subsequently looked much less like extemporized revolt and bore closer resemblance to political resistance in a grim struggle against the criminal justice system. There is no suggestion that the uprisings in Handsworth, Brixton and Broadwater Farm were conspiratorially planned, only that the nature of mobilization had changed (Broadwater Farm Defence Campaign 1987, Broadwater Farm Residents' Association 1987).

Again it is important to distinguish between the political symbolism of such events and the analytical understanding of why they occurred. The events of 1981 were politically that much more significant than the events of 1985 notwithstanding the escalation in violent disorder that the latter events involved. This was precisely because of the place the 1981 riots assumed in the development of the political landscape of Thatcher's Britain. They were, like the Falklands War and the coal disputes, major crises that appeared to shake the government but in hindsight can be seen to have provided both the need and the justification for a new law-and-order politics of the strong state.

Such subtleties, however, were rarely discussed at the time in state

RACIALIZATION AND CRIMINALIZATION INTO THE 1990s

reaction to the disorders. Instead the "riot" was firmly installed as a realistic policing contingency and the council estate replaced the derelict Front Line ("the street") as the icon of Black insurgency (Richards 1985). In the attempts to map Broadwater Farm by painting the buildings to make them more recognisable from the air, in the contingency modelling of Riot City Public Order training, right up to a Safer Cities Programme in which public order considerations provide rhetorical capital in the bids for regeneration monies (Robins 1992), the estate and the tower block became the natural site for both possible insurrection and a new form of policing (Jefferson 1990).

Following such naturalization of disorder it was perhaps unsurprising that in 1991 and 1992, when many predominantly White estates saw collective violence, that there was relatively little surprise expressed in the press coverage, certainly in comparison with the shocked reactions to the events a decade before. The precedents of rioting in Black communities, regardless of any causal similarities or differences, had conditioned both the British public and the British police to expect disorder.

Again the particular had become universal, not that "riot" was freed of its racialized connotations, but instead, that disorder itself had been naturalized. As was suggested in Chapter 3 the existence in the 1990s of incidents of civil disorder caused by many different factors should not be taken as an excuse to collect the disparate events of poll tax rioting, football hooliganism, and community insurrection under the rubric of a single social problem of disorder.

Likewise, the probable rise in levels of crime across racial distinctions do not detract from the power of discussions of criminality to connote a racialized imagery. It is not that the trinity of race, crime and disorder exhaust a description of each other in the discursive field outlined in this chapter; it is instead the case that they each become a constitutive element of the others. The power of cultural constructions of race, crime and public order to work together was thus seen in public reactions in the UK to the major uprising in Los Angeles in 1992 following the acquittal of the police officers caught on video beating Rodney King. The immediate assumption that a potential contagion effect might spread across the Atlantic mirrored the reactions to the long hot summers of the 1960s, but also emphasized the continuing power of notions of race, criminality and rioting to substitute one for another in a frightening cultural shorthand. This does not mean that they always do so, only that an invocation of one necessarily draws on the vocabulary of the other two.

But there are some lessons of the Rodney King beating and the Los Angeles riot that should not be ignored in Britain. Los Angeles quite clearly demonstrated that there is no simple equivalence between an

INTO THE FUTURE?

absence of rioting and an improvement in public support for the police. The absence in recent years of massive scenes of racialized uprisings in Britain on the scale of the events of 1985, and their possible displacement in public consciousness by other expressions of riot, should in no way be taken as an unproblematic diminution of police/Black antagonism.

Equally significantly it is precisely the connotative power of the King incident that should prompt reflection about the salience of policing issues that speaks across Black diasporic experiences. In this context it is no coincidence that in 1992 Spike Lee should use film footage of such an incident in the 1990s in his film about Malcolm X and the 1960s.

The 1990s have already witnessed an increasing incidence of civil disorder that has transcended any reduction to police/Black confrontation. This should not be taken to suggest either that such confrontations are now of less significance or that other forms of uprising or riot should be considered equivalent. Both left and right wing interpretations of these disparate events have again and again tended to bracket them together unproblematically. If this book has only one message it is that both the individuals who take to the streets, and the police delegated to respond to them, deserve better than this.

Notes

1. In this way, the debates between Miles and the authors connected with the CCCS at various points over the last few years might be seen as much about whether the migrant labour paradigm or the "authoritarian statism" of racial politics constitute the dominant force of racialization in post-war British society as they are about the analytical status of the concept of "race".

APPENDIX

A variable catalogue: lists of "riots" in London in 1981

The following very different catalogues were all offered as lists of the 1981 summer disturbances:

GLC Policing London Report, March 1982, stated that "the situation in Lambeth was far from unique" (p. 5):

Acton, Balham, Battersea, Barnet, Brixton, Camberwell, Chelsea, Chiswick, Dalston, Ealing, Hackney, Paddington, Peckham, Putney, Shepherd's Bush, Southall, Stoke Newington, Streatham, Sydenham, Walthamstow.

Commissioner of the Metropolitan Police (Annual Report for the year 1981):

Wood Green, Lewisham, Woolwich, Hounslow, Tooting, Brixton, Paddington, Fulham, Stoke Newington, Chingford, Peckham, Wembley, Hampstead, Southall, Croydon.

Kettle & Hodges (1982) stated that "there was an orgy of looting, and for a while it seemed that a sort of civil war had broken out" (p. 155):

Brixton, Southall, Woolwich, Balham, Lewisham, Stoke Newington, Fulham, Dalston, Battersea.

Joshua & Wallace (1983) stated that "the incidence of violence in London was too widespread to recount" but cited places where there was "particular" trouble although in fact there was only very minor disorder in the latter two locations (see Ch. 3):

Tooting, Dalston, Fulham, Woolwich.

The Home Office:

Notting Hill, Paddington, Fulham, Hackney, Limehouse, Chingford, Walthamstow, Dagenham, Chigwell, Newham, Brixton, Southwark, Penge, Lewisham, Brent, Bexleyheath, Woolwich, Golders Green, Chiswick, Hounslow, Tooting, Battersea, Acton, Southall, Wood Green, Croydon, Sutton.

BIBLIOGRAPHY

Adams, J. S. 1982. The geography of riots and civil disorders in the 1960s. *Economic Geography* **42**, 221–45.

Albritton, R. B. 1979. Social amelioration through mass insurgency. *American Political Science Quarterly* **73**, 1003–1011.

Alderson, J. 1979. *Policing freedom.* London: MacDonald & Evans.

Alderson, J. 1981. Written evidence submitted to the Scarman Inquiry into the Brixton disorders. Kew: Public Records Office.

Alderson, J. 1984. *Law and disorder.* London: Hamish Hamilton.

Alderson, J. & P. J. Stead (eds) 1973. *The police we deserve.* London: Wolfe.

Anderson, B. 1983. *Imagined communities.* London: Verso.

Anderton, J. 1981. Comments on Moss Side Riots, quoted in *The Times*, 9 July 1981.

Ardrey, R. 1961. *The territorial imperative.* London: Fontana.

Ascoli, D. 1979. *The Queen's Peace: the origins and development of the metropolitan peace.* London: Hamish Hamilton.

Banham, J. 1988. Urban renewal and ethnic minorities; the challenge to the private sector. *New Community* **15**(1), 15–30.

Banton, M. 1955. *The coloured quarter.* London: Jonathan Cape.

Banton, M. 1973. *Police community relations* London: Collins.

Barthes, R. 1967. *Elements of semiology.* London: Cape.

Barthes, R. 1973. *Mythologies.* London: Paladin.

Barthes, R. 1979. *The Eiffel Tower.* New York: Hill & Wang.

Becker, H. 1971. *Outsiders.* New York: Free Press.

Belson, W. A. 1975. *The public and the police: an extended summary of the aims, methods and findings of a three part enquiry into the relations between the london public and the metropolitan police force.* London: Harper & Row.

Benn, M. & K. Worpole 1987. *Death in the city, (deaths in police custody 1970–85)* [inquest]. London: Canary Press.

Benyon, J. (ed.) 1984. *Scarman and after* Oxford: Pergamon.

Benyon, J. 1986. *A tale of failure: race and policing.* CRER Policy Papers in Ethnic Relations 3, University of Warwick.

Benyon, J. & C. Bourn (eds) 1986. *The police, powers, procedures and proprieties.* Oxford: Pergamon.

Benyon, J. & J. Solomos (eds) 1987. *The roots of urban unrest.* Oxford: Pergamon.

Berk, R. 1974. *Collective behaviour.* Dubuque, Iowa: Brown.

Berkowitz, L. 1982. Violence and rule-following behaviour. In *Aggression and violence*, D. Marsh & A. Campbell (eds). Oxford: Basil Blackwell.

Bhavnani, R., J. Cooke, P. Gilroy, S. Hall, H. Ouseley, K. Vaz 1986. *A different reality.* Birmingham: West Midlands Council.

Bibliography

Black Unity and Freedom Party 1985. *Introducing the Black unity and freedom party* (mimeo).

Bloombaum, M. 1968. The conditions underlying race riots. *American Sociological Review* 33, 76–91.

Blumer, H. 1933/1969. In *Readings in collective behaviour*, R. E. Evans (ed). Chicago: Rand McNally.

Boddy, M. & Fudge, C. (eds) 1984. *Local socialism?* Basingstoke: Macmillan.

Box, S. 1983. *Power, crime and mystification.* London: Tavistock.

Bradley, D., N. Walkern, R. Wilkie 1986. *Managing the police: law organisation and democracy.* Brighton: Wheatsheaf.

Brewer, J. D., A. Guelke, E. Moxon-Browne, R. Wilford 1988. *The police, public order and the state.* London: Macmillan.

Bridges, L. & L. Fekete 1985. Victims, the urban jungle and the new racism. *Race and Class* XXXII, 45–62.

Bridges, L. 1983. Policing the urban wasteland. *Race and Class* XXV, 31–48.

Bridges, L. & Gilroy, P. 1982. Striking back: race and crime. *Marxism Today*, June.

Brindley J. M. 1982. Disruptive crowd behaviour – a psychological perspective. *Police Journal* LV, 28–39.

Brixton Domino and Social Club 1981. *Evidence to the Scarman Inquiry.* Kew: Public Records Office.

Brixton Neighbourhood and Community Association 1981. *Submission to Lord Scarman.* Kew: Public Records Office.

Brixton Rastafarian Collective 1981. *Submission to Lord Scarman.* Kew: Public Records Office.

Broadwater Farm Defence Campaign 1987. *The Burnham Report, of international jurists in respect to Broadwater Farm Trials.* London: Broadwater Farm Defence Campaign.

Broadwater Farm Residents Association 1987. *Manifesto Of the Movement for Civil Rights and Justice London.* Broadwater Farm Defence Campaign.

Brogden, M. 1982. *The police, autonomy and consent.* London: Academic Press.

Brogden, M., T. Jefferson, S. Walklate 1988. *Introducing policework.* London: Unwin Hyman.

Brookfield, H. 1971. *Interdependent development.* London: Methuen.

Brown J. & G. Howes (eds) 1975. *The police and the community.* Farnborough, England: Saxon House.

Brown, C. 1984. *Black and white britain: the third psi survey London:* Heinemann.

Brown, J. 1977. *Shades of grey.* Cranfield: Cranfield Institute of Technology.

Bunyan, T. 1976. *The history and practice of the political police in Britain.* London: Friedmann.

Bunyan, T. 1977. *The history and practice of the political police in Britain,* revised edn. London: Quartet.

Bunyan, T. 1981. The police against the people. *Race and Class* XXIII, 153–71.

Burgess, J. 1985. News from nowhere. In *Geography, the media and popular culture,* J. Burgess & J. Gold (eds). London: Croom Helm.

Burnham, M. 1987. *The Burham Report, of international jurists in respect to*

Bibliography

Broadwater Farm Trials.

Butler, A. J. P. (nd). *An examination of the influence of training and work experience on the attitudes and perceptions of police constables*. Mimeo: Bramshill.

Button, J. W. 1978. *Black violence: political impact of the 1960s riots*. New Jersey: Princeton University Press.

Cain, M. 1973. *Society and the policeman's role*. London: Routledge & Kegan Paul.

Cambridge, R. 1978. Criminal procedure and the Black masses in the United Kingdom. *The Black Liberator* 1, 1–5.

Canetti, E. 1962. (1973). *Crowds and power*. Harmondsworth, England: Penguin.

Cansdale, D. 1983. *The development of the community/police consultative group for lambeth*. MSc thesis, Cranfield Institute of Technology.

Caplan, N. J. J. M. Paige 1968. A study of ghetto rioters. *Scientific American* **219**, 15–21.

Card, R. 1987. *Public order, the new law*. London: Butterworth.

Carter, B., C. Harris, S. Joshi 1987. The 1951–55 Conservative Government and the racialisation of Black immigration. *Immigrants and Minorities* **6**, 335–47.

Cashmore, E. & Troyna, B. 1982. *Black youth in crisis*. London: Allen & Unwin.

Centre for Contemporary Cultural Studies 1982a. *The empire strikes back*. London: Hutchinson.

Centre for Contemporary Cultural Studies 1982b. *Making histories studies in history-writing and politics* London: Hutchinson.

Chesshyre, R. 1989. *The force: inside the police*. London: Sidgwick & Jackson.

Christian, L. 1983. *Policing by coercion*. London: Greater London Council.

Clare, J. 1984. Eyewitness in Brixton. See Benyon (1984).

Clutterbuck, R. 1983. *The media and political violence*. London: Macmillan.

Cohen, A. 1980. Drama and politics in the development of a London carnival. *Man* **15**, 65–87.

Cohen, A. 1982. A polytechnic London carnival as a contested cultural performance. *Ethnic and Racial Studies* **5**, 23–41.

Cohen, N. E. (ed.) 1970. *The Los Angeles riots: a socio-psychological survey*. New York: Praeger.

Cohen, P. 1979. Policing the working-class city. In *Capitalism and the rule of law*, B. Fine et al. (eds). London: Hutchinson.

Cohen, S. 1972. *Folk devils and moral panics*. London: Paladin.

Cohen, S. 1985. *Visions of social control*. Cambridge: Polity.

Colman, A. & L. P. Gorman 1982. Conservatism, dogmatism and authoritarianism in British police officers: a comment. *Sociology* **16**, 1–11.

Commission for Racial Equality 1981. *Submission to the Scarman inquiry*. Kew: Public Records Office.

Concern 1981. *Evidence given to the Scarman inquiry*. Kew: Public Records Office.

Connery, R. H. (ed.) 1969. *Urban riots*. New York: Columbia University Press.

Cooke, P. 1988. Modernity, postmodernity and the city. *Theory, Culture and Society* **5**, 475–92.

Cooper, P. 1985. Competing explanations of the 1981 riots. *British Journal of Criminology* **25**, 60–69.

Bibliography

Corrigan, P. 1979. *Schooling the Smash Street kids*. London: Macmillan.

Coulter, J., R. Miller, M. Walker (eds) 1984. *A state of siege, politics and the policing of the coalfields, the miners' strike 1984*. London: Canary Press.

Critchley, T. A. 1978. *A history of the police in England and Wales*. London: Constable.

Cross, M. 1986. *Space and racial equality in British cities*. Unpublished.

Cross, M. & M. Keith (eds) 1993. *Racism, the city and the state*. London: Routledge.

Davies, J. C. (ed.) 1971. *When men revolt and why*. New York: Free Press.

Demuth, C. 1978. *Sus: a report on Section 4 of the Vagrancy Act 1824*. London: Runnymede Trust.

Deutsch, F. 1982. *Street crime in London, 1981*. London: Commission for Racial Equality.

Dollard, J., J. Doob, W. Miller, W. Mowrer, R. Sears 1939. Frustration and aggression. See Davies (1971).

Dorn, N., K. Murji, N. South 1991. *Traffickers: drug markets and law enforcement*. London: Routledge.

Downes, D. 1966/1970. *The delinquent solution*. London: Routledge & Kegan Paul.

Dummett, A. 1973. *A portrait of English racism*. Harmondsworth, England: Penguin.

Eco, U. 1979. *A theory of semiotics*. Bloomington: Indiana University Press.

Eco, U. 1985. *Reflections on The Name of the Rose*. London: Secker & Warburg.

Edelman, M. 1971. *Politics of symbolic action: mass apraisal and quiescence*. Chicago: Markham.

Edelman, M. 1985. Political language and political reality. *Political Studies* **XXIII**(1) 10–19.

Edgar, D. 1988. Festivals of the oppressed. *Race and Class* **XXIX**(4), 61–76.

Egbuna, O. 1978. *Destroy this temple*. London: MacGibbon & Kee.

Feagin, J. R. & H. Hahn 1973. *Ghetto revolts*. New York: Macmillan.

Field, S. 1982. *Urban disorders in Britain and America*. London: HMSO.

Fielding, N. 1988. Competence and culture in the police. *Sociology* **22**(1), 45–65.

Fine, B. & R. Millar (eds) 1985. *Policing the miners strike*. London: Lawrence & Wishart.

Fogelson, R. M. 1969. *Violence as protest*. New York: Doubleday.

Fogelson, R. M. & R. B. Hill 1968. *Who riots? A. study of participation in the 1967 riots*. Washington: US Government Printing Office.

Foucault, M. 1979. *The history of sexuality*. London: Allen Lane.

Foucault, M. 1982. The subject and power. In *Michael Foucault: beyond structuralism and hermeneutics*, R. Dreyfus et al. (eds). Brighton: Harvester Wheatsheaf.

Freud, S. 1922. *Group psychology and the analysis of the ego* London: Hogarth Press.

Freud, S. 1975. *The Pelican Freud Library*. Harmondsworth, England: Penguin.

Friedland 1982. *Power and crisis in the city*. London: Macmillan.

Bibliography

Fryer, P. 1984. *Staying power*. London: Pluto.

Fyfe, N. 1989. Contesting consultation: the local political response to S. 106 Pace in the MPD. In *The geography of crime*, D. T. Herbert & D. Evans (eds), London: Routledge.

Fyfe, N. 1990. *Policing consultation: a political geography of policing*. PhD thesis, University of Cambridge.

Gaffney, J. 1987. *Interpretations of violence: the Handsworth riots of 1985*. CRER Policy Papers 10, University of Warwick.

Gamble, A. 1988. *The free economy and the strong state: the politics of Thatcherism*. London: Macmillan.

Gans, H. 1969. The ghetto rebellions and urban class conflict. See Connery (1969).

Gaskell, G. & R. Benewick (eds) 1987. *The crowd in contemporary Britain*. London: Sage.

Geertz, C. 1973. *The interpretation of cultures*. London: Hutchinson.

Geertz, C. 1982. *Local knowledge*. London: Hutchinson.

Giddens, A. 1979. *Central problems in social theory*. London: Macmillan.

Giddens, A. 1981. *A contemporary critique of historical materialism*. London: Macmillan.

Giddens, A. 1984. *The constitution of society*. Cambridge: Polity.

Giddens, A. 1985. Time–space regionalisation. In *Social relations and spatial structures*, D. Gregory & J. Urry (eds). London: Macmillan.

Gifford, Lord A. [chair] 1986. *The Broadwater Farm inquiry*.

Gifford, Lord A. [chair] 1987. *Broadwater Farm revisited: 2nd report of the independent inquiry into disturbances in October 1985 at the Broadwater Farm estate, Tottenham*.

Gifford, Lord A. & T. Richards 1984. *Political policing in Wales*. Cardiff: Welsh Campaign for Civil and Political Liberties.

Gilroy, P. 1981. You can't fool the youths: race and class formation in the 1980s. *Race and Class* **XXIII**, 112–20.

Gilroy, P. 1982a. Police and thieves. In CCCS *The empire strikes back*. London: Hutchinson.

Gilroy, P. 1982b. The myth of Black criminality. *Socialist Register* 1982, 47–56.

Gilroy, P. 1987. *There ain't no Black in the Union Jack*. London: Hutchinson.

Gilroy, P. & J. Sim 1985. Law, order and the state of the left. *Capital and Class* **25**, 15–21.

GLC Police Committee 1982. *Making the police accountable to the public*. (Report PC. 47). London: Greater London Council.

GLC Police Committee 1983. *Neighbourhood watch: an interim report*. London: Greater London Council.

GLC 1985. *Racial attacks in London*. London: Greater London Council.

Goffman, E. 1959. *The presentation of self in everyday life*. New York: Doubleday.

Goffman, E. 1963. *Stigma*. Harmondsworth, England: Penguin.

Goffman, E. 1971. *Relations in public*. New York: Basic Books.

Goffman, E. 1972. *Interaction ritual*. London: Allen Lane.

Goffman, E. 1981. *Forms of talk*. Oxford: Basil Blackwell.

Bibliography

Gordon, P. 1983. *White law: racism in the police, courts and prisons*. London: Pluto.

Gordon, P. 1985. Police and Black people in Britain: a bibliographic essay. *Sage Race Relations Abstracts* 10, 3–33.

Gough, I. 1982. The crisis of the British welfare state. In *Urban policy under capitalism*, N. Fainstein & S. S. Fainstein (eds). London: Sage.

Graef, R. 1990. *Talking blues: the police in their own words*. London: Fontana.

Graham, H. D. & T. R. Gurr (eds) 1979. *Violence in America*. London: Sage.

Gramsci, A. 1971. *Selections from prison notebooks*. London: Lawrence & Wishart.

Grimshaw, G. & T. Jefferson 1987. *Interpreting policework*. London: Allen & Unwin.

Gurnah, A. 1987. Gatekeepers and caretakers: Swann, Scarman and the social policy of containment. In *Racial inequality in education*, B. Troyna (ed.). London: Tavistock.

Gurr, T. R. 1968. Urban disorder – perspectives from the study of civil strife. In *Riots and rebellion*, L. Masotti & D. Bowen (eds). Los Angeles: Sage.

Gurr, T. R. 1970. *Why men rebel*. New Jersey: Princeton University Press.

Gurr, T. R. 1978. Alternatives to violence in a democratic society. See Graham & Gurr (1979).

Gutzmore, C 1983. Capital, "Black Youth" and crime. *Race and Class* XXV, 13–21.

Gutzmore, C. 1978. Carnival, the state and the Black masses in the United Kingdom. *Black Liberator* 1, 8–27.

Gutzmore, C. 1982. The Notting Hill Carnival. *Marxism Today* (August), 31–3.

Hackney Council for Racial Equality (HCRE) 1983. *Policing in Hackney a record of HCRE's experience – 1978–1982*. London: Hackney Council for Racial Equality.

Hain, P (ed.) 1979. *Policing the police*. London: Calder.

Hain, P., M. Kettle, D. Campbell, J. Rollo (eds) 1980. *Policing the police 2*. London: Calder.

Hall, S. 1979. *Drifting into a law and order society*. London: Cobden Trust.

Hall, S. 1980a. Race, articulation and societies structured in dominance. In *Sociological theories: race and colonialism*, UNESCO (ed.). Paris: UNESCO.

Hall, S. 1980b. Popular democratic versus authoritarian populism. In *Marxism and democracy*, A. Hunt (ed.). London: Lawrence & Wishart.

Hall, S. 1982. The lessons of Lord Scarman. *Critical Social Policy* 2, 66–72.

Hall, S. 1983. The Great Moving Right Show. In *The politics of Thatcherism*, S. Hall & M. Jacques (eds). London: Lawrence & Wishart.

Hall, S. 1988. *A hard road to renewal*. London: Verso.

Hall, S., C. Critcher, T. Jefferson, J. Clarke, B. Roberts 1978. *Policing the crisis*. London: Macmillan.

Hamnett, C 1983. The conditions of England's inner cities on the eve of the 1981 riots. *Area* 15, 7–13.

Harre, R. 1979. *Social being*. Oxford: Basil Blackwell.

Harris, C. 1987. British capitalism, migration and relative surplus population. *Migration* 1, 47–90.

Harris, C. (forthcoming). *No Blacks please, we're British* London: Macmillan.

Harrison, P. 1983. *Inside the inner city*. Harmondsworth, England: Penguin.

Bibliography

Herbert, P. & I. Omambala 1990. *Policing in the 1990s: a Black perspective*. London: Society of Black Lawyers.

Hesse, B., D. K. Rai, C. Bennett, P. McGilchrist 1992. *Beneath the surface: racial harrassment*. Aldershot, England: Avebury.

Hobsbawm E. J. 1983. Mass-producing traditions: Europe, 1870-1914. In *The invention of tradition*, E. J. Hobsbawm & T. Rainger (eds). Cambridge: Cambridge University Press.

Hobsbawn, E. J. 1959. *Primitive rebels*. Manchester: Manchester University Press.

Holdaway, S. (ed.) 1979. *The British police*. London: Edward Arnold.

Holdaway, S. 1979. The reality of police-race relations: towards an effective race relations policy. *New Community* **VI**(3), 258-67.

Holdaway, S. 1983. *Inside the British police*. Oxford: Basil Blackwell.

Holdaway, S. 1987. Themes and isssues in police/race relations policy. *New Community* **XIV**, 142-50.

Home Office Statistical Unit 1982. *Arrests in the 1981 riots*. London: HMSO.

Horowitz, D. 1983. Racial violence in the United States. In *Ethnic pluralism and public policy*, N. Glazer & K. Young (eds). London: Heinemann.

Howe, D. 1981. *From Bobby and Babylon*. London: Race Today Collective.

Hume D. 1748. Of liberty and necessity. In *Fundamental problems in philosophy*, O. Hanfling (ed.; 1978). Oxford: Basil Blackwell.

Humphry, D. 1972. *Police power and Black people* London: Panther.

Hunte, J. 1966. *Nigger hunting in England?* London: Institute of Commonwealth Studies.

Hytner, B. [chair] 1981. *Report of the committee of enquiry into the moss side disturbances*. Manchester: Greater Manchester Council.

Ignatieff, M. 1979. Police and the people; the birth of Mr Peel's blue locusts. *New Society*, 30 August 1979.

Institute of Race Relations 1979. *Police against Black people: evidence submitted to the Royal Commission on criminal procedure by the Institute of Race Relations*. London: Institute of Race Relations.

Institute of Race Relations 1987. *Policing against Black people*. London: Institute of Race Relations.

Jackson, P. 1989. Street life: the politics of Carnival. *Environment and Planning D:* **6**, 248-61.

James, C. L. R. 1981. An accumulation of blunders. *New Society* **3**, December 1981.

James, D. 1979. Police-Black relations: the professional solution. In *The British police*, S. Holdaway (ed.). London: Edward Arnold.

Janowitz, M. 1979. Collective racial violence: a contemporary history. See Graham & Gurr (1979).

Jefferson, T. & R. Grimshaw 1984. *Controlling the constable: accountability in England and Wales*. London: Muller.

Jefferson, T. 1990. *The case against paramilitary policing*. Milton Keynes: Open University Press.

Jefferson, T. 1988. Race, crime and policing: empirical, theoretical and methodo-

Bibliography

logical issues. *International Journal of the Sociology of Law* 16(4) 521–39.

Jenkins, R. & J. Solomos (eds) 1987. *Racism and equal opportunity policies in the 1980s*. Cambridge: Cambridge University Press.

Jessop, B., K. Bonnett, S. Bromley, T. Ling 1988. Authoritarian populism, two nations and Thatcherism. *New Left Review* 147, 32–60.

John, A. 1970. *Race and the inner city*. London: Runnymede Trust.

Jones, D. 1982. *Crime, protest, community and police in 19th-century Britain*. London: Routledge & Kegan Paul.

Joshua, H. & T. Wallace 1983. *To ride the storm*. London: Heinemann.

Katznelson, I. 1981. *City trenches* Chicago: University of Chicago Press.

Keith, M. 1984. To ride the storm: a review. *Environment and Planning A* 17, 1003–1005.

Keith, M. 1986. *The 1981 riots in London*. DPhil dissertation, University of Oxford.

Keith, M. 1987. Something happened: explanations of the 1981 riots. In *Race and racism*, P. Jackson (ed.). London: Allen & Unwin.

Keith, M. 1988a. Riots as a "social problem" in British cities. In *Social problems in the city*, D. T. Herbert & D. M. Smith (eds). Oxford: Oxford University Press.

Keith, M. 1988b. Squaring circles? Consultation and inner-city policing. *New Community* 15(1) October, 63–77.

Keith, M. 1989. Misunderstandings? Policing, reform and control, co-optation and consultation. In *Black politics in Britain*, H. Goulbourne (ed.). Aldershot, England: Gower (Avebury).

Keith, M. 1991. Policing a perplexed society?: no-go areas and the mystification of police–Black conflict. In *Out of order? Policing Black people*, E. Cashmore & E. McClaughlin (eds). London: Routledge.

Keith, M. 1992. Angry writing: (re)presenting the unethical world of the ethnographer. *Environment and planning D* 10, 551–68.

Keith, M. 1993. From punishment to discipline? Racism, racialisation and social control. See Cross & Keith (1993).

Keith, M. & M. Cross 1993. Racism and the postmodern city. See Cross & Keith (1993).

Keith, M. & K. Murji 1990. Reifying crime, legitimising racism: Left realism and the local politics of policing. In *Race and local politics*, W. Ball & J. Solomos (eds). London: Macmillan.

Keith, M. & A. Rogers 1991. Hollow promises: policy, theory and practice in the inner city. In *Hollow promises: rhetoric and reality in the inner city*, M. Keith & A. Rogers (eds). London: Mansell.

Kerner, O. [chair] 1968. *Report of the National Advisory Commission on Civil Disorders*. Washington: US Government Printing Office.

Kettle, M & L. Hodges 1982. *Uprising*. London: Pan.

Killian, L. 1981. The perils of race and racism as variables. *New Community* IX, 378–80.

Kinsey, R., J. Lea, J. Young 1986. *Losing the fight against crime*. Oxford: Basil Blackwell.

Kornhauser, W. 1959. *The politics of mass society*. New York: Free Press.

Bibliography

Laclau, E. & C. Mouffe 1985. *Hegemony and socialist strategy*. London: Verso.

Lambert, J. L. 1970. *Crime, police and race relations* Oxford: Oxford University Press.

Lambert, J. L. 1986. *Police powers and accountability*. London: Croom Helm.

Lambeth Council 1981. *Police/black relations in Lambeth*. London: Lambeth Council.

Lang, K. & S. Lang 1969. Racial disturbance as collective protest. In *Riots and rebellion*, L. Masotti & J. Bowen (eds). Los Angeles: Sage.

Lawrence, E. 1982. In the abundance of water the fool is thirsty. Social and Black "pathology". In *The empire strikes back*, CCCS (eds). London: Hutchinson.

Le Bon, G. 1960. *The crowd: a study of the popular mind*. New York: Viking.

Lea, J & J. Young 1982. Riots in Britain. In *Policing the riots*, G. Cowell, T. Jones, J. Young (eds). London: Junction Books.

Lea, J. 1987. Left realism: a defence. *Contemporary Crises* 11, 357–70.

Lea, J. & J. Young 1984. *What's to be done about law & order*. Harmondsworth, England: Penguin.

Lea, J., T. Jones, J. Young 1986. *Saving the inner city: Broadwater Farm a strategy for survival*. London: Middlesex Polytechnic.

Lea, J., R. Matthews, J. Young 1987. *Law and order five years on*. London: Middlesex Polytechnic Centre for Criminology.

Lefebvre, H. 1991. *The production of space*. Cambridge: Polity.

Lewis, R. 1988. *Anti-racism a mania exposed* London: Quartet.

Libman-Rubinstein, R. E. 1972. *Rebels in Eden: mass political violence in the United States*. Boston: Harvard University Press.

Libman-Rubinstein, R. E. 1979. Group violence in America: its structure and limitations. See Graham & Gurr (1979).

Lieberson, S & A. R. Silverman 1965. The precipitants and underlying conditions of race riots. *American Sociological Review* 30, 887–98.

Lipsky, M & D. J. Olsen 1969. Riot Commission politics. See Rossi (1969).

Lipsky, M. & D. J. Olsen 1977. *Commission politics, the processing of racial crisis in America* New Brunswick: Transaction Books.

Little K. 1948. *Negroes in Britain*. London.

Lukes, S. 1974. *Power: a radical view*. London: Macmillan.

Macdonald, I. 1973. Black people and the police. *Race Today* December, 331–43.

Machiarola, R. J. 1969., The social impact of the urban riots. See Connery (1969).

Manning, P. 1977. *Police work: the social organisation of policing*. Cambridge, Mass.: MIT Press.

Marsh, P., E. Rosser, R. Harré 1978. *The rules of disorder*. London: Routledge & Kegan Paul.

Marshall, P. 1975. Urban stress and policing. See Brown & Howes (1975).

Matthews, R. 1987. Taking realist criminology seriously. *Contemporary Crises* 11 371–98.

Matthews, R. & J. Young 1986. *Confronting crime*. London: Sage.

McCabe, S. & P. Wallington (with J. Alderson, L. Gostin, C. Mason) 1988. *The police, public order and civil liberties*. London: Routledge.

McClelland, J. S. 1989. *The crowd and the mob*. London: Unwin Hyman.

McConville, M. & D. Sheperd 1992. *Watching police, watching communities*.

Bibliography

London: Routledge.

McPhail, C. 1971. Civil disorder participation: a critical examination of recent research. *American Sociological Review* **36**, 1058–1073.

McPhail, C. & D. Miller 1973. The assembling process: a theoretical and empirical examination. *American Sociological Review* **38**, 721–35.

Metropolitan Police 1985. *The principles of policing and guidance for professional behaviour*. London: Metropolitan Police.

Metropolitan Police 1986. *Public order review, civil disturbances 1981–85*. London: Metropolitan Police.

Miles, R. 1982. *Racism and migrant labour*. London: Routledge & Kegan Paul.

Miles, R. 1984a. Marxism versus the sociology of race relations. *Ethnic and Racial Studies* **7**, 217–37.

Miles, R. 1984b. The riots of 1958. *Immigrants and Minorities* **3**, 252–75.

Miles, R. 1989. *Racism* London: Routledge.

Miller, J. (ed.) 1983. *States of mind*. London: BBC.

Moore, B. 1978. *The social bases of obedience and revolt*, 2nd edn. London: Macmillan.

Morgan, R. & C. Maggs 1984. *Following Scarman*. Bath: University School of Social Policy.

Morgan, R. & C. Maggs 1985. *Setting the pace: police/community consultation: arrangements in England and Wales*. Bath: School of Social Policy.

Moscovici, S. 1985. *The age of the crowd*. Cambridge: Cambridge University Press.

Moss Side Defence Committee 1981. *The Hytner myths; a preliminary critique of the Hytner Report*. Manchester: Moss Side Defence Committee.

Murdock, G. 1984. Reporting the riots: images and impacts. See Benyon (1984).

Murphy, R. J. & J. M. Watson 1970. The structure of discontent. See Cohen (1970).

NCCL 1980. *Report of the Dummett Inquiry into the Southall disorders*. London: National Council for Civil Liberties.

Newman, K. 1983a. "Policing London post-Scarman." Sir George Bean Memorial Lecture, 30 October 1983.

Newman, K. 1983b. "Public order in free societies." Speech given to the European Atlantic Group, 24 October 1983.

Newman, K. 1983c. *Policing and social policy in multi-ethnic areas in Europe*. Cambridge: Cropwood.

Newman, K. 1986a. "Police–public relations – the pace of change." Police Foundation Annual Lecture.

Newman, K. 1986b. *Report of the Commission of the Metropolitan Police for the year 1985*. London: HMSO.

Northam, G. 1988. *Shooting in the dark*. London: Faber & Faber.

North Kensington Law Centre 1982. *Police and the Notting Hill community*. London: North Kensington Law Centre.

Oakley, R. 1988. *Employment in police forces: a survey of equal opportunities*. London: Campaign for Racial Equality.

Oakley, R. 1989. Community and race relations training for the police: a review

Bibliography

of developments. *New Community* **16**(1), 61–79.

Omi, M. & H. Winant 1986. *Racial formation in the United States*. London: Routledge.

Pearson, G., A. Sampson, R. H. Blagg, P. Stubbs, D. Smith 1989. *Policing racism.* In *Coming to terms with policing*, R. Morgan & D. J. Smith (eds). London: Routledge.

Pilkington, E. 1988. *Beyond the mother country*. London: Tauris.

Piven, F. F. & R. D. Cloward 1979. Electoral instability, civil disorder and relief rises. *American Political Science Review* **73**, 1012–9.

Piven, F. F. & R. D. Cloward 1969. The urban crisis and the consolidation of national power. See Connery (1969).

Piven, F. F. & R. D. Cloward 1971. *Regulating the poor: the functions of public welfare*. New York: Vintage.

Piven, F. F. & R. D. Cloward 1975. *The politics of turmoil*. New York: Pantheon.

Piven, F. F. & R. D. Cloward 1977. *Poor people's movements*. New York: Pantheon.

Police Training Council 1983. *Community and race relations training for the police* London: HMSO.

Policy Studies Institute 1983. *Police and people in London* [4 vols]. London: Policy Studies Institute.

Popular Memory Group 1982. Popular memory: theory, politics, method. In *Making histories: studies in history-writing and politics*, Centre for Contemporary Cultural Studies (eds). London: Hutchinson.

Prashar, U. 1984. The need for positive action. See Benyon (1984).

Pred, A. 1981. Of paths and projects. In *Behavioural geography revisited*, R. Golledge & K. Cox (eds). London: Methuen.

Profitt, R. 1984. Equal respect, equal treatment and equal opportunity. See Benyon (1984).

Pryce, E. 1985. The Notting Hill Gate carnival – Black politics, resistance and leadership 1976–1978. *Caribbean Quarterly* **31**(2) 35–52.

Pryce, K. 1979. *Endless pressure*. Harmondsworth, England: Penguin.

Pulle, S. 1973. *Police/immigrant relations in Ealing*. London: Runnymede Trust.

Railton Road Youth and Community Centre 1981. *Submission to the Scarman Inquiry*. Kew: Public Records Office.

Raine, W. 1970. The perception of police brutality in south central Los Angeles. See Cohen (1970).

Reicher, S. 1984. The St Paul's riot: an explanation of the limits of crowd action in terms of a social identity model. *European Journal of Social Psychology* **14** 1–21.

Reicher, S. & J. Potter 1985. Psychological theory as intergroup perspective: a comparative analysis of "scientific" and "lay" accounts of crowd events. *Human Relations* **30**, 167–87.

Reiner, R. 1978. *The blue-coated worker*. Cambridge: Cambridge University Press.

Reiner, R. 1980. Fuzzy thoughts: the police and law-and-order politics. *Sociological Review* **28**, 377–413.

Reiner, R. & J. Shapland (eds) 1987. Why police? [special issue on policing]. *British Journal of Criminology* **27**(1).

Bibliography

Reiner, R. 1981. Black and blue: race and the police. *New Society* 17 September.

Reiner, R. 1985. The police and race relations. In *Police,the constitution and the community*, J. Baxter & L. Koffman (eds). London: Professional Books.

Reiner, R. 1985. *The politics of the police*. Brighton: Wheatsheaf.

Rex, J. 1981. *Social conflict*. Harlow, England: Longman.

Rex, J. 1982. The 1981 urban riots in Britain. *International Journal of Urban and Regional Research* **6**, 88–113.

Rex, J. 1984. Disadvantage and discrimination in cities. See Benyon (1984).

Richards M. D. [Deputy Assistant Commissioner] 1985. *Serious public disorder in Tottenham*. London: Metropolitan Police.

Richmond, A. 1954. *Colour prejudice in Britain: a survey of West Indian workers in Liverpool*. London: Routledge & Kegan Paul.

Roach, J. & J. Thomacek (eds) 1985. *Police and public order in Europe*. London: Croom Helm.

Roach Family Support Committee (The) 1989. *Policing in Hackney, 1945–1984*. London: Karia Press.

Robins, D. 1992. *Tarnished vision: crime and community relations in the inner city*. Oxford: Oxford University Press.

Robins, D & P. Cohen 1978. *Knuckle sandwich*. Harmondsworth, England: Penguin.

Rock, P 1981. Rioting. *London Review of Books* July, 17–30.

Rollo, J. (ed.) 1980. *Policing the police*, vol. 2: *the politics of policing and the policing of politics (society under surveillance)*. London: John Calder.

Rossi, P. H. (ed.) 1970. *Ghetto revolts*. Chicago: Aldine Press.

Rossi, P. H., R. A. Berk, B. K. Eidson 1974. *The roots of urban discontent*. New York: John Wiley.

Rude, G. 1964. *The crowd in history*. New York: John Wiley.

Runciman, W. G. 1960. *Relative deprivation and social justice*. London: Routledge & Kegan Paul.

Runciman, W. G. 1983. *A treatise on social theory*. Cambridge: Cambridge University Press.

Runnymede Trust 1981. *Evidence given to Scarman inquiry*. Kew: Public Records Office.

Runnymede Trust 1982. Crime and criminal statistics. *Race and Immigration* **143**.

Rushdie, S. 1983. *Shame*. London: Cape.

Russell, B. 1912. *The problems of philosophy*. Oxford: Oxford University Press.

Russell, B. 1946. *History of Western philosophy*. London: Allen & Unwin.

Ryan M. & T. Ward 1986. Law and order: Left realism against the Rest. *The Abolitionist* 1986, no. 2.

Ryan M. & T. Ward 1987. Left realism and the politics of law and order in Britain. Paper presented to the XIVth conference of the EGSDSC on "Justice & ideology" 10–13 September.

Sack, R. D. 1983. Human territoriality. *Association of American Geographers, Annals* **173**, 55–75.

Said, E. 1978. *Orientalism* London: Peregrine.

270

Bibliography

Sayer, A. 1984. *Method in social science*. London: Allen & Unwin.

Scarman, Lord 1981. *The Brixton disorders*. London: HMSO.

Scarman, Lord 1987. Foreword. See Gaskell & Benewick (1987).

Scraton, P. 1985. *The state of the police*. London: Pluto.

Sears, D. O. & J. B. McConahay 1970. Riot participation. See Cohen (1970).

Sherman, L. 1983. After the riots: police and the minorities in the United States, 1970–1980. In *Ethnic pluralism and public policy*, N. Glazer & K. Young (eds). London: Heinemann.

Sherwoord, M. 1984. *Many struggles: West Indian workers and service personnel in Britain 1939–45*. London: Karia Press.

Siegel, B. J. 1979. Defensive cultural adaptation. See Graham & Gurr (1979).

Silver, A. A. 1969. Official interpretation of racial riots. See Connery (1969). J. 1982. Scarman: the police counter-attack. *Socialist Register 1982*, 57–78.

Sivanandan, A. 1976. Race, class and the state. In Sivanandan (1982).

Sivanandan, A. 1982. *A different hunger*. London: Pluto.

Sivanandan, A. 1983. Challenging racism: strategies for the 80s. *Race and Class* XXV, 1–13.

Sivanandan, A. 1985. RAT, the denigration of Black struggle. In *Communities of resistance*, A. Sivanandan (ed.) (1990). London: Verso.

Skolnick, J. 1966. *Justice without trial: law enforcement in democratic society*. New York: John Wiley.

Smelser, N. J. 1962. *A theory of collective behaviour*. New York: Free Press.

Smith, B. L. R. 1969. The politics of protest: how effective is violence? See Connery (1969).

Smith, D. J. & J. Gray 1983. *The police in action*. London: Policy Studies Institute.

Smith, P. T. 1985. *Policing Victorian London: political policing, public order and the London Metropolitan Police*. London: Greenwood Press.

Smith, S. J. 1982. *Race and crime statistics*. London: Board for Social Responsibility, Church of England.

Smith, S. J. 1986a. Police accountability and local democracy. *Area* 18(2), 49–57.

Smith, S. J. 1986b. *Crime, space and society*. Cambridge: Cambridge University Press.

Smith, S. J. 1989. *The politics of race and residence: citizenship, segregation and White supremacy in Britain*. Cambridge: Polity.

Soja, E. 1985. The spatiality of social life: towards a transformative retheriorisation. In *Social relations and spatial structures*, D. Gregory & J. Urry (eds). London: Macmillan.

Soja, E. 1989. *Postmodern geographies*. London: Verso.

Solomos, J. 1984. *The politics of Black youth unemployment*. Warwick: Centre for Research in Ethnic Relations.

Solomos, J. 1986. *Riots, urban protest and social policy: the interplay of reform and social control*. CRER Policy Papers in Ethnic Relations 7, University of Warwick.

Solomos, J. 1988. *Black youth, racism and the state the politics of ideology and policy*. Cambridge: Cambridge University Press.

Southgate, P. 1982. *The disturbances of July 1981 in Handsworth, Birmingham*. London: HMSO.

Bibliography

Southgate, P. (ed.) 1984. *Racism awareness training for the police* London: Home Office.

Spilerman, S. 1970. The causes of racial disturbances: a comparison of alternative explanations. *American Sociological Review* 35, 627–49.

Spilerman, S. 1971. The causes of racial disturbances: tests of an explanation. *American Sociological Review* 36, 427–42.

Stark, M., W. Rance, S. Burbeck, K. Davidson 1974. Some empirical patterns in a riot process. *American Sociological Review* 39, 865–76.

Stead, P. J. 1985. *The police of Britain*. London: Macmillan.

Stevens, P. & C. F. Willis 1979. *Race, crime and arrests*. London: HMSO.

Stevenson, D. & P. Wallis 1970. Survey of young West Indians. *Race Today* August, 278–80.

Strachey, L. 1918. *Eminent Victorians*. Harmondsworth, England: Penguin.

Stubbs P. 1987. Crime, community and the multi-agency approach: a critical reading of the Broadwater Farm Inquiry Report. *Critical Social Policy* 20, 30–45.

Taylor, S. 1984. The Scarman Report and explanations of riots. See Benyon (1984).

Thackrah, J. 1985. Reactions to terrorism and riots. In Bramshill Police College *Contemporary policing*. Bramshill: Police College. London: Sphere Reference.

Tilly, C., L. Tilly, R. Tilly 1975. *The rebellious century, 1830–1930*. Cambridge, Mass.: Harvard University Press.

Tilly, C., L. Tilly, R. Tilly 1978. *From mobilization to revolution*. Reading, Mass.: Addison-Wesley.

Tilly, C., L. Tilly, R. Tilly 1979. Collective violence in European perspective. See Graham & Gurr (1979).

Tomlinson, T. M. & D. O. Sears 1970. Negro attitudes towards the riot. See Cohen (1979).

Trevizias E. 1983. Crowd dynamics and the prevention and control of collective disorders. *Police Journal* LVI 142–63.

Tumber, H. 1982. *Television and the riots*. Aston: Broadcasting Research Unit.

Turner, R. H. & L. Killian 1957. *Collective behaviour*. Englewood Cliffs, New Jersey: Prentice Hall.

Uglow, S. 1988. *Policing liberal society*. Oxford: Oxford University Press.

Vick C. F. J. 1982. Ideological responses to the riots. *Police Journal* LV, 262–78.

Vogler, R. 1982. Magistrates and civil disorder. *LAG Bulletin* November, 12–15.

Vogler, R. 1990. Magistrates courts and the struggle for local democracy. In *Censure, politics and criminal justice*, C. S. Sumner (ed.). Milton Keynes: Open University Press.

Vogler, R. 1991. *Reading the riot act: the magistracy, the police and the army in civil disorder*. Milton Keynes: Open University Press.

Waddington, D. 1987. The summer of '81 revisited: an analysis of Sheffield's Haymarket fracas. See Gaskell, G. & R. Benewick (eds).

Bibliography

Waddington, D. 1992. *Contemporary issues in public disorder*. London: Routledge.

Waddington, D., K. Jones, C. Critcher (eds) 1989. *Flashpoints: studies in public disorder*. London: Routledge.

Waddington, P. A. J. 1982. Racism and the police - the making of a myth. *Police* (October), 18–21.

Waddington, P. A. J. 1984a. Conservatism, dogmatism and authoritarianism in British police officers: a comment. *Sociology* 16(4), 591–4.

Waddington, P. A. J. 1984b. Uniform standards of law enforcement. *Police* (June), 28.

Waddington, P. A. J. 1991. *The strong arm of the law: armed and public order policing*. Oxford: Oxford University Press.

Waller, P. J. 1981. The riots in Toxteth, Liverpool: a survey. *New Community* IX, 344–53.

Wanderer, J. 1969. An index of riot severity and some correlates. *American Journal of Sociology* 74, 500–505.

Weatheritt, M. 1986. *Innovations in policing*. London: Croom Helm.

Wells, R. 1987. The will and the way to move forward in policing. See Benyon & Solomos (1987).

Willis, C. 1983. *The use, effectiveness and impact of police stop and search powers*. London: HMSO.

Willmott, P. (ed.) 1987. *Policing and the community*. London: Policy Studies Institute.

Wright, N. 1986. The new Metropolitan Police Strategy and its implications for the campaign for police accountability. *Critical Social Policy* 17, 75–8.

Young, J. 1974. New directions in sub-cultural theory. In *Approaches to sociology*, J. Rex (ed.). London: Routledge & Kegan Paul.

Young, J. 1987. The task facing a realist criminology. *Contemporary Crises* 11, 337–56.

Young, M. 1991. *Inside job: policing and police culture in Britain*. Oxford: Oxford University Press.

INDEX OF AUTHORS CITED

Alderson, J. 196, 211, 213, 222, 227, 249
Anderson, B. 182, 244
Anderton, J. 90, 93, 207, 213
Ardrey, R. 218

Banton, M. 10, 209, 210, 227
Barthes, R. 53, 117, 164, 197, 218
Becker, H. 198, 243
Benyon, J. 77
Bhavnani, R. 166
Blumer, H. 79
Box, S. 215, 226, 233
Brewer, J. D. 205
Bridges, L. 16, 248
Brogden, M. 14, 212, 215, 226, 233
Brown, C. 32
Brown, J. 210
Bunyan, T. 10, 91, 204
Burgess, J. 58

Cashmore, E. 89
Chesshyre, R. 12
Christian, L. 159, 195, 249
Cloward, R. D. 87
Cohen, A. 48, 124
Cohen, N. 86
Cohen, P. 117, 204
Cohen, S. 57, 249–51

Davies, J. C. 80
Dorn, N. 48, 128

Edelman, M. 72, 172, 213

Feagin, J. R. 75, 86, 88
Field, S. 3, 9, 53, 75, 83–6, 92, 132, 164, 213, 218, 220–23, 227, 233, 234, 240, 242, 245, 251, 254
Fogelson, R. M. 74, 86, 87
Foucault, M. 220, 227, 249, 250
Freud, S. 79

Fryer, P. 44, 91, 124
Fyfe, N. 179, 182

Giddens, A. 155, 160, 164
Gifford, A. 77, 183, 195
Gilroy, P. 16, 84, 90, 91, 159, 179, 190, 206, 223, 236, 237, 241, 243, 244, 248, 250
Goffman, E. 70, 106, 155, 164, 165, 167, 198, 243
Gordon, P. 9, 12, 237
Graef, R. 12, 13, 48
Gray, J. 12, 154, 155, 157, 160, 191
Grimshaw, G. 13, 14, 172, 179, 206, 218
Gurr, T. R. 79, 80, 87
Gutzmore, C. 16, 48, 124

Hall, S. 36, 57, 65, 77, 93, 136, 150, 171, 174–6, 180, 188, 201, 202, 226, 236, 237, 240, 241, 243, 244, 248
Harre, R. 156, 167
Harris, C. 250
Harrison, P. 35, 152
Hesse, B. 64
Holdaway, S. 9, 12, 13, 155, 157, 159, 160, 218
Howe, D. 27, 46, 47, 90, 93, 124
Humphry, D. 9
Hunte, J. 24, 25, 28, 29

Jefferson, T. 9, 13, 14, 172, 173, 179, 204–206, 218, 254
Joshua, H. 19, 29, 90, 96, 117, 136

Kettle, M. 72, 89, 90, 100, 200
Kinsey, R. 16

Laclau, E. 242
Lawrence, E. 10, 72, 116, 130, 209
Lea, J. 16, 17, 89
Lefebvre, H. 147, 188, 200

INDEX

Lipsky, M. 74, 75

Maggs, C. 172, 173, 183
Miles, R. 38, 44, 90, 92, 150, 240, 241
Morgan, R. 172, 173, 175, 183
Murji, K. 16, 223

Northam, G. 202, 203

Olsen, D. J. 74, 75

Pearson, G. 14
Pilkington, E. 44
Piven, F. F. 87
Prashar, U. 89
Profitt, R. 89

Reiner, R. 9, 10, 12, 16, 179, 196, 212,
216, 222, 225, 227, 233
Robins, D. 117, 254
Rude, G. 79, 98, 99, 104
Runciman, W. G. 80, 97

Scraton, P. 10, 204
Sim, J. 190, 206, 223, 237, 243
Sivanandan, A. 15, 93, 252
Smelser, N. J. 79
Smith, D. J. 12, 154, 155, 157, 160, 191
Smith, S. J. 16, 159, 184, 221
Solomos, J. 10, 11, 15, 72, 73, 172, 202,
213, 240, 247
Southgate, P. 15, 89

Taylor, S. 48, 79, 104, 135, 136
Thackrah, J. 212

Vogler, R. 97, 98, 238

Waddington, D. 81, 168, 205–206
Waddington, P. A. J. 191, 197,
203–205, 211
Wallace, T. 75, 90, 96, 117, 136
Wanderer, J. 81, 84, 109–111

Young, J. 16, 89, 198
Young, M. 12, 157

SUBJECT INDEX

All Saints Road 20, 21, 44, 46–8, 122, 124–9, 132, 149, 150, 159, 160, 162, 165, 166, 173, 215
America 16, 46, 52, 57, 74, 75, 77, 78, 81, 83–6, 88, 89, 99, 100, 109, 245
amnesia 9, 18, 19, 53, 216, 220, 229
Anderton, James 90, 93, 207, 213
assimilation 10
Atlantic Road 27–9, 102
authoritarian populism 234, 237, 243, 248

Barr, Chief Superintendent 135–9, 141, 142, 193, 194
baton rounds 197, 203
behaviourism 78, 81, 82, 85, 88, 94, 168
Black Panthers 29, 46
Black Unity and Freedom Party 29, 33
Black Watch 128
Black Youth 5, 15, 46, 47, 68, 89, 97, 116, 117, 152, 181, 196, 197, 210, 234, 243, 246, 247, 250
blues parties 12, 28, 35, 48, 142
Bramshill 193, 211, 212, 216, 227
Brixton 20, 22–33, 37, 52, 55, 56, 64, 70, 71, 77, 78, 101–105, 108–113, 116, 117, 122, 129–34, 142, 143, 150, 152–4, 160–62, 165, 169, 173, 174, 176, 177, 180, 188, 191–5, 197, 198, 203, 211, 232, 243, 253
Brixton Rastafarian Collective 31, 160
Broadwater Farm Defence Campaign 253
Broadwater Farm Estate 38, 77, 144, 197
Brockwell Park 174, 243

cannabis 32, 36, 41, 126, 133, 136, 143, 146, 161
carceral 249
carnival 48, 123–5, 127, 214

CCCS 21, 57, 58, 241, 248
city, inner 38, 52, 58, 69, 70, 73, 76, 78, 86, 89, 100, 106, 117, 128, 136, 172, 179, 180, 185, 189, 204, 208, 209, 212, 215, 218–20, 243, 249–52, 254
Clapham 243
Clark, Kenneth 46, 74
cocaine 136, 161, 214
Cochrane, Kelso 45
Coldharbour Lane 25, 28, 63, 102
collective behaviour 70, 79, 80, 83, 85, 87, 88, 111, 118
combustion 63, 67, 76, 106
commissions 9, 74–6, 83, 100, 172, 179
"community" 2, 5, 13, 17, 18, 20–22, 24–7, 29–35, 37–42, 45, 47, 48, 50, 60, 61, 63, 65, 66, 77, 92, 93, 100, 108, 109, 111, 118, 123, 124, 126, 128–30, 133, 135, 139–43, 145, 148, 150, 152, 156, 161, 169, 171–5, 177–82, 184, 185, 193, 194, 199, 210, 216, 223, 225, 228, 231, 233, 234, 236, 241–3, 244, 245, 249–54
  involvement 31, 139, 140, 228
  relations 13, 33, 39, 48, 60, 61, 63, 139–41, 143, 177, 193, 210
consensus 6, 72, 91, 129, 141, 215, 216, 221, 222, 225, 233, 234, 237, 244
consultation 34, 41, 171–3, 176, 178–82, 184, 185, 223
contagion 4, 64, 68, 71, 87, 149, 254
copycat 52, 57, 58, 68, 149
crack 58
Critchlow, Frank 47, 48, 126
crowds 32, 53, 58, 62, 64, 65, 78–80, 88, 91, 97–101, 104, 109, 114, 115, 117, 118, 130, 138, 144–6, 149–51, 161, 162, 167, 168, 192, 202, 204, 205, 211, 212, 216
crowd psychology 79, 80, 99, 104, 118, 167, 205, 211, 216

277

INDEX

CS gas 203

Dalston 33–6, 38–40, 42, 60, 141, 142, 144, 150, 156, 162, 193, 194
Dalston Lane 35
de Freitas, Michael 46
discourse 3, 53, 73, 81, 92, 201, 207, 208, 212–14, 216, 218–20, 223–9, 232, 234, 236, 238, 239–41, 245, 246, 250–52
disorder 3–5, 7, 20, 21, 37, 48, 53, 54, 57, 58, 60, 61, 64, 67–70, 72, 73, 76–86, 88, 89–94, 96–9, 101, 102, 106, 108–111, 113, 114, 116–18, 122, 123, 129, 135, 144, 145, 147, 149, 150, 152, 154, 159, 160, 164, 168–70, 172, 173, 179, 190, 191, 196, 197, 201–206, 209, 211, 213, 216–18, 220, 232–4, 236, 238, 245–7, 251-5
District Support Units 31, 146, 190, 191
dogs 24, 30, 35, 37, 38, 52, 61, 64, 70, 137, 191, 192, 193
drugs 27, 28, 32, 39–41, 43, 48, 125, 126, 128, 133, 134, 136, 139, 141, 142, 177, 193, 217

empiricism 82, 96, 104

Falklands 3, 236, 253
fishing raids 132, 161, 195
flashpoints 81, 168
Four Aces 35, 42, 43
Francis, Joshua 19, 29
Front Line 20, 21, 25–9, 31–3, 36, 39, 41, 91, 104, 131–3, 136, 138, 141, 142, 145, 146, 159–62, 165, 166, 177, 192–5, 199, 200–202, 215, 217, 220, 245, 253, 254
front line deviancy 131, 136, 138, 145, 146, 161, 195

ganja 32, 40
ghetto 31, 52, 76, 83, 84, 86, 88, 243, 251
Gibbs, Asquith 60
Greaves, George 24
guilt 72, 77, 81, 83, 113, 200

Handsworth 13, 48, 70, 72, 77, 89, 93, 188, 197, 205, 253
Hassan, Tunay 33

heroin 161
historicity 161
Holly St 144, 145, 191
Home Office 11, 55, 56, 60, 61, 64–7, 89, 96, 97, 99, 102, 107, 109–111, 113, 117, 118, 171, 172, 181–3, 192, 239, 248, 249
Howe, Darcus 27, 46, 47, 90, 93, 124
human awareness training 15
Hunte, Joseph 24, 25, 28, 29
Hurd, Douglas 34, 172, 192

imagined community 244
Imbert, Sir Peter 123, 197, 202, 219, 223
Immediate Response Units 31, 125, 132, 190, 197
inquiries 25–7, 31–3, 37, 74, 75, 77, 78, 81, 93, 132, 164, 176, 192, 228
inscription 21, 24, 50, 95, 166, 177, 253
institutional racism 6, 8, 22, 25, 50, 78, 94, 189, 199, 200, 207, 242
Irish 242

"the job" 6, 129, 131, 139, 144, 156–9, 223, 227, 228
JJ's 36–9, 136, 137, 146, 150, 165
Johnston's 35, 36, 41, 135, 142
Jones, G. W. 135
juvenile 30, 66, 72, 106, 108, 150

Kafka, Franz 206, 228
Kerner Inquiry 74–8, 81, 84, 86, 100, 106, 211
King, Martin Luther 91, 173, 254, 255
knock-on 33, 130, 145, 198

Laws, Courtney 24, 26
Leander, Tony 46
Lee, Vincent 48, 255
Left realists 16, 17, 101
Liverpool 7, 20, 58, 63, 99, 180, 207
looting 13, 52, 62, 66, 67, 69, 72, 101–105, 107–111, 114–16, 117, 138, 150–152, 169, 231
Los Angeles 86, 254

Malcolm X 255
Maltese 242
Mangrove 46, 47, 124–7, 129, 148, 149,

278

SUBJECTS

160
marginalization 22, 159, 244
Marnoch, Alex 24, 132, 133, 173–8, 184, 193, 194
Mayall Road 25, 29, 102
miners 137, 205, 206, 253
Monerville, Trevor 33
monitoring 179, 204
Moorlands Estate 25, 191
moral panic 4, 42, 52, 57, 58, 70, 232
mugging 15, 16, 57, 159, 226, 228, 231, 243, 245
Muirhead, Michael 40
multi-agency 128, 132, 133, 194, 223, 225, 233
myth 53, 70, 87, 88, 117, 172, 197, 201, 221, 222, 225, 247

nation 2, 76, 77, 86, 185, 206, 236, 244
nationalism 3, 226, 236, 241, 243
naturalization 3, 7, 203, 234, 237, 238, 252–4
New Cross 60
Newham 55, 56, 61, 62
Newman, Sir Kenneth 7, 20, 39, 41, 49, 50, 122, 123, 135, 140, 196, 202, 210, 211, 215–17, 218, 219, 221–3, 225, 227, 228, 249
no-go areas 37, 125, 193, 214–216, 219, 220
Notting Hill 20, 22, 33, 44–8, 112, 113, 122–7, 129, 131, 142, 148, 149, 160, 162, 165, 166, 173, 191, 193–6, 214
Nottingham 44

Operation
  Condor 26, 177
  Lucy 41–3, 214
  Swamp 132, 228
  Trident 48, 128

paramilitarism 202–205
Parkinson, Astel 32, 174–8
pathologies 12, 15, 18
Patten, John 249
Pearman, Chief Superintendent 128
Penge 67, 112, 113
plastic bullets 93, 197
Plowman, Detective Chief

Superintendent 27, 32, 132
Plus Programme 184
police
  discourse 201, 207, 208, 213, 216, 218–20, 223–7, 229
  racism 4, 6, 11, 14, 15, 17, 18, 74, 118, 154, 171, 189
poll tax 238, 254
Powell, Enoch 54, 245
professionalism 14, 59, 123, 138, 141, 154, 157, 158, 212, 224, 229
public
  inquiry 25, 176
  knowledge 54, 57, 59, 60, 68, 69, 97, 213, 242, 249

race
  awareness training 15
  relations 11, 15, 16, 52, 75, 85, 93, 182, 240
racialization 31, 34, 118, 167, 189, 231, 232, 234, 235, 238–42, 243, 244, 245, 246–8, 250–52, 254
racism 3–6, 8–12, 14–18, 22, 24, 25, 42, 45, 50, 54, 74–8, 84, 90, 94, 98, 101, 118, 141, 154, 159, 163, 171, 188, 189, 198–200, 207, 210, 224, 232, 234, 237, 239, 241, 242, 244, 250, 252
racist 2, 3, 6, 8, 10–15, 28, 35, 42–4, 46, 60, 62–5, 68, 84, 111, 115, 130, 131, 149, 159, 166, 170, 176, 185, 188, 197–200, 206, 207, 209, 210, 219, 224, 232, 234, 236, 237, 239–51
Railton Road 20–22, 25–9, 31–3, 101, 102, 104, 122, 131–4, 152, 154, 159–62, 165, 166, 173, 174, 176, 177, 191, 192, 199, 215, 253
Rastafarian 27, 31, 38, 160
rebellion 4, 92, 147, 167, 170, 232, 247
recipe 76–8, 82, 83, 85, 87, 122
riot 3, 4, 7, 13, 22, 25, 26, 30, 37, 52, 53, 54, 57–63, 64, 66, 67–73, 74, 75, 76, 78, 80, 82–94, 96, 97, 98, 99, 100–105, 107–118, 122, 132, 133, 136, 138, 145, 146, 148, 149, 152, 161, 164, 167, 168, 169, 170, 173, 179, 190, 197–9, 200, 202–205, 212, 213, 216, 219, 231, 232, 234, 238, 246, 247, 253, 254, 255

279

INDEX

average rioter 5, 97, 98, 100, 101, 106, 108, 109, 116, 247
severity 111–113, 114, 115
rites of passage 117, 238
Roach, Colin 33, 37, 137, 138, 142, 194, 222
Roots Pool 38–42, 140, 141, 143, 192
rotten-apple racism 11
Rushdie, Salman 8, 9, 91, 93, 95, 236

Sandringham 20, 21, 33, 35–8, 40, 41, 43, 44, 122, 134–43, 146, 150, 151, 156, 159, 160, 161, 162, 165, 191–4, 199, 203, 215
Scarman, Lord 13, 15, 22, 24–7, 31–3, 37, 60, 68, 76–8, 81, 84, 102–104, 106, 132, 160, 164, 168, 172, 173, 178–80, 192, 195, 205, 211, 227, 228
shabeens 28, 35–9, 132, 142
Shepherds 29–32, 133
Sims, Assetta 33
slag 157
social movements 53, 85, 87, 88, 90, 179, 245
Somerleyton Road 24, 25
Southall 55, 56, 58, 59, 63, 64, 110–13, 115, 150, 204, 245, 252
space 16, 30, 31, 61, 95, 106, 122, 139, 147, 154, 157, 159, 164, 169, 188, 189, 199, 200–202, 204, 212, 215, 220, 223, 236, 239, 240, 245, 248–51
spatiality 154, 164, 169, 249, 250
Special Branch 29, 134, 140
spontaneity 5, 90, 91, 92, 94, 144, 154, 170, 190, 201, 203, 253
stage 28, 43, 50, 70, 71, 74, 75, 88, 113, 142, 144, 147, 164, 165, 166, 175, 178, 196, 197, 200, 211, 215, 216, 243, 244
Stalker, John 13, 227
Stockwell Park 25, 26
Stoke Newington 20, 33, 34, 36, 37, 39, 40, 42–4, 55, 123, 134, 135, 137–9,

141, 150–52, 162, 192, 194, 198, 214, 217, 226, 228
street 15, 26, 31, 32, 38, 42, 45, 46, 59, 62, 66, 67, 69, 77, 89, 91, 93, 101, 104, 109, 118, 135, 140, 143–6, 149–52, 157, 159, 173, 175, 191, 193, 198, 217, 228, 250, 253, 254

subculture 12–14, 142, 157, 191, 203
surveillance 126, 133, 135, 136, 140, 195, 196, 204, 246, 249

targeting 126, 133, 135, 136, 195, 196
Taylor, Robert 48, 79, 104, 135, 136
Terkel, Studs 12
Thatcher, Margaret 72, 234, 235, 243, 248, 253
Thatcherism 234, 236, 237
Tottenham 70, 77, 144, 169, 211
Toxteth 59, 175
trigger 84, 150, 164, 167–9

uprising 3, 4, 7, 8, 16, 26, 48, 49, 53, 54, 71, 72, 77, 82–4, 87, 89–91, 92, 93, 95, 96, 99, 101, 104, 108, 118, 152, 168, 169, 171, 188, 198, 200, 201, 203–205, 211, 213, 214, 219, 238, 246, 247, 253–5
USA 9, 79, 83–5, 99
Utopia 12, 156, 225

Walthamstow 60, 64–6, 112, 113, 115
Wapping 137, 237, 253
water canon 93, 197
West Ham 55, 61–3, 112, 113, 115
Whitfield, Chief Superintendent 125–8, 173, 193, 194

Yardies 41, 42, 43, 44, 214, 226, 245
"youth" 5, 15, 17, 21, 24, 29–33, 36, 38, 46, 47, 52, 53, 66–9, 89, 91, 92, 97, 109, 116, 117, 140, 152, 174, 181, 196, 197, 205, 206, 210, 234, 243, 245, 246, 247, 248, 250, 252